High/Scope Buyer's Guide to Children's Software

1992

Forsyth Library

Related High/Scope Materials

Young Children & Computers
(Book exploring the potential of computer learning)

Computer Learning for Young Children
(Videotape on using computers in the early childhood classroom)

High/Scope's Extensions
(High/Scope curriculum newsletter featuring a regular computer column)

The High/Scope Preschool Curriculum

Young Children in Action
(Manual of the High/Scope Preschool Curriculum)

The Daily Routine
(videotape)

Small-Group Time Video Series

The Plan-Do-Review Process
(Preschool Videotapes)

High/Scope K–3 Curriculum Series

Language & Literacy
Mathematics
Science
(K–3 Curriculum Guides)

Active Learning
Classroom Environment
Language & Literacy
Mathematics
(K–3 Videotapes)

Related Publications of the High/Scope Press

The Teacher's Idea Book: Daily Planning Around the Key Experiences
Supporting Young Learners—Ideas for Preschool and Day Care Providers
A School Administrator's Guide to Early Childhood Programs
Round the Circle: Key Experiences in Movement for Children
Good Beginnings: Parenting in the Early Years

Available from

THE HIGH/SCOPE PRESS
600 North River Street, Ypsilanti, MI 48198-2898   (313)485-2000   FAX (313)485-0704

High/Scope Buyer's Guide to Children's Software

1992

Annual Survey of
Computer Programs
for Children
Aged 3 to 7

By Warren Buckleitner

High/Scope® Press
Ypsilanti, Michigan

Published by
HIGH/SCOPE® PRESS

A division of the
High/Scope® Educational Research Foundation
600 North River Street
Ypsilanti, MI 48198-2898
(313)485-2000, FAX (313)485-0704

Editors: Kathy Gibbons, Marge Senninger, Lynn Taylor
Interior Design and Production: Margaret FitzGerald
Cover Design: Linda Eckel

The following products are mentioned in the *High/Scope Buyer's Guide to Children's
Software 1992* and are registered trademarks of the companies indicated:

Apple Computer Company: Apple II, IIe, IIc, IIGS, Macintosh, Macintosh II, Imagewriter, Imagewriter II
Atari, Inc.: Atari 400, 800, ST
Commodore Business Machines: PET, C64/128, Amiga, Vic-20
Covox, Inc.: Covox Speech Adapter
Dunamis Corp.: PowerPad, WonderWorker
Edmark, Inc.: TouchWindow
International Business Machines, Inc.: IBM Personal Computer
Josten's Learning Corporation: Ufonic Speech Synthesizer
Koala Technologies Corporation: Koala Pad
Milton Bradley Co.: Chutes & Ladders
Nintendo of America: Nintendo
RC Systems: Slotbuster II
Street Electronics Corp.: Echo II, II+, IIb, Cricket
Sunburst Communications, Inc.: Muppet Learning Keys
Tandy, Inc.: Radio Shack TRS-80 Models
Walt Disney Computer Software, Inc.: The Sound Source

ISBN 0-929816-37-4
ISSN 1060-9504

Printed in the United States of America

CONTENTS

INTRODUCTION

Welcome to the *High/Scope Buyer's Guide to Children's Software 1992: The Annual Survey of Computer Programs for Children Aged 3 to 7*. Now in its eighth year of publication, this buyer's guide to children's software is specially designed to save you time and money as you make decisions about purchasing software for young children. This year's edition has been updated and expanded, offering reviews of 501 titles currently on the market, including 77 brand new reviews.

What's New?

More high-quality software. Software programs developed recently are easier to use; are more likely to incorporate speech, sounds, and clear graphics; and generally take better advantage of the computer's potential. Two computers—the color Macintosh LC and the low-cost IBM compatible—have been keeping software developers (and us) busy in the last year, presenting exciting new programs for use with children. See the graph illustrating the number of programs available for each computer brand on page 26.

More IBM software. This year's edition identifies 202 programs that run on IBM or IBM-compatible computers—that's up from 160 last year and 147 in 1990. We also list the latest programs for Apple II, Macintosh, Commodore, Atari, and Apple IIGS computers. For special listings by computer brands, see page 243.

ShareWare and special education software. We've included 52 programs designed for use in special education (see page 239). For a listing of distributors of ShareWare, a low-cost resource for software, see Appendix 2.

Award-winning titles. Of all 501 titles in this guide, just 4 receive the annual High/Scope Early Childhood Software Award of Excellence. See page 9 for complete descriptions of this year's award-winners.

Tips for buying software. We've included some software buying tips to help you find the best prices and get off to a successful start. See page 5.

Why Does High/Scope Review Computer Software?

The High/Scope Educational Research Foundation has been studying and supporting the development of young children since 1962. We began exploring the use of computers with young children in the late 1970s and have been carefully integrating computer technology into the early childhood curriculum at our demonstration school in Ypsilanti, Michigan, ever since. Today, visitors can see young children at our school using computers as routinely as they use blocks and art materials. We've learned that the success of using computers with young children is directly linked to software quality. By publishing these software reviews, we can share our experience with others.

High/Scope, a nonprofit organization, receives no fees or monetary consideration from either publishers or distributors for reviewing their software.

For more information: If you produce early childhood software and are interested in having your products and company listed in the 1993 Buyer's Guide, contact us before August 31, 1992. If you have questions about our reviews or want information about our programs for young children, write to the *High/Scope Buyer's Guide to Children's Software 1992*, High/Scope Educational Research Foundation, 600 North River Street, Ypsilanti, Michigan 48198-2898, (313)485-2000, or FAX (313)485-0704.

1

FINDING THE BEST SOFTWARE

This chapter contains (1) software purchasing tips, including quality criteria for choosing good software to use at home or school with young children, and (2) discussions of the programs receiving the 1992 High/Scope Early Childhood Software Award of Excellence.

SOFTWARE PURCHASING TIPS

It's happened to thousands of us—well-intentioned teachers, parents, or grand-parents who want to use our computers with young children. We eagerly open a colorful box containing a software program that promises "unlimited fun and learning" as an eager child waits. But when we insert the program disk into the computer an "INSUFFICIENT MEMORY ERROR" message flashes on the screen.

Matching Software to Your Computer

Unfortunately, purchasing software is not a simple task. There are countless variations of computer hardware, and the software has to match it to work. If it's any comfort, software vendors are also frustrated! Sally Carr Hannafin of Weekly Reader Software (the *Stickybear* folks) once made an entire Halloween costume out of the thousands of special hardware stickers she's required to put on various program boxes.

Here are some tips to help you avoid problems when buying software.

1. **Identify your computer's hardware components before you buy any software.** This is especially important if you have a pre-1989 IBM or compatible. If you are a computer novice, find a knowledgeable friend or consult your computer dealer. One teacher kept the advertise-ment for his computer to use as easy reference. (Hardware require-ments for specific programs are included in the software descriptions sections in Chapter 3.) In general, before you purchase a software program, learn these things about your computer's capabilities.

   • *Amount of RAM (random access memory).* Programs vary in the amount of RAM required to run them.

   • *Type of graphics display* (especially important for IBM or com-patibles). Early childhood software depends on crisp, colorful graphics. An increasing number of programs require specialized hardware to provide special graphics.

   • *Type of printer* you have (if any).

- *Type of speech- or sound-enhancement hardware* you have (if any). Many programs depend on a separate speech synthesizer to produce special speech or sound effects.
- *Version of DOS or operating system* you use. Some programs require special versions.
- *Size of hard disk drive* (if any) and amount of space available. Not only do more software programs require a hard disk, but some programs also use up to 3 megabytes of space because of digitized sound effects and detailed graphics.
- *Type of input device in addition to the keyboard.* Do you have a mouse or any other kind of auxiliary input device? A mouse is becoming a common option in early childhood software and is required in some programs.
- *Type of disk drives on your computer.* Software is delivered on disks that your computer must be able to read, so it is important to have a perfect match. There are two sizes—the older 5.25-inch "floppy" drives, and the newer 3.5-inch higher capacity drives (the Macintosh standard). Most newer IBM or compatible computer systems are equipped with both.

2. **Once you have a title in mind, make sure it will work with your computer.** There are generally two ways to do this:

- Study the box or advertisement. Software vendors commonly list hardware requirements on the package.
- Contact the software producer directly to describe your computer configuration and insure a match. For a listing of producers, see Appendix 1.

Getting the Best Price

If you think software seems a little expensive, you're right. The average "suggested retail price" of single-title packages in this guide is $42.53. However, here are some ways to get the best price possible:

1. **Use software mail-order companies.** You'll save the cost of state and local taxes, and these prices are often the best because mail-order companies purchase in volume. Advertisements for larger mail-order companies are usually found in popular computer magazines.

2. **Investigate ShareWare.** ShareWare is a software distribution method that allows anyone to copy the program disks and pass them on to others. The original author benefits through "registration fees" collected for either updates or documentation. There are several commercial sources of ShareWare that carry early childhood titles we've reviewed for $3 to $5 (for example, see *Software Excitement!* page 218).

3. **Check software specialty stores.** Software specialty stores are becoming more common. Because they also buy in bulk from software producers, these specialty stores often have low prices. See listings in Appendix 2.

4. **Investigate libraries.** Some college or university libraries have software preview centers; also, contact your public library to see if it has such a center.

5. **Share with a friend!** It is perfectly legal to swap titles with others—just don't make copies (that's not legal). Organizations for computer-users provide an excellent source for sharing software.

6. **Don't buy more than you need.** If you're a teacher, you don't necessarily have to buy a "school edition." Some vendors charge schools more for software titles so they can provide backup disks and lesson ideas. If you're interested in the software only, ask for the lower-priced "consumer" version.

Keep in mind that owning a few good titles is far wiser than owning many mediocre ones. Like a favorite toy, a well-designed program will be used over and over by young children.

Quality Criteria

In Chapter 4, you can read about the detailed software evaluation instrument that we used in rating the 501 software programs described in this year's *Buyer's Guide*. However, a much handier reference for your own use in judging software is the following "quality checklist," which we distilled from our detailed evaluation instrument. You should look for software with these characteristics:

Easy to use The program should start as soon as the computer is turned on, or the program should begin with a simple picture menu. Program formats should use a mouse or else only a few keys (if the child must use the keyboard). Instructions should be clear.

Interactive The best programs are the ones that require frequent reactions, decisions, or creative input from the child. The computer's response to the child's input should not involve delays.

Childproof The designers of good software know that children will experiment with all the keys. Good programs can handle busy fingers and an occasional elbow without "locking up."

Designed with features for teachers and parents   Look for special menus adults can use to control the sound, add new challenges, or review what a child has done while using the program. Well-designed programs not only have such options but also have clearly written instructions describing the options.

Strong in content   If you can't put your finger on the content, it's probably weak. Worthwhile programs give the impression that they're about something: language, patterns, classification, numbers. Programs that offer a range of topics or challenges within a topic are preferable over those with a limited scope.

Child-controlled   A program should not leave the child feeling trapped in an activity: It should be easy to pause, finish up quickly, go on to another activity, or stop altogether (for example, by using the ESCAPE key). "Child-controlled" software also gives a child many appropriate choices.

Designed to aid learning   Clear pictures and interesting sounds related to the learning activity—not just displays of color and fanfares of sound—are signs of good design for learning. Programs that offer novel challenges each time they are used and that provide instant feedback on a child's responses are superior. Automatic adjustment— moving up or down in degree of challenge—in response to the child's performance is another design feature that aids learning.

Worth the price   The price of the program must be weighed against what you get for your money. Check whether the price is above or below the average price of software, how many activities you get for your money, and what the program "package" includes. Consider also the longevity of a program—how long it might hold a child's interest or how much classroom use it will get—to decide if a program is worth its price.

If a program has most of the qualities we've just listed, there's a good chance children will both benefit from and enjoy using it. Though a checklist can help to identify good software, there is no substitute for actual testing by young children. The programs we describe next are ones that will survive both the checklist and child testing.

1992 AWARD-WINNERS

Of the 501 programs evaluated in the *Buyer's Guide*, we have selected 4 to receive High/Scope's "Best Early Childhood Software" award for 1992. The following programs are award-winners because they meet most of the criteria on our checklist and because we have observed children in the three- to seven-year age-range enjoying and benefiting from each of them.

High/Scope's 1992 Award-Winners

KidPix by Broderbund Software
Kids Works by Davidson and Associates
The Playroom by Broderbund Software
The Treehouse by Broderbund Software

High/Scope Award-Winners in Previous Years

Color Me by Mindscape, Inc. (1988, 1990)
Color 'n' Canvas by Wings for Learning (1991)
Counting Critters by MECC (1990)
Explore-a-Story by D.C. Heath (1988)
Exploring Measurement, Time, & Money by IBM Educational Systems (1990)
KidsTime by Great Wave Software (1990, 1991)
Mask Parade by Springboard (1988)
Math and Me by Davidson and Associates, Inc. (1988)
Muppets on Stage by Sunburst Communications, Inc. (1988)
Observation and Classification by Hartley Courseware, Inc. (1988)
Picture Chompers by MECC (1991)
Playroom, The by Broderbund Software (1990, 1991)
Stone Soup by William K. Bradford Publishing (1990, 1991)
Ted Bear Games by Baudville (1991)

KidPix

Produced in 1991, *KidPix* by Broderbund is a slightly wacky drawing program you simply must try. While it is easy enough for three-year-olds to operate, it seems to enthrall adults as well. *KidPix* successfully turns your computer into a (self-cleaning) art corner, complete with unlimited supplies of paper, glitter, rubber stamps, patterned paint rollers, confetti, paint—even melting ice cream cones.

Originally designed by a father for his three-year-old son, this program captures the spirit of a curious child. The *KidPix* drawing screen appears immediately when the program is started. The drawing area resembles a blank sheet of paper, bordered above by 3 pull-down menus; on the left, by 12 drawing tools; and below, by a tool-options menu bar. You draw by selecting a tool and then holding the mouse button and moving the mouse. As with other good children's drawing programs, such as *Color Me* or *Color 'n' Canvas*, nothing is hidden from view. When the drawing is printed, everything seen in the drawing area appears in the same size on the printed paper.

A sample screen from *KidPix* (Mac)

Those who've tinkered a bit with *MacPaint* or *Color Me* are familiar with drawing program "basics": lines, shapes, a paintbrush with a variety of tip sizes, spray paint, cut-and-paste tools, fill tools, erasers, different shapes, and a palette of basic colors. *KidPix* has these and more, which is what makes it stand out from earlier drawing programs. Consider these features:

- *Colored stamps* (112) so children can easily add a herd of dinosaurs to a picture and can edit or create their own stamps.

- *A range of exciting sound effects*, i.e., the noise of an explosion when erasing a screen, the noise of a diesel truck when cutting and pasting, or the sound of gurgling paint when filling in an area. (Don't worry teachers—these sounds can be turned off, too).

- *An electric mixer* that allows children to miniaturize, scramble, animate, or slice up their pictures to the beat of African drums.

- *A "Wacky Brush"* that enables children to draw with dribbling ice cream, branching lines, linked pretzel shapes, dripping slime, squiggles, symmetrical forms, number lines (can be used to make and print dot-to-dot puzzles), and letter strings that can be customized to include any text (ideal for a child's name).

- *A random paint mixer* that cycles through the color palette as the brush is moved across the drawing screen, creating colorful blends and patterns.

- *A "small kids' mode"* that allows an adult to eliminate the pull-down menu bar so there's less chance of a small child opening a menu and choosing an item accidentally.

The only drawback we've seen with *KidPix* is that there are so many powerful choices children can quickly clutter the screen before they fully understand all the possibilities. Some adult support during the initial introduction is helpful. We would also like *KidPix* to have a better text-generation capacity. While a set of capital-letter stamps is available, the time-consuming process of choosing each letter made it difficult for children to add much text to their pictures. In this, *KidPix* passes up an opportunity to provide language experiences appropriate for young children. A drawing program that does have this feature is *Easy Color Paint* by MECC (reviewed in Chapter 3).

The IBM and Macintosh versions of *KidPix* have only minor differences in design and performance. The IBM version has a Spanish-language option and a music library of six sound effects, and works with the "Sound Blaster," PS/1 Audio Card, Tandy Digital Sound, and Disney Sound Source for quality sound. The Macintosh version makes use of the Macintosh's built-in sound capacities, offering twice as many colors on its palette and having the ability to record sounds. It should also be noted that the IBM version requires a hard disk drive (also recommended for the Macintosh) a mouse, VGA, MCGA, EGA, or Tandy graphics. Another good drawing program for the Macintosh is *Easy Color Paint* by MECC, which puts more emphasis on artistic features but is more complicated. For the IIGS, we suggest *Color 'N' Canvas* by Wings for Learning. For the older Apple IIs with a mouse, the best drawing program is *Color Me* by Mindscape.

Because there are multiple ways to succeed at any time and it is easy to "undo" any action, a child feels in control and competent. *KidPix* meets all our criteria for age-appropriate childhood software.

Kid Works

A kindergarten teacher recently described her ideal software package: "Someone should combine three programs into one—the 'friendly' word processing capacity of *Muppet Slate* (see page 126) with the creative drawing capacities and ease-of-use of *Color Me* (see page 56), with the speech capacity of *Dr. Peet's TalkWriter* (page 66). This would give my children the chance to connect meaningful illustrations with their writing." Well, it is clear that someone at Davidson and Associates has been talking to kindergarten teachers! The result is *Kid Works*.

This 1991 program by Davidson and Associates starts simply: turn on the computer and see "Story

A sample Kid Works screen (IBM)

Writer," a blank pad that resembles a sheet of primary school paper and lists a range of options via two picture-menu bars. This is exactly what is needed in a word-processing program for young children—the child simply turns on the computer and is presented with writing space just waiting to be filled. An online "help" option is available (by clicking the "?" button at any point), although the program's design rarely necessitates its use. A scroll bar allows the page to be moved up and down. The program's "Story Writer" word-processor has all the basics: word wrap; large (20-column) or small (40-column) letters; upper and lower case letters; responsive keyboard action; insert or typeover modes; and the ability to easily clear the screen, print, or save work.

After a little practice, our kindergarten children found it easy to move words or pictures around with the mouse and the "move" button. There are two other noteworthy features to this part of *Kid Works*: the icon libraries and use of synthesized speech. The icon selections consist of four libraries of 245 color icons, or picture stamps, classified into *things, actions, descriptions/locations,* and *my words*, which features a custom list of word-pictures that can be created using the icon editing option. The point-and-click interface makes it easy to mix pictures and text. Speech is used throughout the program. In addition to the talking "help" menus, speech can be set so that the computer "reads" each word or sentence as it is entered. At any time, a word or sentence can be highlighted with the mouse and read by clicking on a mouth-shaped icon. The speech quality is quite dependent on the external speech adapter. While the program will run without it, the speech sounds scratchy and is difficult to hear using only the PC's internal speaker.

A finished story can be illustrated with the "Story Illustrator," a drawing program easy enough for preschoolers to use that allows the creation of half-screen pictures for the story. The "Story Illustrator" contains these basic art tools: 16 colors; a drawing crayon; and buttons for drawing straight lines, undoing, erasing, filling, making circles and squares, and spray painting. In addition, text can be incorporated into the pictures, and 66 black and white picture stamps are available. Moving back to the "Story Writer" is easily achieved by clicking on the "Story Writer" button. When the picture is finished, it is saved and the child is asked if the picture should be put in the story. If so, a miniature version of the illustration (similar to a slide) is incorporated into story text and can be moved around for use in the "Story Player," which is described next. The program comes with 12 background pictures.

The "Story Player" handles the performance function of the story. It divides the screen into two halves—the top for illustrations and the bottom for text. Clicking on the "GO" button causes the story to be read by the computer, showing the illustrations on the top half of the screen at the points where they should be inserted in the story text. Stories and illustrations can also be printed on paper at this time. The "Story Player" promotes a sense of personal accomplishment, offering children the opportunity to see their work "brought to life."

To reach the *Kid Works* control panel, all an adult has to do is press the F1 key. This feature allows adults to change text sizes, access the various activities, make adjustments to speech volume, access the disks, and control the features of the speech synthesizer. It also permits the use of phonetic spelling for children's names and other words the synthesizer may not recognize. The control panel meets the needs of both parents and classroom teachers. The program user's guide is also very useful, clearly illustrating each feature of the program.

To run *Kid Works*, you will need an IBM or compatible computer with VGA graphics; at least 2MB of hard disk space; a mouse; and an operating speed of at least 8 Mhz. An external speech device is not required, but highly recommended. Devices supported on the installation menu—one of the most complete available—are the Ad Lib Card; Sound Blaster; Tandy with a Sound System; PS/1 Audio Card; Echo PC II; Hearsay 11, 500, or 1000; Covox Speech Thing; and IBM Speech Adapter. A color printer is also recommended.

Kid Works capitalizes on the power of less-expensive IBM-compatible computers and makes the IBM option more viable for schools. We'd been looking for this kind of program for the IBM family of computers for quite awhile, and we are pleased to see that the gap has been filled. This is an outstanding early literacy activity for young children.

The Playroom

This 1989 program by Broderbund Software defies simple description. It impresses us especially with its variety of content, its ease of use, and its high degree of child-control. The content ranges from language, math, and time concepts to fantasy play with animated toys—a variety of activities that provides something for any child in the three- to seven-year age-range. The program format—each object in the playroom is the key to an activity—was the first in giving children an easy and enticing way to interact with the computer.

The Playroom's main menu

The designers of *The Playroom* were obviously aware of young children's ability to (1) use a mouse and (2) understand consistent icon menus. The playroom scene, which contains more than a dozen toys—books, a computer, a one-eyed monster, to name just a few—is the program's menu. For example, clicking the mouse button on the one-eyed monster causes the monster to keep its eye on you as you move around the playroom. If you click on the ABC book, you're transported to a street scene where letters are turned into related objects that can be moved—an "A" may turn into an apple, for example (we've seen children as young as three enjoy this activity). The playroom's spinner toy leads to activities allowing both exploration and, if desired, practice with numbers. To change to a new activity, you simply return to the playroom scene by clicking the mouse on the ever-present playroom icon.

With this type of picture menu, three-, four- and five-year-olds using the program in the High/Scope demonstration classroom discovered their way, without any adult introduction, into most of *The Playroom*'s activities. However, adult assistance was needed to help them discover some of the deeper challenges of the program.

For older children, *The Playroom* includes a "Mousehole Game," which we've seen six- and seven-year-olds use and enjoy. It is a three-level board game in which children roll dice and count to advance on a playing board; the game can incorporate other number strategies, such as adding and subtracting, as well.

Although *The Playroom*'s choice of content is rather standard—beginning letter, number, and clock-reading concepts—the program presents these in novel ways and does so at least as well as other programs dealing with this content. Most important, the program's rewarding process of discovery encourages children to stick with its activities.

The Playroom's wide variety of topics and ease of use make it a good starter program for the preschool or kindergarten classroom. These features make it a good choice for children's home use, as well. For older children, *The Treehouse* (see next review) offers a similar kind of program with expanded content and challenge.

The Treehouse

Most treehouses are found in backyards and are places where children go to have fun, escape from parents, and be in control. Now there's an indoor "treehouse" that also fits this description. Designed with the same easy-to-use interface as *The Playroom* (see previous review), this 1991 program by Broderbund represents the state-of-the-art in children's software. *The Treehouse* contains many colorful, exciting activities presented in a variety of attractive formats. It is well suited to the six- to eleven-year age range, and several of the activities are appropriate for some kindergartners. Educational content covers using various quantities of money, adding and subtracting, drawing, comparing pitch, producing musical notation, reproducing the sounds of instruments in an orchestra, and reviewing history, word order, and animal facts.

The first screen of *The Treehouse* reveals two 'possums (a male and a female) asleep on a branch. Children use a mouse to select one of the 'possums, causing it to wake up and climb into the treehouse. This 'possum assumes the role of a child—playing games, asking for help, and even getting hungry and tired. Twenty different routines, or games, are available once the 'possum is "inside" the treehouse. Each routine provides a cleverly animated activity sequence. There is also a chalkboard with four colors and an eraser for drawing, and a calendar that displays different historical facts about the current day. A digital clock shows the current time (taken from the computer's internal clock).

Some of the animated routines are surprisingly vivid—a spider eats a fly, an owl offers help if needed, and a peanut falls down on the ground only to be consumed by a hoard of hungry ants. A telescope near the window provides a look at the outside world. Clicking on a nest causes a bird to fly in and feed its babies. A fluffy cloud outside the window changes into different shapes. We observed children activating these little routines over and over again; they seemed to take a personal interest in their 'possum, as it periodically requested food or a nap.

A look inside
The Treehouse

Four of *The Treehouse* items—a board game ("Road Rally Games"), a musical keyboard ("Musical Games"), a puppet theater ("Treehouse Theater"), and an animal book ("Backyard Zoo Games")—lead the user out of the treehouse into separate game areas where fun and learning activities continue. An important design note: returning to the treehouse at any point is as easy as pressing the ESCAPE key or clicking on a small "treehouse" button. Following are descriptions of each of the main activities.

"Road Rally Games" is a board game that provides experience with base 10 and units of money. Children can play against a friend or the computer. A 24-intersection roadmap has a car for each player. Clicking on the dice icon determines the number of "blocks" that can be moved. With each roll, the player is asked to solve a simple addition problem; correctly solving the problem wins more points. The first player to get to the goal wins a trophy, which appears in the treehouse. Our children found this activity to be a little confusing at first and needed help to get started.

"Musical Games" offers three musical activities: a 17-key keyboard with a song library, an orchestra tour, and a maze game in which the child matches a short melody to written notes and moves through passageways to win a trophy. It's easy for children to create music on the keyboard by clicking on the keys with the mouse or by pressing the middle or lower row of letter keys. As a note is played, it automatically appears on the staff line—an excellent way for children to experiment with musical notation. Children's music can be saved or printed, as can any of the 40 short tunes in the songbook. In the tour of the orchestra, the child can click on an orchestra seating-chart to see each instrument and learn about its history. An accompanying cassette tape includes a song featuring each orchestra section. "Musical Games" is an excellent activity for what can be a typically barren curriculum area in some schools.

"Treehouse Theater" fosters creation of short, animated, and scripted sequences, in which a child constructs sentences using elements of "who/what," "does what," "where," and "when." Any combination of eight actors (e.g., "a baby"), eight actions (e.g., "eats pickles"), six background scenes (e.g., "at the beach"), and four times (e.g., "at night") can be combined on the screen, creating a broad range of possibilities. One child created and printed one sequence and used it as a greeting card. Clicking on the "director" button activates the corresponding animated sequence. This activity also contains a "prop" option with 48 colorful items (e.g., a beachball) that can be pasted onto the scene. The resulting scripts can easily be saved or printed. The best part of this activity is that children don't seem to have the slightest idea they are learning about grammar!

In "Backyard Zoo Games," children categorize and learn facts about 45 animals native to the United States. By clicking on seven categories (i.e., "warm-blooded," or "eats plants"), a child views the animals in each category, along with fact cards. The animals can then be moved onto a backyard scene that can be saved or printed. In a second activity, a mystery animal is hidden and the child uses category clues to guess its identity. It is possible to play this game with a friend or against the computer. The child who makes the fewest guesses receives a prize that shows up back at the treehouse.

The Treehouse is the largest and most technically advanced program we've reviewed. It requires an IBM or compatible computer with 640K; VGA, EGA, MCGA or Tandy graphics; and a hard disk drive with at least 3MB of available memory. It can be used with a regular keyboard, although a mouse or joystick is recommended. A separate sound device is also recommended. *The Treehouse* version we reviewed supports the Disney Sound Source, the AdLib card, the Sound Blaster, the PS/1 Audio card, and Tandy digital sound. We reviewed the program using the Disney Sound Source device and were very impressed with its clever sounds and clear speech. Apple II and Macintosh versions will be released in the spring of 1992. It is important to note that several activities ("Animal Album," "Treehouse Theater," and half of the chip game) are not included in the Apple II version.

The only major problem we encountered in using this program concerned the copy protection puzzle, which requires reference to the user's guide to match a shape every fifth time the program is loaded. But the user's guide is clear and concise. In fact, as a separate book for children, it contains information about real 'possums and songs sung in the activity sequences. Also included with the guide is a cassette tape with three songs related to *The Treehouse* activities.

Like *The Playroom*, *The Treehouse* is a program children will want to use again and again. We've seen how it successfully captures a child's imagination, mixing real-world experiences and meaningful problem solving with the types of fantasies children love. Once again, the team at Broderbund has come up with a program that advances children's software to a new level.

Where to Obtain More Details

More information about these award-winning programs, along with information about all the other programs High/Scope has surveyed, can be found in

Chapter 3, Software Descriptions. A software description gives you such specific information as a program's price and quality ratings. Chapter 2 introduces the software descriptions and the High/Scope rating system.

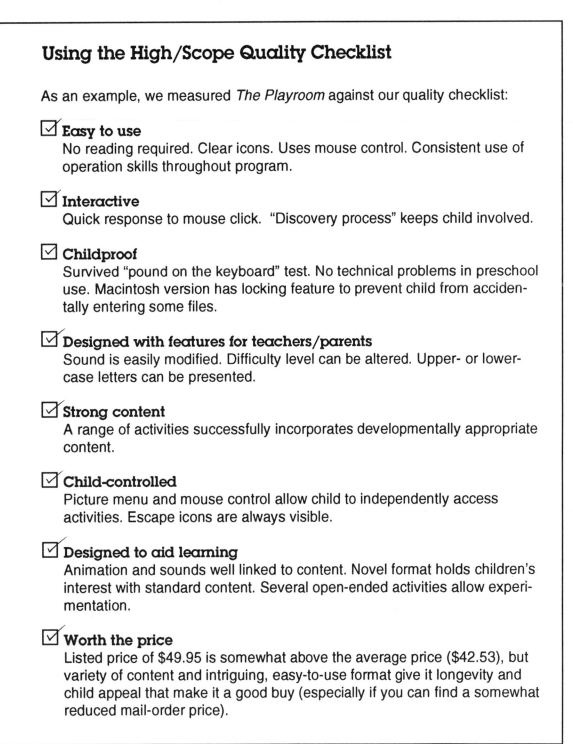

Using the High/Scope Quality Checklist

As an example, we measured *The Playroom* against our quality checklist:

☑ **Easy to use**
No reading required. Clear icons. Uses mouse control. Consistent use of operation skills throughout program.

☑ **Interactive**
Quick response to mouse click. "Discovery process" keeps child involved.

☑ **Childproof**
Survived "pound on the keyboard" test. No technical problems in preschool use. Macintosh version has locking feature to prevent child from accidentally entering some files.

☑ **Designed with features for teachers/parents**
Sound is easily modified. Difficulty level can be altered. Upper- or lowercase letters can be presented.

☑ **Strong content**
A range of activities successfully incorporates developmentally appropriate content.

☑ **Child-controlled**
Picture menu and mouse control allow child to independently access activities. Escape icons are always visible.

☑ **Designed to aid learning**
Animation and sounds well linked to content. Novel format holds children's interest with standard content. Several open-ended activities allow experimentation.

☑ **Worth the price**
Listed price of $49.95 is somewhat above the average price ($42.53), but variety of content and intriguing, easy-to-use format give it longevity and child appeal that make it a good buy (especially if you can find a somewhat reduced mail-order price).

2

INTRODUCTION TO THE
SOFTWARE DESCRIPTIONS

This chapter contains (1) a guide to interpreting the software descriptions and ratings in Chapter 3; (2) a summary of software information; and (3) an alphabetical index of software titles, indicating the page numbers of the program descriptions in Chapter 3.

INTERPRETING THE SOFTWARE DESCRIPTIONS AND RATINGS

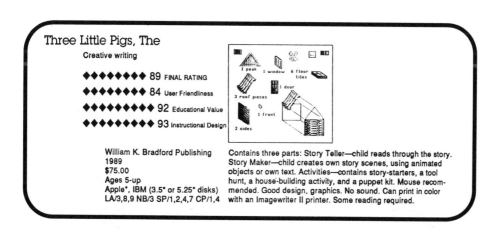

Three Little Pigs, The

Creative writing

◆◆◆◆◆◆◆◆ 89 FINAL RATING

◆◆◆◆◆◆◆◆ 84 User Friendliness

◆◆◆◆◆◆◆◆◆ 92 Educational Value

◆◆◆◆◆◆◆◆◆ 93 Instructional Design

William K. Bradford Publishing
1989
$75.00
Ages 5-up
Apple*, IBM (3.5" or 5.25" disks)
LA/3,8,9 NB/3 SP/1,2,4,7 CP/1,4

Contains three parts: Story Teller—child reads through the story. Story Maker—child creates own story scenes, using animated objects or own text. Activities—contains story-starters, a tool hunt, a house-building activity, and a puppet kit. Mouse recommended. Good design, graphics. No sound. Can print in color with an Imagewriter II printer. Some reading required.

Title: The program's title

Date: The program's most recent copyright date.

Company: The program's publisher. This is not necessarily the name of a software distributor. The address and phone number of the program's publisher are given in Appendix 1: Early Childhood Software Producers.

Price: The publisher's list price for the version of the program evaluated. Prices often vary with the type of computer and source of software. If the program is part of the ShareWare distribution system, it will be noted.

Age: The publisher's recommended age-range for the users of the program. Many software packages contain more than one game or activity, and the specified age-range takes into account the difficulty levels of all the various games or activities available. We mention in our comments if the publisher's recommended age-range seems inappropriate.

Computer: A listing of the computers for which versions of the program are available. A star (*) is placed after any versions used in evaluating the program. Any additional hardware a program requires or can utilize, such as a speech synthesizer, a mouse, additional memory, a printer, is listed.

Apple—Apple II family with at least 48K of memory

IIGS—Apple IIGS specific software. Note that this software will not run on the Apple IIe or IIc computers.

Amiga—Commodore Amiga

Atari—Atari 400, 800, or 1200

Atari ST—Atari ST

C64—Commodore 64

Nintendo—Nintendo

IBM—IBM Personal Computer or compatible with color graphics adapter, IBM PS/2 series, IBM PCjr

Mac—Macintosh

TRS 80—TRS 80 computer

TI—Texas Instruments

If more specific computer information is required, e.g., 3.5-inch disk availability, we make every attempt to list this information in this space. However, it is safest to call the producer directly before ordering. See Appendix 1 for a listing of producers' phone numbers.

Conceptual Area: A listing, from strongest to weakest, of the conceptual areas present in a program. The codes used refer to the chart found in Chapter 4. For example, CL/1 refers to the first item under the conceptual area of Classification, "Identifying attributes." (High/Scope Curriculum users will recognize the Conceptual Area lists as incorporating the curriculum's "key experiences.") The line under the title contains a short description of the computer program's goals or objectives as stated by the producer.

Comments: An overview of the program, what the child does when using the program, its strengths and weaknesses, and any special equipment requirements.

Interpreting the Ratings: The Early Childhood Software Evaluation Instrument (Chapter 4) rates each program with an *overall score*, which is the mean of nine component scores; with three *summary scores*, which are means of selected component scores; and with nine *component scores*. (Each of these elements is defined, starting on the next page.) The diagram on the following page indicates how the three levels of scoring are related.

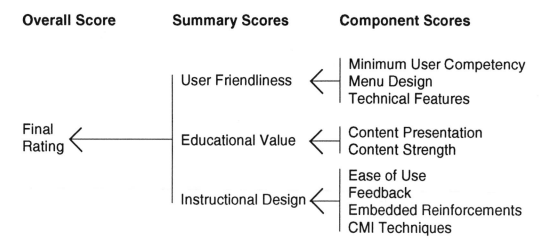

All scores are percents from 1 to 100 based on a program's performance on the evaluation instrument (Chapter 4). The scores are displayed in numerical form and as a bar graph with a row of 1 to 10 diamonds. (For example, 47% = ◆◆◆◆.) An "nr" is listed if the title is not rated. The software was evaluated with the assistance of the children and teachers in the High/Scope demonstration classroom at the High/Scope Educational Research Foundation in Ypsilanti, Michigan. Scoring was done by Warren Buckleitner.

Overall Score **Final Rating:** The mean score of all nine component scores.

Summary Scores **User Friendliness:** The mean score of Minimum User Compe-
Selected component tency, Menu Design, and Technical Features.
scores are combined
into the following scores **Educational Value:** The mean score of Content Presentation and Content Strength.

Instructional Design: The mean score of Ease of Use, Feedback, Embedded Reinforcements, and CMI techniques.

Component Scores **Minimum User Competency:** A measure of the degree of computer skill a child needs to use the program independently. A program that allows the user to enter information via picture menus and arrow keys is more suitable for a young child than is a program that requires typing words or using SHIFT keys, the CONTROL key, or the function keys. This scale covers only the parts of the program intended for the child's use. It does not consider features designed for the teacher (e.g., setting difficulty levels). The higher the score, the easier it is for preschoolers and kindergartners to use the program.

Menu Design: A rating of the ease-of-use of the menu(s). A menu is a point in the program when choices are listed and a child selects one of them and enters this choice into the computer. If the child can use and access a program menu, she or he can usually control the program without adult help. Using some menus, however, requires skills preschool children may not have, such as reading skill. The higher the score in this category, the easier the menu is for preschoolers or kindergartners to use.

Component Scores (continued)

Technical Features: A rating of technical features of the program. Does the program permit a child to experiment with *all* the keys without "locking up?" Can a teacher easily use the program in a classroom situation where there is little time to review the program instructions? Does the program make effective use of the computer's capabilities?

Content Presentation: A rating of how well content is presented, including whether the program maintains a level of challenge; whether a child controls the functioning of the program; whether the content is free from gender, racial, or ethnic bias; whether there are demonstrations; whether the program is free from unnecessary stimulation; and whether the central outcome is educational.

Content Strength: A rating of the accuracy and depth of the program's conceptual content.

Ease of Use: A rating of the program's ease of use by a first-time user. Higher scores mean easier first-time use.

Feedback: A rating of the feedback techniques employed by the program. This measures such factors as correlation between the keystrokes and screen events, appropriateness of feedback for preschool and kindergarten children, and reinforcement of content by feedback.

Embedded Reinforcements: A rating of how well graphics and sounds used for rewards complement and reinforce content.

Computer-managed Instruction Techniques: A rating of the level of computer-managed instruction (CMI) techniques employed by the program. This score includes consideration of whether the program changes levels as the child progresses and whether the program keeps ongoing records. This score is not counted if (1) the program is completely open-ended (e.g., a drawing activity) or (2) the program permits the child or adult to set the difficulty level.

A SUMMARY OF THE SOFTWARE

Background Information: Some interesting facts about the 501 programs
we reviewed—

Copyright dates range from 1980 to 1992.
Prices range from $3.00 to $16,800.00.
$42.53 is the average price for a one-title package.
68% is the average overall rating.
93% is the highest overall rating.
22% is the lowest overall rating.
64.4 is the average user friendliness rating.
75.9 is the average educational value rating.
66.6 is the average instructional design rating.
92 companies produce early childhood software.
123 programs are open-ended in nature or are used by
 a child to create a product of some kind.
74 programs incorporate speech.
57 programs utilize an Echo speech synthesizer.
93 programs can utilize a printer.
43 programs can utilize a color printer.

User Interface: This *Buyer's Guide* contains
137 programs that use the arrow keys.
105 programs that can work with a mouse.
78 programs that can work with a joystick.
26 programs that can work with a TouchWindow.
22 programs that can work with the Muppet Learning Keys.

Computer Types: Percent of reviewed software available for various brands of
computers—

Apple	376/501	75%
IBM	202/501	40%
C64	97/501	19%
Macintosh	56/501	11%
Apple IIGS	48/501	10%
Atari	28/501	6%
Amiga	14/501	3%

Software by Computer Brand

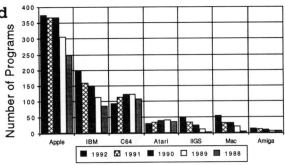

Software by Price

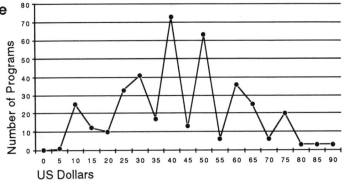

Software by Final Rating

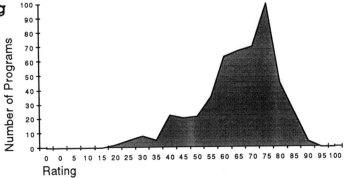

INDEX OF SOFTWARE TITLES

The following list contains the title of each program reviewed in Chapter 3 along with the page number on which it can be found.

3

SOFTWARE DESCRIPTIONS

This chapter contains an alphabetical listing of software descriptions.

1-2-3 Sequence Me

Sequencing skills

◆◆◆◆◆◆ 75 FINAL RATING

◆◆◆◆◆◆ 67 User Friendliness

◆◆◆◆◆◆◆ 84 Educational Value

◆◆◆◆◆◆ 75 Instructional Design

Sunburst Communications, Inc.
1988
$65.00
Ages 5-7
Apple
TI/2,6 LA/5

Child sees three pictures or phrases that form an ordered sequence but are placed out of order, e.g., a snowman progressively melting. By putting a 1, 2, or 3 under each box, child restores the pictures to correct order. Some reading required. Works with Muppet Learning Keys or regular keyboard.

ABC's

Coloring pictures

◆◆◆◆◆◆◆ 80 FINAL RATING

◆◆◆◆◆◆ 79 User Friendliness

◆◆◆◆◆◆ 73 Educational Value

◆◆◆◆◆◆◆ 84 Instructional Design

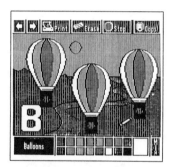

Merit Software
1986
$14.95
Ages 3-up
Apple* (128K), IBM, C64
CP/1,4 SP/4

A coloring program with 26 pictures, one per letter (e.g., an acrobat for "a"). Child moves cursor with mouse, joystick, or arrow keys to fill in sections of a picture with 1 of 16 available colors. Prints in color. Mouse and color monitor recommended. Very easy to use. Prints picture with calendar.

ABC-123 Activities for Learning

Matching, alphabetical order

◆◆◆◆ 48 FINAL RATING

◆◆◆ 39 User Friendliness

◆◆◆◆◆ 56 Educational Value

◆◆◆◆◆ 50 Instructional Design

Educational Activities, Inc.
1984
$39.95
Ages 3-7
Apple*, C64
LA/4

Two activities on one disk: Copycats—child matches three to five random or teacher-picked words by typing the letters and pressing RETURN. ABC—four activities to teach alphabet order. Reading required.

OT = Other topics   **SE** = Seriation   **SP** = Spatial relations   **TI** = Time   * = Version reviewed

Action/Music

Using the computer for speech output

◆◆◆◆◆◆◆◆ 80 FINAL RATING

◆◆◆◆◆◆◆ 77 User Friendliness

◆◆◆◆◆◆◆ 71 Educational Value

◆◆◆◆◆◆◆◆ 89 Instructional Design

P.E.A.L. Software
1985
$150.00
Ages 1.5-5
Apple
LA/8

Designed for severely visually impaired children, this package allows a child to touch a picture and hear a response (Echo speech synthesizer required). Two templates for the Muppet Learning Keys contain 12 sentence parts each, based on action words and music words for sentences like "I want you to help me eat." Intended for use with concrete materials.

Adventures of Dobot, The

Problem solving, critical thinking

◆◆◆◆◆◆◆ 70 FINAL RATING

◆◆◆◆◆◆◆ 77 User Friendliness

◆◆◆◆◆◆◆◆ 87 Educational Value

◆◆◆◆◆ 55 Instructional Design

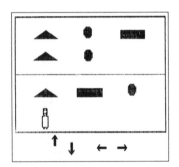

Educational Activities, Inc.
1986
$59.95
Ages 3-7
Apple*, IBM, C64
SP/4 CL/2 SE/2 OT/1

Seven simple games in which child uses arrow keys to move robot to sort letters, arrange rods according to length, match numerals, and practice with the arrow keys. Management tracks the progress of up to 50 children.

Adventures of Jimmy Jumper, The

Prepositional concepts

◆◆◆◆◆◆ 69 FINAL RATING

◆◆◆◆◆◆ 61 User Friendliness

◆◆◆◆◆◆◆◆ 84 Educational Value

◆◆◆◆◆◆ 65 Instructional Design

E.C.S.
1986
$29.95
Ages 2.5-5
Apple
LA/1,8 SP/4

A story program of 12 screens. The story is told using an Echo speech synthesizer while the graphics show prepositional concepts. Children use a game paddle or spacebar to advance the story screen-by-screen. A second version is now available.

CL = Classification   **CP** = Creative projects   **LA** = Language   **NA** = Not applicable   **NB** = Number

Alice In Wonderland

Remembering a sequence of events

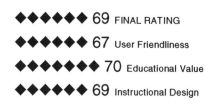

◆◆◆◆◆◆ 69 FINAL RATING

◆◆◆◆◆◆ 67 User Friendliness

◆◆◆◆◆◆◆ 70 Educational Value

◆◆◆◆◆◆ 69 Instructional Design

Queue, Inc.
1985
$49.00
Ages 7-12
Apple
LA/5,8 TI/5

Modeled from the traditional story. Child uses arrow keys and RETURN to select two-word commands to explore Wonderland. How children proceed depends on the options they choose. Requires reading. Could be used as language experience with adult help.

Alphabet Academy, The

Alphabet sequencing, letter recognition and formation

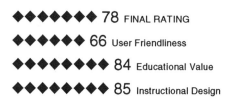

◆◆◆◆◆◆◆ 78 FINAL RATING

◆◆◆◆◆◆ 66 User Friendliness

◆◆◆◆◆◆◆◆ 84 Educational Value

◆◆◆◆◆◆◆◆ 85 Instructional Design

Hartley Courseware, Inc.
1985
$49.95
Ages 5-6
Apple
LA/4,5,6 CL/2

Three activities with clear graphics and digitized speech (Echo or Ufonic speech synthesizer needed): Sequencing—part of the alphabet is displayed and sung; child enters next letter. Letter Recognition—a letter is drawn and named; child enters that letter. Letter Formation—a letter is drawn slowly as strokes are described. Options include individualized lessons and upper/lowercase letters.

Alphabet Arcade, The

Alphabetizing, dictionary skills

◆◆◆◆ 42 FINAL RATING

◆◆◆◆ 48 User Friendliness

◆◆◆◆◆ 52 Educational Value

◆◆◆ 31 Instructional Design

Queue, Inc.
1983
$24.95
Ages 5-9
Apple*
LA/4

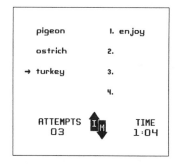

Consists of three games in which child puts letters and short words in correct alphabetical order. No branching. Not recommended.

OT = Other topics   **SE** = Seriation   **SP** = Spatial relations   **TI** = Time   * = Version reviewed

Alphabet Blocks

Letter names and sounds, alphabet, upper/lower case

◆◆◆◆◆◆◆ 85 FINAL RATING

◆◆◆◆◆◆◆ 82 User Friendliness

◆◆◆◆◆◆◆ 83 Educational Value

◆◆◆◆◆◆◆ 89 Instructional Design

Bright Star Technology, Inc.
1987
$59.95
Ages 3-up
Mac (1 MB)
LA/4,5,6

Contains two disks: Letter Names and Letter Sounds. Child sees alphabet and clicks on a letter or presses a key to hear its sound or name and to see a related picture. In another mode, a talking elf asks child to find a letter by saying its name or sound. Includes a raised-letter book, so letters can be felt. Clear speech. Good for exploration of letter sounds.

Alphabet Circus

Letter recognition, alphabet order

◆◆◆◆◆◆ 68 FINAL RATING

◆◆◆◆◆ 54 User Friendliness

◆◆◆◆◆◆◆ 89 Educational Value

◆◆◆◆◆◆ 69 Instructional Design

DLM
1984
$32.95
Ages 4-7
Apple*, IBM, C64
LA/4

Child presses any key to move a hat and presses spacebar to select one of six letter-recognition, alphabetical order, or keyboard-skill activities. Good sound and graphics. Best for age 5. Some reading.

Alphabet Express

Alphabet skills

◆◆◆◆◆◆ 68 FINAL RATING

◆◆◆◆◆◆◆ 73 User Friendliness

◆◆◆◆◆◆◆ 71 Educational Value

◆◆◆◆◆◆ 62 Instructional Design

Gamco Industries, Inc.
1985
$49.95
Ages 5-8
Apple*, C64, TRS 80
LA/4,6

Child uses spacebar to select one of three letters to fill in an alphabet sequence, match upper/lower-case letters, or indicate the beginning letter for a pictured object (26 pictures in all). Allows control over the number of problems. Keeps up to 200 student records. Rather dry presentation.

Alphabet for Everyone

Letter recognition, alphabet order, letter pronunciation

◆◆◆◆◆ 54 FINAL RATING

◆◆◆◆◆ 52 User Friendliness

◆◆◆◆◆◆ 65 Educational Value

◆◆◆◆ 49 Instructional Design

Intellimation
1990
$29.00
Ages 3-up
Mac (Hypercard 1.2.2)
LA/4

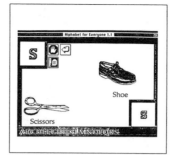

A simple letter recognition activity designed for adult literacy students with content also appropriate for the early childhood age-group. User first clicks on a letter from A-Z to select a lesson consisting of two letter-related pictures. The correct letter key must be pressed to see and hear each word. Very narrow range of content and challenge. No management options. Uses clear speech.

Alphabet Fun: Big and Little Letters

Upper/lower-case letters

◆◆◆◆◆◆ 64 FINAL RATING

◆◆◆◆◆◆ 69 User Friendliness

◆◆◆◆◆◆◆ 71 Educational Value

◆◆◆◆◆ 54 Instructional Design

Troll Associates
1991
$39.95
Ages 5-7
Apple
LA/4

Three simple activities on one disk: (1) Fun on Ice—child uses arrows to select from three upper-case letters and match one lower-case letter shown. (2) Sea Pals—child moves seahorse to make lower-case match to upper-case letter shown. (3) Cat Nap—child selects match from three letters of the alphabet shown in sequence. Entertaining graphics. Slow presentation of content.

Alphabet Fun: Learning the Alphabet

Letter recognition, alphabetical order

◆◆◆◆◆◆◆ 78 FINAL RATING

◆◆◆◆◆◆◆ 73 User Friendliness

◆◆◆◆◆◆◆◆ 88 Educational Value

◆◆◆◆◆◆◆ 75 Instructional Design

Troll Associates
1991
$39.95
Ages 5-7
Apple
LA/4

Three cleverly designed activities on one disk. Child uses the spacebar, arrows, and RETURN to match letters with corresponding pictures (e.g., Y with yo-yo) or to put a series of letters into alphabetical order. Also includes an alphabet book in which child uses arrows to flip pages. Can be set to use upper/lower-case letters.

OT = Other topics   **SE** = Seriation   **SP** = Spatial relations   **TI** = Time   * = Version reviewed

Alphabet Recognition

Letter recognition, upper/lower-case matching

◆◆◆◆ 46 FINAL RATING

◆◆◆◆◆ 56 User Friendliness

◆◆◆◆◆ 52 Educational Value

◆◆◆ 35 Instructional Design

Micro Power & Light Company
1986
$24.95
Ages 4-6
Apple
LA/4

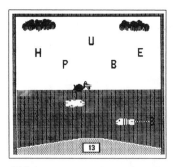

Child uses arrow keys to select one of four letters to match a letter carried by a swimming fish. If the match is correct, a point is earned. Can be set for upper or lower case. Limited content.

Alphabet Sounds

Letter sounds, initial consonants

◆◆ 29 FINAL RATING

◆◆◆ 35 User Friendliness

◆◆◆ 33 Educational Value

◆◆ 23 Instructional Design

Data Command
1984
$84.95
Ages 5-7
Apple
LA/6

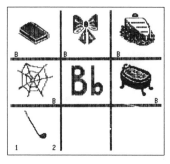

Three disks show eight pictures of each letter of the alphabet, one at a time. For vowels, a child must choose long or short (L or S); for consonants, whether the sound comes at the beginning or end (1 or 2). Smile/frown reinforcements. Low level of child-interaction. Not recommended.

Alphabet Zoo

Letter recognition

◆◆◆◆◆ 51 FINAL RATING

◆◆◆◆◆ 56 User Friendliness

◆◆◆◆◆ 52 Educational Value

◆◆◆◆ 48 Instructional Design

Queue, Inc.
1983
$29.95
Ages 3-8
Apple*, IBM
LA/4,5

Poor menu design makes maze game difficult to use. Child uses joystick or ESDX keys to move a character through randomly generated mazes. Must find each letter in sequence of a model word given above the maze.

CL = Classification   **CP** = Creative projects   **LA** = Language   **NA** = Not applicable   **NB** = Number

Alphabetization & Letter Recognition

Alphabetizing, letter discrimination

◆◆◆◆◆◆ 67 FINAL RATING

◆◆◆◆◆ 54 User Friendliness

◆◆◆◆◆◆◆ 76 Educational Value

◆◆◆◆◆◆ 69 Instructional Design

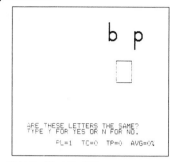

ARE THESE LETTERS THE SAME?
TYPE Y FOR YES OR N FOR NO.

PL=1 TC=0 TP=0 AVG=0%

Milliken Publishing Co.
1980
$75.00
Ages 5-13
Apple
LA/4 CL/2

First of two-disk Language Arts Series for K-8. Contains 63 levels of alphabetizing drills, from letter discrimination (child presses Y if two letters are the same) to alphabetizing to the seventh letter. Uses sophisticated password and record-keeping system.

Alphaget

Letter recognition practice

◆◆◆◆◆ 51 FINAL RATING

◆◆◆◆ 47 User Friendliness

◆◆◆◆◆ 53 Educational Value

◆◆◆◆ 47 Instructional Design

Alphaphonics
1982
$50.00
Ages 5-6
Apple
LA/4,5

Presents simple maze context where child moves "Astro" (using arrow keys) to arrange letters or letter symbols in alphabetical order. Upper/lower-case option available. Effective for practice with alphabetical order.

Amy's First Primer 2.2

Letters, counting, shapes, and spatial relations

◆◆◆◆◆◆◆ 71 FINAL RATING

◆◆◆◆◆◆◆ 70 User Friendliness

◆◆◆◆◆◆◆ 84 Educational Value

◆◆◆◆◆◆ 62 Instructional Design

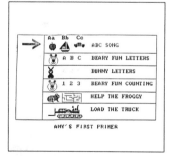

Aa Bb Cc
🦀 ⛵ 🐟 ABC SONG
🐻 A B C BEARY FUN LETTERS
🐰 BUNNY LETTERS
🐻 1 2 3 BEARY FUN COUNTING
HELP THE FROGGY
LOAD THE TRUCK

AMY'S FIRST PRIMER

Software Excitement!
1991
$3.00
Ages 4-8
IBM
LA/4 NB/3 CL/2 SP/4

Six simple activities on one disk allow a child to play an illustrated ABC song, match letters and pictures using the keyboard, draw a line from a picture to the correct letter, count sets of objects from 1 to 9, move a frog through a simple maze using the arrow keys, and create simple shape sets that match a model. An excellent software value for the 3-to-5-year-old age-range.

Animal Alphabet and Other Things

Letter recognition, alphabetical order

◆◆◆◆◆◆◆◆ 81 FINAL RATING

◆◆◆◆◆◆◆◆ 87 User Friendliness

◆◆◆◆◆◆◆◆ 89 Educational Value

◆◆◆◆◆◆◆ 73 Instructional Design

Queue, Inc.
1986
$29.95
Ages 3-6
Apple
LA/1,4,6

Child presses a key, e.g., A, to see that letter on the screen. Pressing A again causes the letter to turn into an alligator. Pressing spacebar causes the next letter in the alphabet to appear. There are 26 pictures on each side of the disk. Side 1 covers upper case; side 2, lower case. Easy to use.

Animal Hotel

Memory skills

◆◆◆◆ 45 FINAL RATING

◆◆◆◆◆ 55 User Friendliness

◆◆◆ 38 Educational Value

◆◆◆◆ 40 Instructional Design

Merit Software
1985
$9.95
Ages 4-8
Apple*, IBM, C64
OT/1

A memory game that shows either three (easy level) or six (hard level) animals and then hides each behind a different door. When shown a door, child selects animal behind that door by pressing a number key. Menu requires reading.

Animal Photo Fun

Animals and their habitats

◆◆◆◆◆◆◆ 70 FINAL RATING

◆◆◆◆◆◆ 62 User Friendliness

◆◆◆◆◆◆◆ 75 Educational Value

◆◆◆◆◆◆◆ 73 Instructional Design

DLM
1985
$32.95
Ages 4-8
Apple
OT/1

Six games in which children match animals with their habitats. Includes Animal Concentration and Animal Rummy. Child uses spacebar and RETURN to play with 36 animals from six habitats. Good graphics, sounds. Color monitor recommended.

CL = Classification   **CP** = Creative projects   **LA** = Language   **NA** = Not applicable   **NB** = Number

Animated Alphabet

Letter recognition

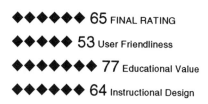 65 FINAL RATING

◆◆◆◆◆ 53 User Friendliness

◆◆◆◆◆◆◆ 77 Educational Value

◆◆◆◆◆◆ 64 Instructional Design

Software Excitement!
1990
$3.00
Ages 3-5
IBM (VGA)
LA/4

Child sees object (e.g., a quarter) and is shown the message, "What letter does this start with?" If "Q" is pressed, an animated sequence is shown (in this example, the face on the coin winks). Contains 26 sequences, each one corresponding to a letter of the alphabet. Objects appear in random order. Clever design. Limited content.

Animated Math

Counting, math facts with sums less than 10

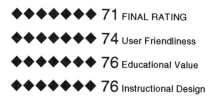 71 FINAL RATING

◆◆◆◆◆◆◆ 74 User Friendliness

◆◆◆◆◆◆◆ 76 Educational Value

◆◆◆◆◆◆◆ 76 Instructional Design

Software Excitement!
1991
Shareware
Ages 3-6
IBM (hard disk and EGA)
NB/3,4,5,6

Six rather dry activities provide practice in counting (child sees a set and clicks on numeral); matching numerals with sets; and adding/subtracting with sets of objects and numerals. Give 10 correct answers and go on to six games that include a dot-to-dot puzzle, a music box, and a rocket construction game. Employs clever, simple graphics. No adult options. Uses mouse or keyboard.

Animated Memory

Matching, memory practice, animation

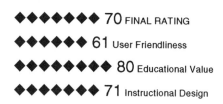 70 FINAL RATING

◆◆◆◆◆◆ 61 User Friendliness

◆◆◆◆◆◆◆◆ 80 Educational Value

◆◆◆◆◆◆◆ 71 Instructional Design

Software Excitement!
1991
Shareware
Ages 5-8
IBM (VGA and hard drive)
OT/1 CL/2 TI/2,3

A concentration game in which children use the mouse or arrow keys and ENTER to match sets of pictures and earn points. When a successful match is made, the pictures animate themselves. Four levels of difficulty ranging from 8 pictures at the simplest to 34 pictures at the most difficult. Menu requires reading. Includes a clever "Mini Movie Theater" option presenting animated sequences that can be viewed slide by slide, illustrating how animation works.

OT = Other topics **SE** = Seriation **SP** = Spatial relations **TI** = Time * = Version reviewed

Animated Shapes

Shapes and colors

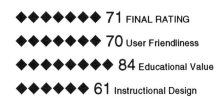

◆◆◆◆◆◆◆ 71 FINAL RATING

◆◆◆◆◆◆◆ 70 User Friendliness

◆◆◆◆◆◆◆◆ 84 Educational Value

◆◆◆◆◆◆ 61 Instructional Design

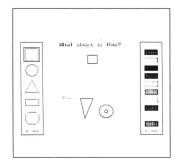

Software Excitement!
1990
$3.00
Ages 4-up
IBM (VGA and hard drive)
SP/8 CL/2

Five shapes (square, circle, triangle, rectangle, and hexagon) appear on one side of the screen; 10 color blocks are shown on the other, with a colored shape appearing between. Children use arrows and ENTER to match shapes with colors to be incorporated into a picture. When several matches are made, the picture is cleverly animated. Limited content. Entertaining graphics.

Arithmetic Critters

Counting, addition, and subtraction

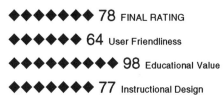

◆◆◆◆◆◆◆ 78 FINAL RATING

◆◆◆◆◆◆ 64 User Friendliness

◆◆◆◆◆◆◆◆◆ 98 Educational Value

◆◆◆◆◆◆◆ 77 Instructional Design

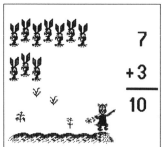

MECC
1986
$59.00
Ages 5-7
Apple (64K)
NB/3,6,7,9

Four well-designed games: adding groups of up to 9, subtracting up to 9 from a group of up to 18, measuring lengths using a worm as units, and counting in groups of 10. Allows teacher modification. Clear sounds and graphics aid the content.

Astro's ABCs

Letter recognition skills

◆◆◆◆◆◆ 62 FINAL RATING

◆◆◆◆◆◆ 63 User Friendliness

◆◆◆◆◆◆◆ 75 Educational Value

◆◆◆◆◆ 54 Instructional Design

Alphaphonics
1984
$175.00
Ages 5-6
Apple
LA/4,5

Consists of seven disks, each covering four letters. Lessons follow fixed sequence, showing alphabet, word pictures, and the letter drawn on the screen. Child then finds letter on keyboard and plays a game with the letter symbols. Child cannot control sequence. Offers effective practice with each letter.

CL = Classification   **CP** = Creative projects   **LA** = Language   **NA** = Not applicable   **NB** = Number

Bake & Taste

Reading skills, following directions

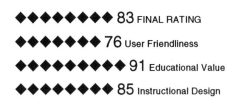 83 FINAL RATING

◆◆◆◆◆◆◆ 76 User Friendliness

◆◆◆◆◆◆◆◆ 91 Educational Value

◆◆◆◆◆◆◆ 85 Instructional Design

MindPlay
1990
$49.99
Ages 7-up
Apple, IBM (VGA)
TI/6 LA/10 CP/4 OT/5

A cooking simulation activity. Children use spacebar and RE-TURN to select recipe; find ingredients; measure out ingredients using cups, tablespoons, and teaspoons; set timers on mixers; select appropriate cooking dishes; and set the oven temperature. When the recipe is finished, the product is "tasted" by a group of friends. Errors are then illustrated. Contains 30 simple recipes that can be printed. A fun program.

Balancing Bear

Comparing amounts, additions, problem solving

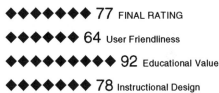 77 FINAL RATING

◆◆◆◆◆◆ 64 User Friendliness

◆◆◆◆◆◆◆◆ 92 Educational Value

◆◆◆◆◆◆◆ 78 Instructional Design

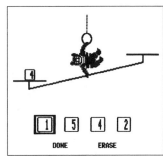

Sunburst Communications, Inc.
1988
$65.00
Ages 5-8
Apple
NB/1,2,3

Introduction to addition and inequalities. Child selects number or set that will make a scale balance. Can involve sums up to 99. Can use regular keyboard, TouchWindow, or Muppet Learning keys. Includes worksheets and classroom lesson ideas.

Bald-Headed Chicken, The

Language experience

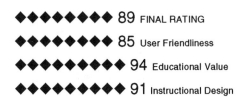 89 FINAL RATING

◆◆◆◆◆◆◆◆ 85 User Friendliness

◆◆◆◆◆◆◆◆ 94 Educational Value

◆◆◆◆◆◆◆◆ 91 Instructional Design

D. C. Heath & Company
1988
$75.00
Ages 5-10
Apple (128K)
LA/2,3,5,9 CP/4 SP/4,7

Children use mouse, Koala Pad, joystick, or arrow keys to select or move objects, backgrounds, words, or characters of a story. They can also add their own words. Resulting stories can be saved and printed in color. Includes four copies of the storybook. Good design. Fun to use.

Bank Street Writer III, The

Word processing

◆◆◆◆◆◆◆ 71 FINAL RATING

◆◆◆◆ 49 User Friendliness

◆◆◆◆◆◆◆ 88 Educational Value

◆◆◆◆◆◆◆ 80 Instructional Design

Scholastic Software, Inc.
1986
$79.95
Ages 7-up
Apple*, IBM
LA/9

Easy-to-use word processor with large (20-column) text. Effective for writing preschool experience stories. Stories can be saved, printed, and edited. Price also includes small print (40- and 80-column) version with more word processing features.

Base Ten Blocks

Develop understanding of number patterns

◆◆◆◆◆◆◆ 86 FINAL RATING

◆◆◆◆◆◆◆ 84 User Friendliness

◆◆◆◆◆◆◆◆ 92 Educational Value

◆◆◆◆◆◆◆ 82 Instructional Design

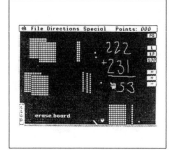

The Learning Box
1991
$59.00
Ages 5-12
IIGS
NB/1,2,3,4,5,6,7,8 SP/1,2

A range of activities in which children use the mouse to move base ten blocks to illustrate numbers, solve addition and subtraction problems, duplicate mosaic-like patterns, and guess a hidden number. Well designed. Easy to use. Offers a range of options. High in child-control. Can be interfaced with an Appleshare network. An excellent program for grades K-3.

Beginning Reading Skills

Beginning reading skills

◆◆◆◆◆ 57 FINAL RATING

◆◆◆◆◆ 53 User Friendliness

◆◆◆◆◆◆ 61 Educational Value

◆◆◆◆◆ 57 Instructional Design

MicroED, Inc.
1986
$89.95
Ages 3-6
Amiga (512K)
LA/5,6

A four-disk series that presents (using computer voice) a sentence, e.g., "A man ran." Each word of the sentence also appears randomly in one of nine boxes. The child identifies, in order, each word in the sentence by clicking the mouse on the appropriate word box. Contains 1000 words, as hard as "delve" and "gauze."

CL = Classification   **CP** = Creative projects   **LA** = Language   **NA** = Not applicable   **NB** = Number

Berenstain Bears Fun With Colors, The

Coloring and creating with stickers

◆◆◆◆◆◆◆◆ 86 FINAL RATING

◆◆◆◆◆◆◆◆ 86 User Friendliness

◆◆◆◆◆◆◆◆ 86 Educational Value

◆◆◆◆◆◆◆◆ 87 Instructional Design

Compton's NewMedia
1991
$39.95
Ages 3-9
IBM (VGA, hard disk)
CP/1,4

A 24-page computerized coloring book in which a child can use a mouse (required) to fill in the colors from a 48-color palette. Includes 95 "stickers" and cartoon-style word balloons which can be easily incorporated into a picture. Nineteen of the stickers become animated and move once they are selected. Pictures can be printed or saved. Similar to the Polarware, Inc. programs, but with more features.

Berenstain Bears Junior Jigsaw, The

Spatial problem solving

◆◆◆◆◆◆◆ 71 FINAL RATING

◆◆◆◆◆◆ 65 User Friendliness

◆◆◆◆◆◆◆ 78 Educational Value

◆◆◆◆◆◆◆ 72 Instructional Design

Compton's NewMedia
1990
$24.95
Ages 4-7
IBM
SP/1,2,4,7,9

Ten bear pictures which can be divided and scrambled into 8, 15, 40, or 60 even square-shaped parts. The child uses the mouse to click twice—once on the piece selected and next on the new location. A timer keeps track of speed and records the fastest time. Includes pull-down menus that young children will need help using. For a better puzzle program, see "Mickey's Jigsaw Puzzles."

Berenstain Bears Learn About Counting, The

Counting to 9 and other early math skills

◆◆◆◆◆◆◆ 76 FINAL RATING

◆◆◆◆◆◆◆ 77 User Friendliness

◆◆◆◆◆◆◆◆80 Educational Value

◆◆◆◆◆◆◆74 Instructional Design

Compton's NewMedia
1990
$39.95
Ages 4-7
IBM (VGA, CGA)
NB/3,4,6,7 SE/1 CL/4

Eight simple and rather dry activities in which a child matches a set to an illustrated numeral; counts sets; counts parts of a set according to one attribute; uses units to measure a line, selects the larger of two sets; and solves addition and subtraction problems with sets. Adult menu allows nice degree of control over presentation, speech, and scorekeeping options. Feedback employs speech. No speech adapter required.

Berenstain Bears Learn About Letters, The

Letter recognition, alphabet

◆◆◆◆◆◆◆ 73 FINAL RATING

◆◆◆◆◆◆ 67 User Friendliness

◆◆◆◆◆◆◆ 79 Educational Value

◆◆◆◆◆◆◆ 74 Instructional Design

Compton's NewMedia
1991
$39.95
Ages 3-7
IBM* (CGA, VGA, 2.6MB of hard
   disk space)
LA/4,5,6

Child uses mouse, joystick, or arrows to direct a skateboarding bear through a maze of forest trails. Occasionally, the child must answer a question to pass down a trail (e.g., "What letter does NET start with?") or play one of five letter-recognition games. Limited content. Uses digitized speech. Setup options allow upper/lower-case selection or control over games.

Big and Small

Concepts of big and small

◆◆◆◆◆◆ 66 FINAL RATING

◆◆◆◆◆◆ 69 User Friendliness

◆◆◆◆◆◆◆ 72 Educational Value

◆◆◆◆◆ 59 Instructional Design

Access Unlimited
1988
$25.00
Ages 3-6
Apple
SE/1

Presents two or three objects of varying size. Child indicates which object is largest (or smallest) by pressing any key when an arrow moves next to that object. Management options allow for control over sound or input method (can also be used with single switch). Designed for handicapped users. Color monitor advised.

Big Book Maker

Printing utility program

Not rated

Queue, Inc.
1990
$49.95
Ages 6-12
Apple
CP/4 LA/9

A useful printing utility program for creating book pages. Two double-sided disks. Requires the use of layers of word menus and frequent disk swapping; young children will need help. Pages can be saved or printed in color. Contains five fonts and can produce five page sizes, the largest measuring 25 by 33 inches (sheets must be taped together). Art selection includes 237 items and 22 backgrounds based on popular fairy tales.

CL = Classification   **CP** = Creative projects   **LA** = Language   **NA** = Not applicable   **NB** = Number

Big Red Hat, The

Short "a" sound and reading comprehension

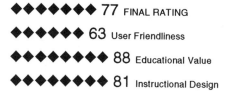 77 FINAL RATING

63 User Friendliness

88 Educational Value

81 Instructional Design

Hartley Courseware, Inc.
1989
$39.95
Ages 3-6
Apple
LA/5,6,8

Contains 10 lessons on one disk. Each lesson consists of a short story (four to seven paragraphs) and comprehension questions. Child can hear sentences or words with an optional Echo or Ufonic speech synthesizer. Makes use of animated graphics to illustrate stories. Vocabulary builds on the short "a" sound , using C-V-C Dolch words. Includes diagnostic record keeping.

Bike Hike

Memory, recall of objects

 41 FINAL RATING

57 User Friendliness

35 Educational Value

32 Instructional Design

Merit Software
1985
$9.95
Ages 4-8
Apple*, IBM, C64
OT/1 NB/3

Child first watches objects pass a bicycle, then uses number keys to select objects from a list shown at the end of the ride. Reading required. Two difficulty levels available. Inflexible design allows little child-control.

Bird's Eye View

Perspective and positional relationships

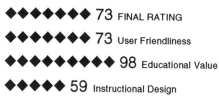 73 FINAL RATING

73 User Friendliness

98 Educational Value

59 Instructional Design

Hartley Courseware, Inc.
1987
$49.95
Ages 5-8
Apple*, IBM
SP/3,4 LA/1

A scene is shown with a bird. Views possibly seen by bird appear in a box. Child uses spacebar to select which view bird sees, based on the bird's location. Other activities allow moving the bird to correspond to a view shown. Management keeps records and allows teacher-control over the presentation.

OT = Other topics   **SE** = Seriation   **SP** = Spatial relations   **TI** = Time   * = Version reviewed

Bears Tell Time, The

Clock skills

◆◆◆◆◆◆ 68 FINAL RATING

◆◆◆◆◆◆ 64 User Friendliness

◆◆◆◆◆◆◆◆ 82 Educational Value

◆◆◆◆◆◆ 63 Instructional Design

Queue, Inc.
1987
$29.95
Ages 3-7
Apple
TI/9 NB/4

Three activities: Telling Time—child sees clock and must type in the time shown. Setting The Clock—child sees a digital time and must set the clock hands to match. Time Trials—a faster version of the first activity, keeps score. Clear, colorful graphics. Some reading required.

Body Awareness

Location of body parts

◆◆◆◆◆ 64 FINAL RATING

◆◆◆◆◆◆◆◆ 82 User Friendliness

◆◆◆◆◆◆ 65 Educational Value

◆◆◆◆◆ 50 Instructional Design

Mindscape, Inc.
1983
$61.00
Ages 3-6
Apple
SP/5 LA/5

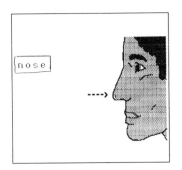

Three games on body parts. Child selects Y, N, ?, or ESCAPE for each problem. Provides practice with body part locations, names of body parts, and seasonal clothing. Provides performance summary and allows selection for number of rounds, season, and timing of cursor movement. No reading required.

Bouncy Bee Learns Letters 1.0

Letter recognition

◆◆◆◆◆◆◆ 72 FINAL RATING

◆◆◆◆ 42 User Friendliness

◆◆◆◆◆◆◆◆◆ 97 Educational Value

◆◆◆◆◆◆◆◆ 81 Instructional Design

IBM Educational Systems
1985
$51.00
Ages 4-8
IBM
LA/4

Four games: Game 1 introduces a letter. Games 2-4 provide practice with the letter in a game context using the spacebar and arrows. Management can track up to 225 children and automatically adjusts difficulty. Independent of "Writing to Read." Speech attachment optional.

Bouncy Bee Learns Words 1.0

Word knowledge

◆◆◆◆◆◆ 62 FINAL RATING

◆◆◆◆ 44 User Friendliness

◆◆◆◆◆◆◆ 87 Educational Value

◆◆◆◆◆◆ 61 Instructional Design

IBM Educational Systems
1985
$51.00
Ages 5-10
IBM
LA/5

Four activities using common words in game context. Child uses arrow keys and spacebar to match words with pictures, pick a word from one or more distractors, or identify a word as it is formed by marching ants. Management system can track 150 children. Menu requires reading. Speech synthesizer is optional.

Bozons' Quest

Cognitive strategies, left/right skills

◆◆◆◆◆◆◆ 78 FINAL RATING

◆◆◆◆◆◆◆◆ 83 User Friendliness

◆◆◆◆◆◆ 71 Educational Value

◆◆◆◆◆◆◆ 79 Instructional Design

Laureate Learning Systems
1989
$65.00
Ages 4-up
Apple
SP/4 TI/5 NB/3

Enjoyable game in which child uses left and right arrows to move creature through a grid. A voice labels each move with the direction "left" or "right" (Echo speech synthesizer required). Points are scored by capturing certain objects and avoiding obstacles. Can be used with variety of input devices, including TouchWindow. For one or two players.

Brand New View, A

Language experience

◆◆◆◆◆◆◆◆ 89 FINAL RATING

◆◆◆◆◆◆◆ 85 User Friendliness

◆◆◆◆◆◆◆◆◆ 94 Educational Value

◆◆◆◆◆◆◆◆ 91 Instructional Design

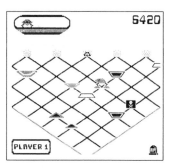

D. C. Heath & Company
1988
$75.00
Ages 5-10
Apple (128K)
LA/2,3,5,9 CP/4 SP/4,7

Children use mouse, Koala Pad, joystick, or arrow keys to select or move objects, backgrounds, words, or characters of a story. They can also add their own words. Resulting stories can be saved and printed in color. Includes four copies of the storybook. Good design. Fun to use.

Brandon's Bigbox

Letter recognition

◆◆◆◆◆ 51 FINAL RATING

◆◆◆ 35 User Friendliness

◆◆◆◆◆◆◆ 71 Educational Value

◆◆◆◆◆ 52 Instructional Design

Software Excitement!
1989
Shareware
Ages 3-7
IBM (CGA)
LA/4,5 OT/1 NB/3

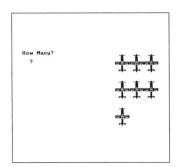

Twenty-two simple activities on one disk: matching letters; upper/lower-case matching; counting up to 9; addition facts with sums to 9; flash card word drill (custom words can be entered); matching words; counting by 2s and 4s; and concentration. Rather dry presentation at times. Menu requires adult help. A range of activities at a low price.

Bremen Town Musicians

Homonyms, context clues, comprehension

◆◆◆◆ 45 FINAL RATING

◆◆◆◆◆ 53 User Friendliness

◆◆◆◆◆ 54 Educational Value

◆◆◆ 35 Instructional Design

Troll Associates
1987
$39.95
Ages 5-8
Apple
LA/5,7 SP/4

Three games: Rebus—child places pictures on blank lines in text of story to complete the tale. Stepping Stones—child moves along a path, selecting homonyms to earn moves, e.g., "Bremen was weigh/way off." Mystery—child solves rebus puzzle. Best for ages 6 and up. Includes book.

Bumble Games

Plotting (x,y) points on a grid

◆◆◆◆ 49 FINAL RATING

◆◆◆◆◆ 55 User Friendliness

◆◆◆◆◆ 50 Educational Value

◆◆◆◆◆ 51 Instructional Design

The Learning Company
1982
$59.95 (school edition)
Ages 5-10
Apple
NB/1

Six games from easy to hard provide practice for plotting points on grid. Whether or not content is applicable to early childhood is at issue. Menu requires reading. School edition includes curriculum materials.

CL = Classification   **CP** = Creative projects   **LA** = Language   **NA** = Not applicable   **NB** = Number

Cat 'n Mouse

Relational concepts

◆◆◆◆◆◆ 65 FINAL RATING

◆◆◆◆◆◆◆ 74 User Friendliness

◆◆◆◆◆ 55 Educational Value

◆◆◆◆◆◆ 63 Instructional Design

MindPlay
1984
$49.99
Ages 5-12
Apple*, IBM
LA/6

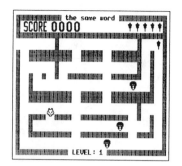

A maze game in which child earns points by moving a mouse (with joystick, mouse, or arrow keys) away from a hungry cat and correctly matching homonyms, antonyms, and picture words. Adult can add own words or change other features of the program.

Caveman Clockwork

Time concepts

◆◆◆◆ 45 FINAL RATING

◆◆◆◆ 43 User Friendliness

◆◆◆◆◆◆ 65 Educational Value

◆◆◆◆ 42 Instructional Design

BL Educational Software
1988
$39.95
Ages 4-8
IBM (VGA)
TI/9

Two parts: tutoring and practice. Tutoring describes the rationale for keeping time and illustrates 5-, 10-, 15-, 30-, and 60-minute time units, also showing the syntax for writing time. In the practice component, the child must type in the correct time on the clock shown. Rather dry presentation. Reading required.

CCC Instructional System

Instructional practice in all curriculum areas

◆◆◆◆◆◆ 78 FINAL RATING

◆◆◆◆◆◆ 75 User Friendliness

◆◆◆◆◆◆◆ 88 Educational Value

◆◆◆◆◆◆ 74 Instructional Design

Computer Curriculum Corp.
1989
Starts at $1400.00
Ages 5-17
Atari (1040ST) and other
    customized hardware
LA/1-10, NB/1-8 CL/2 SP/1,4
    OT/1,3

A networked computer system providing individualized instruction in math, reading, and language arts for K-12. Contains around 2200 hours of instruction. Management system adjusts to student's level and keeps records of progress. Prints individualized worksheets. Quality graphics, sound, and speech. We reviewed only K-1 levels.

OT = Other topics   **SE** = Seriation   **SP** = Spatial relations   **TI** = Time   * = Version reviewed

Charlie Brown's 1-2-3's

Numeral recognition, counting

◆◆◆◆◆◆ 67 FINAL RATING

◆◆◆◆◆◆ 60 User Friendliness

◆◆◆◆◆◆◆ 78 Educational Value

◆◆◆◆◆◆ 69 Instructional Design

Queue, Inc.
1985
$29.95
Ages 3-7
Apple
NB/3,4,8

Child selects a numeral and then uses spacebar or number keys to count out the number. Correct response makes 1 of 16 animated Peanuts scenes appear. Good sound and graphics. Enjoyable program.

Charlie Brown's ABC's

Letter recognition & association

◆◆◆◆◆◆ 64 FINAL RATING

◆◆◆◆ 47 User Friendliness

◆◆◆◆◆◆◆ 70 Educational Value

◆◆◆◆◆◆◆ 71 Instructional Design

Queue, Inc.
1984
$29.95
Ages 3-7
Apple*, IBM, IIGS
LA/4

Child presses any letter to see tutorial screen on the letter (letter and picture). Finding and pressing the letter again on the keyboard animates the picture with Peanuts Gang characters. Disk must be turned over to access entire alphabet. Fun to use. Potential starter program. IIGS and IBM version have speech capacity (IBM requires Digispeech Card).

Children's Switch Progressions

Cause and effect, progressions

◆◆◆◆◆◆ 65 FINAL RATING

◆◆◆◆◆ 59 User Friendliness

◆◆◆◆◆◆ 65 Educational Value

◆◆◆◆◆◆ 69 Instructional Design

R. J. Cooper & Associates
1987
$75.00 (Free preview copy)
Ages 2-up
Apple
TI/1,6

Child controls an eight-step animated sequence, such as crossing the street or changing channels on a TV, by using a single switch, the open APPLE key, or a TouchWindow. Use of an Echo speech synthesizer allows instructions to be spoken. Setup options allow control of reaction time and use of sign language (ASL) prompts. Menu requires reading.

Children's Writing & Publishing Center

Creative writing, creating printed material

◆◆◆◆◆◆◆◆ 86 FINAL RATING

◆◆◆◆◆◆◆◆ 80 User Friendliness

◆◆◆◆◆◆◆◆◆ 98 Educational Value

◆◆◆◆◆◆◆◆ 87 Instructional Design

The Learning Company
1988
$89.95 (school edition)
Ages 7-up
Apple*, IBM
LA/9 CP/4 OT/4

An easy-to-use two-disk program for use by older chldren or early childhood teachers. Combines word-processing features with a 159-picture graphics library. Picture menus allow user to select fonts (8 available), add pictures, save files on disk, or print (in color, with Imagewriter II). Compatible with "The Print Shop" graphics. Great for teachers.

Chip 'n Dale

Entertainment

◆◆◆◆◆ 53 FINAL RATING

◆◆◆◆◆◆ 69 User Friendliness

◆◆◆◆ 46 Educational Value

◆◆◆◆ 45 Instructional Design

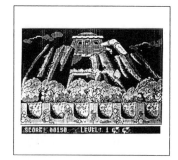

Hi Tech Expressions
1990
$14.95
Ages 5-up
IBM (CGA or EGA)
TI/1,3,4

An arcade-style game in which children use arrows or joystick to move chipmunks through nine screens of obstacles (e.g., dogs, fire balls, and grabbing hands). Each successful screen earns one part for a spaceship, which is completed at the end of the game. Good graphics. Fun game. Slow in loading from disk drive. Limited learning value.

Chutes and Ladders

Counting

◆◆◆◆◆ 58 FINAL RATING

◆◆◆◆◆◆ 65 User Friendliness

◆◆◆◆◆ 59 Educational Value

◆◆◆◆◆ 50 Instructional Design

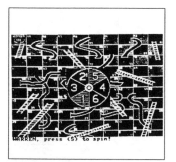

GameTek/IJE, Inc.
1988
$11.96
Ages 4-7
IBM
NB/3

A computerized version of the Milton Bradley board game. Child first spins a spinner to move a playing piece on a 100-space game board with ladders (which move a player ahead) or chutes (which set a player back). Play is for one to four players, or against the computer. Some technical problems, e.g, no control over sound.

City Country Opposites

Word meanings through context

◆◆◆◆◆◆◆ 78 FINAL RATING

◆◆◆◆◆◆◆ 74 User Friendliness

◆◆◆◆◆◆◆◆ 87 Educational Value

◆◆◆◆◆◆◆ 76 Instructional Design

Queue, Inc.
1986
$29.95
Ages 3-7
Apple
SE/1 TI/1

Presents and illustrates 20 antonym pairs. Child uses left and right arrows to alternate between pictures illustrating antonyms, e.g., push/pull. Easy to use. Good level of child-control. Includes scenes from city and country environments. Limited content.

Clock Works

Clock-reading skills, units of time

◆◆◆◆◆◆◆ 72 FINAL RATING

◆◆◆◆◆◆◆◆ 80 User Friendliness

◆◆◆◆◆◆◆◆ 83 Educational Value

◆◆◆◆◆ 56 Instructional Design

Nordic Software, Inc.
1986
$39.95
Ages 4-10
Mac
TI/9 NB/3

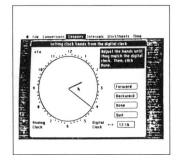

Contains five clock lessons on analog and digital watches, using time expressions and time units. Prints worksheets to go with lessons. Offers a variety of content and lesson setups. Includes a game, called 4 in a Row, that is a strategy game played against a friend or the computer.

Clue in on Phonics

Practice with letter sounds

◆◆◆◆◆◆◆ 71 FINAL RATING

◆◆◆◆◆◆ 61 User Friendliness

◆◆◆◆◆◆◆◆ 82 Educational Value

◆◆◆◆◆◆◆ 72 Instructional Design

Gamco Industries, Inc.
1989
$49.95
Ages 5-8
Apple*, C64, TRS
LA/4,5,6,7

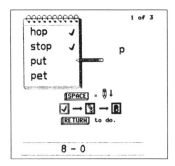

Child uses spacebar, RETURN, and arrows to move a marker to identify a blend, digraph, or dipthong in a word; to create a word by combining the correct clusters of letters; to move the letter "e" to an appropriate word; or to match vowel sounds. Keeps up to 200 student records. Good scores are rewarded with a chance to play an arcade-style game.

CL = Classification   **CP** = Creative projects   **LA** = Language   **NA** = Not applicable   **NB** = Number

Coin Works

Value of coins

◆◆◆◆◆◆◆ 71 FINAL RATING

◆◆◆◆◆◆◆◆ 81 User Friendliness

◆◆◆◆◆◆◆ 69 Educational Value

◆◆◆◆◆◆ 63 Instructional Design

Nordic Software, Inc.
1986
$39.95 (Free preview copy)
Ages 4-12
Mac
NB/3,7 TI/3,4,5

Uses a set of U.S. coins to provide practice counting money, making change, and comparing coin value. For a given coin, child can click mouse to hear computer say value. Teacher options include control over presentation and generation of worksheets. Also includes a game in which child moves mouse to deflect a bouncing ball to earn points.

Color 'n' Canvas

Visual art, drawing, painting, symmetry

◆◆◆◆◆◆◆◆◆ 91 FINAL RATING

◆◆◆◆◆◆◆◆ 86 User Friendliness

◆◆◆◆◆◆◆◆◆ 91 Educational Value

◆◆◆◆◆◆◆◆◆ 95 Instructional Design

Wings for Learning
1990
$99.00 (school edition)
Ages 6-up
IIGS (1 mb)
CP/1,4 SP/4,8 LA/9

An easy-to-use drawing program with powerful features. Ideal for elementary classrooms. Drawing tools include geometric shapes, cut-and-paste, lines and rays, fill, magnify, and a variety of brush sizes. Allows "mixing" of color elements. Teacher options include adjustment for different grade levels. Text can be added in a range of styles and sizes. Pictures can be printed or saved.

Color Find

Matching colors

◆◆◆◆◆◆ 69 FINAL RATING

◆◆◆◆◆◆◆ 77 User Friendliness

◆◆◆◆◆◆ 69 Educational Value

◆◆◆◆◆◆ 63 Instructional Design

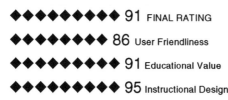

E.C.S.
1985
$19.95
Ages 2.5-5
Apple
CL/2

A simple drill-and-practice program on nine colors. When a color fills the screen, child presses correspondingly colored sticker on the keyboard. (Stickers included.) Responses are recorded. Echo speech synthesizer optional to say "press a color."

OT = Other topics   **SE** = Seriation   **SP** = Spatial relations   **TI** = Time   * = Version reviewed

Color Me

Drawing, creating

◆◆◆◆◆◆◆ 89 FINAL RATING

◆◆◆◆◆◆◆ 88 User Friendliness

◆◆◆◆◆◆◆◆ 91 Educational Value

◆◆◆◆◆◆◆ 87 Instructional Design

Mindscape, Inc.
1986
$55.00
Ages 3-10
Apple*, IBM, C64
CP/1,4 LA/3

Easy-to-use program. Our youngest children could use this program with success. Requires Koala Pad, mouse, or joystick. Child can draw, select colors, or write. Pictures can be printed in color and saved. Includes book, puppet, and picture disk.

Colors and Shapes

Color ID, visual discrimination

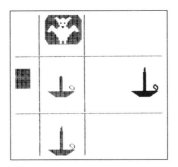

◆◆◆◆◆◆◆ 76 FINAL RATING

◆◆◆◆◆◆◆ 84 User Friendliness

◆◆◆◆◆◆◆ 88 Educational Value

◆◆◆◆ 59 Instructional Design

Hartley Courseware, Inc.
1984
$35.95
Ages 3-6
Apple
CL/1 SE/1

Consists of four activities based on matching of shapes and colors. Makes use of picture menus. Options for speed, sound, and three levels of difficulty for each activity, selected by child. Well-designed program.

Comparison Kitchen

Compare and categorize pictures

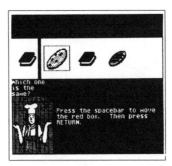

◆◆◆◆◆◆◆ 72 FINAL RATING

◆◆◆◆◆◆ 62 User Friendliness

◆◆◆◆◆◆◆◆ 89 Educational Value

◆◆◆◆◆◆◆ 70 Instructional Design

DLM
1985
$32.95
Ages 4-8
Apple*, IBM
CL/1,2 SP/8 NB/1

Six games provide experience matching shapes, colors, and sizes. Child uses spacebar and RETURN to make selections. Menu requires reading. Color monitor recommended.

Computergarten

Keyboard skills, computer terms

◆◆ 27 FINAL RATING

◆◆◆ 34 User Friendliness

◆◆ 28 Educational Value

◆◆ 21 Instructional Design

Scholastic Software, Inc.
1984
$54.95
Ages 4-6
Apple*, C64
OT/1,2,3 LA/4

A workbook set, 4' by 8' keyboard-on-the-floor, teacher's edition, and game disk are designed to teach children keyboard skills, parts of the computer, and programming in LOGO and BASIC. Includes 53 lessons. Ratings apply to software only.

Concentrate!

Short-term memory skills

◆◆◆◆◆◆ 60 FINAL RATING

◆◆◆◆◆◆ 68 User Friendliness

◆◆◆◆◆◆◆◆◆ 96 Educational Value

◆◆◆◆◆◆◆ 73 Instructional Design

Laureate Learning Systems
1988
$95.00
Ages 3-up
Apple
OT/1 CL/2 LA/1,5,6

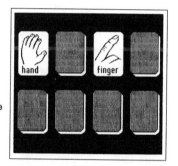

A simple game of Concentration, in which 6, 8, or 12 boxes appear face down on the screen. Child uses TouchWindow (optional) to select two boxes with matching words, which computer reads aloud as they are selected (Echo speech synthesizer, optional). Includes 40 words. Adult setup required. Keeps records. For one or two players.

Conservation and Counting

Counting skills

◆◆◆◆◆◆◆ 71 FINAL RATING

◆◆◆◆◆◆◆ 78 User Friendliness

◆◆◆◆◆◆◆ 81 Educational Value

◆◆◆◆◆ 56 Instructional Design

Hartley Courseware, Inc.
1985
$35.95
Ages 3-6
Apple
NB/1,2,3,4

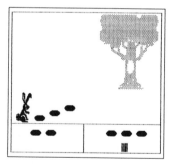

Four games in which child uses spacebar and RETURN to match sets of objects, to match numbers with sets, and to estimate quantities, all with numbers less than 10. Three levels to each game. Child can select own level or activity, using picture menus. Limited teacher options.

Consonant Capers

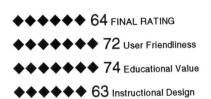

Letter and upper/lower-case recognition

◆◆◆◆◆◆ 64 FINAL RATING

◆◆◆◆◆◆◆ 72 User Friendliness

◆◆◆◆◆◆◆ 74 Educational Value

◆◆◆◆◆◆ 63 Instructional Design

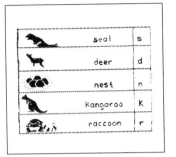

Hartley Courseware, Inc.
1989
$119.95
Ages 5-6
Apple (Echo or Ufonic synthe-
    sizer required)
LA/4,5

Four disks cover 20 consonant sounds. Each disk contains three tutorial-style activities: typing the initial consonant, matching the consonant with a picture, and choosing the picture with a given consonant. A letter matching game is used for application. Good sounds. Blocky graphics. Rigid design is scripted and leaves little child-control. Includes masters of worksheets.

Costume Ball, The

Variety of basic skills

◆◆◆◆◆◆ 62 FINAL RATING

◆◆◆◆◆◆◆ 76 User Friendliness

◆◆◆◆◆◆◆ 76 Educational Value

◆◆◆◆ 43 Instructional Design

DIL, Intl.
1986
$188.00
Ages 2-8
Apple, IBM
CL/2 SP/5 OT/1

Six disks cover a range of topics, such as hot and cold, sharp and not sharp, occupations, transportation, and other thematic material. Provides simple, but limited, activities. Includes overlays to use with WonderWorker touch tablet (recommended).

Cotton Tales

Word processing, language development

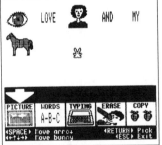

◆◆◆◆◆◆◆ 78 FINAL RATING

◆◆◆◆◆◆ 68 User Friendliness

◆◆◆◆◆◆◆◆ 88 Educational Value

◆◆◆◆◆◆◆◆ 81 Instructional Design

MindPlay
1987
$49.99
Ages 4-8
Apple*, IBM, Mac
LA/3,4,5,8,9 CP/4

Child uses spacebar, arrow keys, RETURN and ESCAPE to manipulate menus to select pictures, select words, or type in own words to create stories. Work can be printed. Library contains 192 pictures and 616 words. Up to 168 additional words can be added. Can be used with a color printer.

Cotton's First Files

Beginning database management, animals

◆◆◆◆◆◆◆ 77 FINAL RATING

◆◆◆◆◆◆ 68 User Friendliness

◆◆◆◆◆◆◆◆ 88 Educational Value

◆◆◆◆◆◆◆ 78 Instructional Design

MindPlay
1988
$49.99
Ages 5-up
Apple
CL/2,3,4,5,6 CP/4

Four activities: Peek and Find—child sees animal (e.g., cat) and picks its category. File Hunt—child sees animal and picks which of 10 categories animal is in. Clue Search—child finds animal, using attribute clues. Custom databases (category sets) can be constructed. Instructions spoken with Echo speech synthesizer. Includes 200 animals. Prints "animal data cards."

Counters

Counting experiences

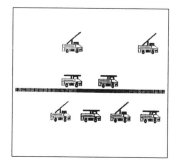

◆◆◆◆◆◆ 69 FINAL RATING

◆◆◆◆ 47 User Friendliness

◆◆◆◆◆◆◆◆ 87 Educational Value

◆◆◆◆◆◆◆ 77 Instructional Design

Wings for Learning
1983
$65.00
Ages 3-6
Apple
NB/2,3,4

Consists of three counting, addition, and subtraction activities, all with numbers less than 10. Child matches sets of objects one at a time using the spacebar or all at once using a number key. Strong content. Adult help required.

Counting and Ordering

1-9 counting, numeral recognition

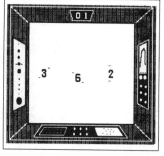

◆◆◆◆◆ 56 FINAL RATING

◆◆◆◆ 45 User Friendliness

◆◆◆◆◆◆◆ 71 Educational Value

◆◆◆◆◆ 56 Instructional Design

Micro Power & Light Company
1986
$29.95
Ages 4-6
Apple
NB/3,6

Contains two games: Crater Jumper—child counts the height of a jump to get a spaceman out of a crater. Enjoyable game. Meteor Shower—two to four numbered meteors pass by the screen. To earn points, child must press the key for the largest of the numbers. Some reading required.

Counting Critters 1.0

Counting and early math concepts

◆◆◆◆◆◆◆◆ 81 FINAL RATING

◆◆◆◆◆◆ 68 User Friendliness

◆◆◆◆◆◆◆◆ 99 Educational Value

◆◆◆◆◆◆◆◆ 81 Instructional Design

MECC
1985
$39.95
Ages 3-6
Apple (64K)
NB/3,4,7,8 CL/2

Five games on one disk. Child uses arrow keys and number keys to match numerals from 1-20, match sets with numerals, create a set corresponding to a given numeral, and use numerical order to fill in a dot-to-dot design. Clear graphics and sounds support content. Allows teacher modification.

Country Combo

Creative experience

◆◆ 26 FINAL RATING

◆◆ 25 User Friendliness

◆◆ 29 Educational Value

◆◆ 24 Instructional Design

Micro Power & Light Company
1982
$29.95
Ages 3-6
Apple
CL/1,3 CP/4

Offers a 25-square grid in which child can place 1 of 37 pieces by (1) selecting the piece and (2) typing the numeral of the location on the grid. Game too hard for young children. Reading required. Clumsy design.

Creature Chorus

Cause & effect, switch use, visual tracking

◆◆◆◆◆◆◆ 78 FINAL RATING

◆◆◆◆◆◆◆ 75 User Friendliness

◆◆◆◆◆◆◆◆ 83 Educational Value

◆◆◆◆◆◆◆ 78 Instructional Design

Laureate Learning Systems
1987
$85.00
Ages "Lower cognitive
       functioning" children and
       adults
Apple
TI/1,2

Six games on one disk. Child uses a TouchWindow, single switch, or spacebar to cause up to eight creatures to move or make sounds. Each reaction of the child yields a reaction of the critter on the screen. Requires an Echo speech synthesizer. Adult setup is required.

CL = Classification   **CP** = Creative projects   **LA** = Language   **NA** = Not applicable   **NB** = Number

Creature Creator

Pattern matching, programming

◆◆◆◆◆◆ 62 FINAL RATING

◆◆◆◆ 46 User Friendliness

◆◆◆◆◆◆◆ 78 Educational Value

◆◆◆◆◆◆ 66 Instructional Design

Compton's New Media
1983
$9.95
Ages 4-8
Apple*, IBM
TI/6 LA/10

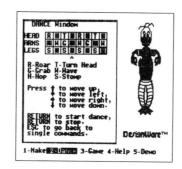

Child chooses parts of monster and makes it dance, or matches the movements of another monster. Child uses spacebar and RETURN to select monster's parts. Monster's movements can be programmed. Some reading required. Similiar in design to "Facemaker." Will not run on the Apple IIGS. Soon to be discontinued.

Curious George Goes Shopping

Classifying into categories, such as food, pets

◆◆◆◆◆◆ 65 FINAL RATING

◆◆◆◆◆ 53 User Friendliness

◆◆◆◆◆◆◆ 73 Educational Value

◆◆◆◆◆◆ 69 Instructional Design

DLM
1989
$24.95
Ages 4-8
Apple (2-sided disk)
CL/2,3,4

Includes three classification activities and an interactive story. Child uses the spacebar to indicate when an object belongs, when it is similar, or when it does not belong. Requires some reading. Good graphics, but limited content.

Curious George in Outer Space

Size comparisons

◆◆◆◆◆◆ 62 FINAL RATING

◆◆◆◆◆◆ 62 User Friendliness

◆◆◆◆◆◆◆ 78 Educational Value

◆◆◆◆◆ 51 Instructional Design

DLM
1989
$24.95
Ages 4-8
Apple
SE/1 CL/2

A computerized storybook in which Curious George blasts off in a rocket for the moon, where he solves multiple-choice size comparison problems (tall and short, long and short, big and small) to get home. Includes a tutorial. Requires switching disk sides. Reading required. Limited content.

Curious George Visits the Library

Position words (up, down, in, out, etc.)

◆◆◆◆◆ 59 FINAL RATING

◆◆◆◆◆ 53 User Friendliness

◆◆◆◆◆◆ 67 Educational Value

◆◆◆◆◆ 58 Instructional Design

DLM
1989
$24.95 ($62.00 for lab version)
Ages 4-8
Apple*, IBM
SP/4

Child indicates when George is illustrating a position word, matches a position word with a scene, or types the position word illustrated in a scene. Good graphics. Requires simple reading for independent operation. Adult help is required to get started.

Daffy Duck, P.I.

Spelling practice

◆◆◆◆◆◆◆ 72 FINAL RATING

◆◆◆◆◆◆◆ 75 User Friendliness

◆◆◆◆◆◆◆◆ 82 Educational Value

◆◆◆◆◆◆ 63 Instructional Design

Hi Tech Expressions
1991
$11.95
Ages 6-8
IBM (CGA or VGA)
LA/5 TI/3

Child uses arrows or joystick to move a duck around a maze and collect missing letters to words while avoiding hazards (e.g., hunters). Correct matches earn points and advance player to more difficult levels. Includes word-search puzzles. A fun game that effectively combines arcade-style play with spelling concepts.

Delta Drawing Today

Drawing, programming concepts

◆◆◆◆◆◆◆ 81 FINAL RATING

◆◆◆◆◆◆ 60 User Friendliness

◆◆◆◆◆◆◆ 88 Educational Value

◆◆◆◆◆◆◆ 89 Instructional Design

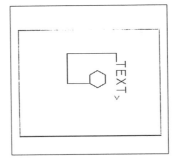

Power Industries LP
1990
$69.95
Ages 5-8
IBM
SP/4 CP/1,3,4

Offers a creative context in which single commands create pictures (e.g., "D" to draw, "R" to turn right). Each command used in drawing picture is stored as a program, which can be edited. Pictures can be printed or saved. Similar to LOGO computer language.

CL = Classification   **CP** = Creative projects   **LA** = Language   **NA** = Not applicable   **NB** = Number

Designasaurus

Dinosaurs

◆◆◆◆◆ 57 FINAL RATING

◆◆◆◆ 47 User Friendliness

◆◆◆◆◆◆ 67 Educational Value

◆◆◆◆◆◆ 60 Instructional Design

Compton's New Media
1987
$39.95
Ages 4-up
Apple*, IBM, Amiga, C64
CP/4 SP/5 TI/5

Three dinosaur-related activities on two disks: Build-A-Dinosaur—child creates a dinosaur by combining the head, body, and tail fossils of eight dinosaurs. Walk-A-Dinosaur—child controls a dinosaur as it survives through four ecosystems. Print-A-Dinosaur—prints dinosaur scenes in two sizes. Printer recommended. Requires reading and adult help. Designasaurus II for ages 7–14 is also available.

Developing Language Skills

Knowledge of words

◆◆◆◆ 45 FINAL RATING

◆◆◆◆◆ 57 User Friendliness

◆◆◆◆ 41 Educational Value

◆◆◆ 38 Instructional Design

Queue, Inc.
1983
$425.00 ($795.00 in Spanish)
Ages 3-6
Apple
LA/1 NB/4 SP/5

Twelve disks and picture books, each with 32 words about toys, clothes, food, furniture, animals, transportation, body parts, action words, outside/inside, play, colors, and numbers. Child uses arrows and RETURN to match words with pictures. Keeps records. Little child-control.

Dino Speller

Alphabetization, letter/word recognition

◆◆◆◆◆◆ 63 FINAL RATING

◆◆◆◆◆ 58 User Friendliness

◆◆◆◆◆◆◆ 75 Educational Value

◆◆◆◆◆◆ 61 Instructional Design

Troll Associates
1992
$39.95
Ages 5-7
Apple
LA/4,5,6

Three activities on one disk: (1) Dino Match shows three words starting with the same letter. Child selects the first alphabetically, using spacebar and RETURN. (2) Dino Spell shows a partially spelled word. Child types in missing letter. (3) Dino Dictionary shows an item (e.g., a bed). Child types starting letter. Contains three 26-word lists that can be interchanged with a teacher's menu. Rather dry presentation.

OT = Other topics   **SE** = Seriation   **SP** = Spatial relations   **TI** = Time   * = Version reviewed

Dinosaur Days Plus

Creation of writing and graphics

◆◆◆◆◆◆ 69 FINAL RATING

◆◆◆◆ 46 User Friendliness

◆◆◆◆◆◆◆◆ 83 Educational Value

◆◆◆◆◆◆◆◆ 81 Instructional Design

Queue, Inc.
1988
$49.95 ($99.95 for lab pack)
Ages 5-up
Apple (128K)
CP/4 LA/3,6,9

Child selects from a variety of clip-art (heads, plants, legs, etc.) to create a dinosaur scene that can be saved or printed in color. Words can be added and pronounced with the Echo speech synthesizer (optional). Our five-year-olds loved the graphics but needed help flipping between the two disks and using written menus.

Dinosaur Discovery Kit, The

Matching, picture-word connections

◆◆◆◆◆◆ 65 FINAL RATING

◆◆◆◆◆◆◆ 77 User Friendliness

◆◆◆◆◆ 54 Educational Value

◆◆◆◆◆ 59 Instructional Design

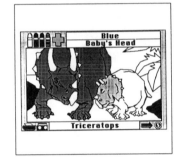

First Byte, Inc.
1988
$39.95
Ages 3-8
IBM*, IIGS, Mac, Amiga
CL/2 LA/8 CP/4

Three activities. Coloring book—a primitive coloring activity in which child uses a mouse to color a dinosaur scene one part at a time. Dinosaur match—concentration game for one or two players. Story maker—child selects endings for five simple sentences and sees them illustrated. Stories and pictures can be printed. Design confuses some children.

Dinosaurs

Reading, math, and memory skills

◆◆◆◆◆◆ 65 FINAL RATING

◆◆◆◆◆◆◆ 77 User Friendliness

◆◆◆◆◆◆◆ 72 Educational Value

◆◆◆◆◆ 51 Instructional Design

Advanced Ideas, Inc.
1984
$39.95 ($34.95 for C64)
Ages 2.5-5
Apple*, IBM, C64
CL/1,2

Games about six dinosaur breeds include matching an outline to its twin; classifying dinosaurs by what they ate, where they lived; and recognizing their written names. Uses a picture menu. Includes stickers and coloring book.

Dinosaurs Are Forever

Coloring pictures

◆◆◆◆◆◆◆◆ 80 FINAL RATING

◆◆◆◆◆◆◆ 79 User Friendliness

◆◆◆◆◆◆◆ 73 Educational Value

◆◆◆◆◆◆◆◆ 84 Instructional Design

Merit Software
1988
$29.95
Ages 3-up
Apple* (128K), IBM, C64
CP/1,4 SP/4

A coloring program with 26 blank dinosaur pictures on one disk. Child moves cursor with mouse, joystick, or arrow keys to fill in sections of a picture with one of 16 available colors. Prints in color. Mouse and color monitor recommended. Very easy to use. Prints picture with calendar, banner, or message.

Diskovery Adding Machine

Counting, addition skills

◆◆◆◆◆◆ 69 FINAL RATING

◆◆◆◆◆ 54 User Friendliness

◆◆◆◆◆◆◆◆ 80 Educational Value

◆◆◆◆◆◆◆ 74 Instructional Design

Queue, Inc.
1984
$39.95
Ages 4-8
Apple
NB/1,3,7,9

Three games: Counting—child counts and combines two sets. Number Matching—child counts two uneven sets to determine the greater. Adding Facts—child practices addition problems. Some reading required. Management prints and records child's performance.

Diskovery Take Away Zoo

Counting, subtraction practice

◆◆◆◆◆◆ 68 FINAL RATING

◆◆◆◆◆ 52 User Friendliness

◆◆◆◆◆◆◆◆ 82 Educational Value

◆◆◆◆◆◆◆ 73 Instructional Design

Queue, Inc.
1984
$39.95
Ages 4-8
Apple
NB/3,4,9

Three games on one disk. Child uses arrow keys to remove animals from sets, illustrating subtraction problems. Progresses to traditional subtraction drill, using numbers up to 9. Management prints and records child's performance.

Donald's Alphabet Chase

Letter recognition, alphabetical order

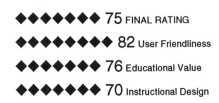

◆◆◆◆◆◆ 75 FINAL RATING

◆◆◆◆◆◆◆ 82 User Friendliness

◆◆◆◆◆◆ 76 Educational Value

◆◆◆◆◆◆ 70 Instructional Design

Walt Disney Software
1990
$14.95
Ages 2-5
Apple*, IBM, C64
LA/4

A simple letter search game. A scene (e.g., a kitchen) with five hidden letters is shown. The same five letters are displayed in alphabetical order at the top of the screen. When child presses one of the visible letters, the alphabet song plays as the matching hidden letter becomes animated and is captured. Keyboard is somewhat unresponsive at times. Upper-case letters only. Our children liked Donald's entertaining, animated routines.

Dot-to-Dot Construction Set

Counting, problem solving

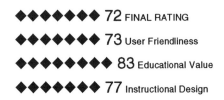

◆◆◆◆◆◆ 72 FINAL RATING

◆◆◆◆◆◆ 73 User Friendliness

◆◆◆◆◆◆◆ 83 Educational Value

◆◆◆◆◆◆ 77 Instructional Design

Chariot Software Group
1986
Shareware
Ages 4-8
Mac
NB/3 SP/7

A simple program for creating and playing dot-to-dot puzzles. A puzzle editor feature allows the creation of puzzles around existing scrapbook clip art. Puzzles can have between 3 and 125 dots, and can be made so that clip art gradually fades in as the puzzle is completed. Puzzles can be printed or saved.

Dr. Peet's Talk/Writer

Language exploration and skills

◆◆◆◆◆◆ 79 FINAL RATING

◆◆◆◆◆ 58 User Friendliness

◆◆◆◆◆◆◆ 98 Educational Value

◆◆◆◆◆◆◆ 88 Instructional Design

Hartley Courseware, Inc.
1986
$69.95
Ages 3-7
Apple
LA/3,4,5,6,7,9 CL/2 CP/4

Consists of two disks. Disk 1 includes the ABC song, finding and matching letters, and creating and listening to words. Disk 2 is an easy-to-use talking word processor that says whatever is typed, in robotic voice. Uses large letters. Echo speech synthesizer required. Stories can be saved and printed.

Dr. Seuss Fix-Up the Mix-up Puzzler

Problem solving

◆◆◆◆◆◆◆ 70 FINAL RATING

◆◆◆◆◆ 51 User Friendliness

◆◆◆◆◆◆◆◆ 83 Educational Value

◆◆◆◆◆◆◆ 79 Instructional Design

CBS Software
1985
$29.95
Ages 4-10
Apple, C64*
SP/1

A puzzle program featuring six Dr. Seuss characters. Each puzzle is randomly designed with five difficulties to choose from. More advanced levels use smaller and/or inverted pieces. Compatible with Muppet Learning Keys.

Dragon Tales

Language development

Not rated

Josten's Learning Corporation
1991
Starts at $7,000
Ages 5-9
Mac LC (CD ROM fileserver
   required)
LA/1-10

A comprehensive whole-language English curriculum consisting of 18 five-day units covering basic English sounds. Each unit contains lesson plans and materials for circle time and the computer, art, and listening centers. Includes big books and puppets, along with parent newsletters and activities. Software reads stories, asks comprehension questions, and allows child to write and illustrate own stories. An exciting language curriculum.

Ducks Ahoy!

Logical reasoning skills

◆◆◆◆◆◆◆ 78 FINAL RATING

◆◆◆◆◆◆◆ 70 User Friendliness

◆◆◆◆◆◆◆◆ 87 Educational Value

◆◆◆◆◆◆◆ 76 Instructional Design

Joyce Hakansson Associates
1984
$34.95
Ages 3-6
C64 (cartridge)
TI/3,5

A game in which children move a boat through canals to pick up ducks. Timing and selection of the best route to avoid a moving obstacle are required to collect all the ducks. Entertaining music and graphics. Joystick required. Discontinued in 1986.

OT = Other topics   **SE** = Seriation   **SP** = Spatial relations   **TI** = Time   * = Version reviewed

Early & Advanced Switch Games

Cause/effect, matching, counting, scanning

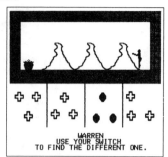

◆◆◆◆◆◆◆ 75 FINAL RATING

◆◆◆◆◆◆◆◆ 86 User Friendliness

◆◆◆◆◆◆◆◆ 87 Educational Value

◆◆◆◆◆◆ 63 Instructional Design

R. J. Cooper & Associates
1987
$75.00 (Free preview copy)
Ages 2-up
Apple
CL/2,4 TI/1 SP/4,8 CP/4

Thirteen clever games. Child uses only single switch or open APPLE key to make noises or visual effects, build a scene, play music, scan, build shapes, count, match shapes and colors, move through a maze, or construct a face that can be printed. Adult setup required. Designed for children with limited motor abilities. Echo speech synthesizer optional. Good child-control.

Early Childhood Learning Program

Conceptual skill development

◆◆◆◆◆ 53 FINAL RATING

◆◆◆ 36 User Friendliness

◆◆◆◆◆ 56 Educational Value

◆◆◆◆◆◆ 67 Instructional Design

Educational Activities, Inc.
1983
$159.00
Ages 3-7
Apple*, C64
CP/3 SP/1 TI/3

A series of five disks, all of which use one-key commands (e.g., F = forward) to move objects. Based on LOGO concepts. Gives open-ended context for exploration in directionality, planning, sequencing, etc. Animation is slow, limiting child's control.

Early Concepts SkillBuilder Series

Matching, prepositions, things that do not belong

◆◆◆◆◆◆ 60 FINAL RATING

◆◆◆◆◆◆◆◆ 89 User Friendliness

◆◆◆◆◆◆ 61 Educational Value

◆◆◆ 36 Instructional Design

Edmark Corporation
1990
$309.95
Ages 3-6
Apple
CL/2 LA/4

Children are directed to find or touch specific items in this multiple-choice-style series. Makes use of TouchWindow and Echo speech synthesizer. Consists of eight lessons that cover 170 words from categories of color, shape, and position. Makes use of clear speech and graphics, although lesson design is rather dry. Content can be altered with the Edmark LessonMaker program.

CL = Classification   **CP** = Creative projects   **LA** = Language   **NA** = Not applicable   **NB** = Number

Early Elementary I

Counting and matching

◆◆ 27 FINAL RATING

◆◆ 26 User Friendliness

◆◆ 23 Educational Value

◆◆◆◆ 40 Instructional Design

Compu-Tations
1982
$34.95
Ages 4-7
Apple*, Atari, IBM
CL/1 NB/4

TYPE THE MISSING LETTER

Presents four activities: Count Shapes, Color Match, Number Drill, and Shape Match. Contains management file and password system. Uses blocky graphics. Presentation can trap child in routines. Not recommended.

Early Elementary II

Letter recognition, counting

◆◆ 28 FINAL RATING

◆◆ 28 User Friendliness

◆◆ 23 Educational Value

◆◆◆ 30 Instructional Design

Compu-Tations
1981
$34.95
Ages 5-7
Apple
LA/4 SP/4 NB/4,8

Contains four games: Upper/Lower-case Match, Alphabet Line, Inside Out, Number Line. Includes management file. No branching. Possible to break the program. Graphics are unclear and sounds are distracting. Not recommended.

Early Games

Counting, letters, and drawing

◆◆◆◆◆◆ 60 FINAL RATING

◆◆◆◆ 44 User Friendliness

◆◆◆◆◆◆◆ 72 Educational Value

◆◆◆◆◆◆◆ 74 Instructional Design

Queue, Inc.
1984
$34.95
Ages 2-6
Apple*, IBM, Mac
CP/1 LA/4 CL/1 NB/3,8

CAN YOU MATCH THIS NUMBER?

Contains nine separate games that are strong in content. Poorly designed menu is easy to use but confusing to children. Successful in providing a variety of activities. Drawing activity pictures can be saved on disk.

OT = Other topics   **SE** = Seriation   **SP** = Spatial relations   **TI** = Time   * = Version reviewed

Early Math

Counting, numerical order, basic skills

◆◆◆◆ 43 FINAL RATING

◆◆◆◆ 43 User Friendliness

◆◆◆◆◆◆ 69 Educational Value

◆◆◆◆ 41 Instructional Design

MicroED, Inc.
1987
$49.95
Ages 3-6
Amiga (512K)
NB/3

Four programs on one disk: child counts from 1-31 objects and enters the number, completes a three-number sequence, finds the sum of two groups of 0-9 objects, or subtracts with sets of 0-9 objects. Blocky graphics. Provides verbal feedback.

Early-On

Case management and program evaluation

Not rated

Agency Systems
1990
Starts at $3,995.00
Ages na
IBM
OT/4

A computerized planning and record-keeping system designed for child care agencies that must maintain background information and individual plans (such as IEP's) for large numbers of children. Contains a built-in statistical module useful in gathering information for planning activities or measuring children's progress. Builds a goals and objectives library as it is used. Designed for networking among several sites, although a single-user version is available.

Early Skills

Shape and word discrimination

◆◆◆◆◆◆ 61 FINAL RATING

◆◆◆◆ 49 User Friendliness

◆◆◆◆◆◆◆◆ 83 Educational Value

◆◆◆◆◆ 58 Instructional Design

Hartley Courseware, Inc.
1986
$39.95
Ages 5-7
Apple
CL/2 SE/4

Child uses spacebar to match objects, colors, or words in this simple, matching, two-disk program. Design permits control over many aspects of the content and includes record keeping and automatic progress report. Menu requires reading.

Easy as ABC

Letter recognition, alphabet order

◆◆◆◆◆◆◆◆ 80 FINAL RATING

◆◆◆◆◆◆◆ 78 User Friendliness

◆◆◆◆◆◆◆◆◆ 91 Educational Value

◆◆◆◆◆◆◆ 77 Instructional Design

Queue, Inc.
1984
$39.95
Ages 3-6
Apple*, Mac, IBM
LA/4,5

Provides five games: Match Letters, Dot-to-Dot, Leapfrog, Lunar Letters, and Honey Hunt. Spacebar, JKIM keys, arrow keys, and joystick make the program easy to use. Can be used with upper/lower-case letters. Reading not required.

Easy Color Paint 2.0

Drawing, creation of visual products

◆◆◆◆◆◆◆◆ 84 FINAL RATING

◆◆◆◆◆◆ 67 User Friendliness

◆◆◆◆◆◆◆◆◆ 96 Educational Value

◆◆◆◆◆◆◆◆◆ 92 Instructional Design

MECC
1991
$89.00
Ages 6-up
Mac
CP/1,4 LA/3,9 SP/4

A full-feature drawing program ideal for K-12 art programs. Includes a full range of art techniques (e.g., brush shapes, shading, lines, geometric shapes, and cut and paste). Can be customized for young children, who will need help in using the pull-down menus. Good capacity for adding text. Includes 24 pictures to color. Products can be saved or printed in color. Recommended.

Easy Street

Classification, matching, and counting

◆◆◆◆◆◆◆◆ 84 FINAL RATING

◆◆◆◆◆◆◆ 79 User Friendliness

◆◆◆◆◆◆◆◆◆ 90 Educational Value

◆◆◆◆◆◆◆◆ 84 Instructional Design

MindPlay
1988
$49.99
Ages 4-8
Apple*, IBM, Mac, IIGS
CL/2,3 SP/4,8 LA/4,5 NB/2,3
    TI/3

Using arrow keys, joystick, or mouse, child moves a boy down a street past various storefronts in search of special objects. "Challenge Upgrade" feature offers a wide range of challenges. Optional speech synthesis makes the program easier to use (Echo speech synthesizer). Enjoyable program.

OT = Other topics   **SE** = Seriation   **SP** = Spatial relations   **TI** = Time   * = Version reviewed

Eco-Saurus

Ecology facts

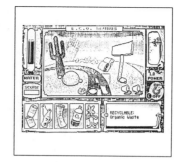

◆◆◆◆◆ 59 FINAL RATING

◆◆◆◆◆◆◆◆ 81 User Friendliness

◆◆◆◆ 49 Educational Value

◆◆◆◆◆◆ 63 Instructional Design

First Byte, Inc.
1991
$39.95
Ages 4-9
Mac, IBM* (VGA, hard disk,
    speechcard, mouse)
SP/7 OT/5

Child uses mouse or arrow keys to move through an island, finding trash and listening to characters who share ecology tips along the way. When trash is correctly sorted in recycling bins, points are earned. Some reading required. Younger children (ages 4-5) will need help. Some of the cartoonish graphics are confusing, especially at first.

Edmark LessonMaker

A utility program

Not rated

Edmark Corporation
1990
$199.95
Ages na
Apple
OT/4

A program for teachers that allows them to create multiple-choice lessons. Designed to work with the TouchWindow and the Echo speech synthesizer. See Early Concepts SkillBuilder Series and Vocabulary SkillBuilder Series for examples of lessons that can be designed with this program.

Edmark Reading Program Level 1

Beginning reading and language development

◆◆◆◆◆◆ 66 FINAL RATING

◆◆◆◆◆◆ 62 User Friendliness

◆◆◆◆◆◆ 68 Educational Value

◆◆◆◆◆◆ 67 Instructional Design

Edmark Corporation
1987
$450.00
Ages 3-up
Apple
LA/4,5,6 CL/2

Consists of 227 lessons on 15 disks, with workbooks and a storybook. Child uses the keyboard, joystick, or TouchWindow to answer multiple-choice questions that range from matching pictures to matching pictures with phrases. Instructions are spoken (Echo speech synthesizer required). Records when a child has mastered each lesson. Rigid presentation.

CL = Classification **CP** = Creative projects **LA** = Language **NA** = Not applicable **NB** = Number

Electric Company: Bagasaurus

Vocabulary development and word recognition

◆◆◆◆◆ 59 FINAL RATING

◆◆◆◆ 41 User Friendliness

◆◆◆◆◆◆◆ 83 Educational Value

◆◆◆◆◆ 59 Instructional Design

Hi Tech Expressions
1988
$9.95
Ages 6-9
Apple (128K)*, IBM, C64
LA/7,8,9

Child uses joystick (recommended) or arrow keys to move a walking dinosaur to select words or pictures that best answer a word puzzle, e.g., Where can a plant grow? Offers a nice range of questions (100) and background scenes (13). No escape from activities. Somewhat hard to control with the arrow keys.

Electric Company: Picture Place

Develop vocabulary and word recognition

◆◆◆◆◆ 58 FINAL RATING

◆◆◆ 37 User Friendliness

◆◆◆◆◆◆◆ 80 Educational Value

◆◆◆◆◆◆ 62 Instructional Design

Hi Tech Expressions
1988
$9.95
Ages 5-9
Apple* (128K), IBM, C64
CP/1 LA/6

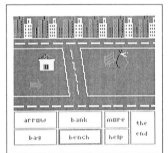

Child uses arrow keys or joystick to select word (e.g., dog) and move it into a scene. Pressing RETURN replaces the word with a picture. Resulting scenes can be saved but not printed. Has six backgrounds and 193 word/pictures. Word menus and blocky graphics limit this program's value.

Electric Company: Roll-A-Word

Word recognition, vowel sounds

◆◆◆◆ 44 FINAL RATING

◆◆◆ 37 User Friendliness

◆◆◆◆◆ 52 Educational Value

◆◆◆◆ 45 Instructional Design

Hi Tech Expressions
1988
$9.95
Ages 5-9
Apple (128K)*, IBM, C64
LA/8

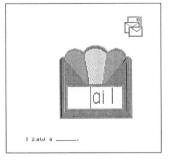

Child sees picture, incomplete sentence, and part of a word. Correctly completing the word (by typing missing letters) causes the word to move into the sentence. Possibility of creating nonsense sentences makes this confusing. Contains 90 word/picture combinations. Menus require reading, which limits child-control. No escape from activities.

OT = Other topics   **SE** = Seriation   **SP** = Spatial relations   **TI** = Time   * = Version reviewed

Electronic Builder

Shapes, spatial thinking

◆◆◆◆◆◆◆ 82 FINAL RATING

◆◆◆◆◆◆◆ 75 User Friendliness

◆◆◆◆◆◆◆ 76 Educational Value

◆◆◆◆◆◆◆◆ 91 Instructional Design

Mobius Corporation
1990
See KidWare 2
Ages 3-5
IBM
CP/4 SP/1,2,8

Child uses mouse to select one of five shape icons and then place shapes on screen to create block designs. Pictures can be filled with color (five colors available). High in child-control; limited in options and design. (For example, once shapes are placed, they cannot be retrieved.) Some teacher options. Pictures can be saved or printed.

Electronic Easel

Drawing pictures

◆◆◆◆◆◆ 73 FINAL RATING

◆◆◆◆◆◆ 74 User Friendliness

◆◆◆◆◆◆ 72 Educational Value

◆◆◆◆◆◆ 72 Instructional Design

Mobius Corporation
1990
See KidWare 2
Ages 3-5
IBM
CP/1 SP/7

Child moves finger on PowerPad (a large touch-tablet) to draw on screen. Eight colors available. Pictures can be saved or printed. Instructions are spoken. Our children were frustrated by the Power Pad's unresponsiveness to their touch. Resulting pictures appeared blotchy. See "KidWare 2."

Emerging Literacy Program

Language, independence, prediction,etc.

◆◆◆◆◆◆◆ 89 FINAL RATING

◆◆◆◆◆◆◆ 85 User Friendliness

◆◆◆◆◆◆◆◆ 94 Educational Value

◆◆◆◆◆◆◆◆ 91 Instructional Design

Jostens Learning Corporation
1991
$8000
Ages 5-6
Apple*, IBM, Mac LC
LA/3,8,9 NB/3 SP/1,3,4 CL/3
　CP/1,4

Includes 50 programs for language and math, each with cassette tapes, books, and toys that relate to themes such as "Little Red Hen" and "The Circle Game." Software is similar in design to the Explore-a-Story series. Speech is employed. Ratings apply to software only. Several titles are available in Spanish.

CL = Classification　　**CP** = Creative projects　　**LA** = Language　　**NA** = Not applicable　　**NB** = Number

ESL Writer

Word processing

◆◆◆◆◆◆◆ 79 FINAL RATING

◆◆◆◆◆ 55 User Friendliness

◆◆◆◆◆◆◆◆◆ 91 Educational Value

◆◆◆◆◆◆◆◆◆ 94 Instructional Design

Scholastic Software, Inc.
1989
$99.95
Ages 6-up
Apple
LA/9 CP/4 OT/4

A two-disk word processor for native speakers of Spanish or Asian languages. Contains a spell-checker designed to find common spelling errors made by English-learning students. Designed so corrections are made as words are typed. Uses 40- or 80-column text. Documents are limited to two pages in length. Well-designed.

Estimation

Estimation of length, area, & time units

◆◆◆◆◆◆◆ 78 FINAL RATING

◆◆◆◆◆◆ 67 User Friendliness

◆◆◆◆◆◆◆◆◆ 92 Educational Value

◆◆◆◆◆◆◆ 79 Instructional Design

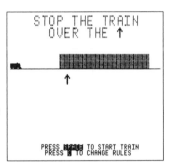

Lawrence Hall of Science
1984
$34.95
Ages 4-6
Apple
TI/1,3,4 NB/5,6

Offers three activities with estimation skills: Choo-Choo—child guesses when a train is over an arrow by pressing spacebar. Junk Jar—child estimates area. Bugs—presents units of "bugs" for child to estimate a line's length.

Exploratory Play

Early language acquisition

◆◆◆◆◆◆◆ 71 FINAL RATING

◆◆◆◆◆◆ 62 User Friendliness

◆◆◆◆◆◆ 69 Educational Value

◆◆◆◆◆◆◆◆ 84 Instructional Design

P.E.A.L. Software
1985
$150.00
Ages 1.5-3
Apple (64K)
LA/1,5 SP/7

Provides two overlays for the Muppet Learning Keys (required). Child first plays with real toys, then presses their pictures on the overlay to hear the associated words in a robotic voice. (Toy kit purchased separately for $54.) Requires Echo speech synthesizer. Covers 24 words. Adult setup required.

OT = Other topics **SE** = Seriation **SP** = Spatial relations **TI** = Time * = Version reviewed

Exploring Measurement, Time, & Money

Units of time, measurement, and money

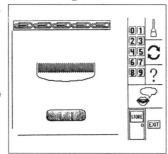

◆◆◆◆◆◆◆ 86 FINAL RATING

◆◆◆◆◆◆◆ 79 User Friendliness

◆◆◆◆◆◆◆◆ 92 Educational Value

◆◆◆◆◆◆◆◆ 87 Instructional Design

IBM Educational Systems
1989
$195.00
Ages 5-7
IBM (3.5")
TI/9 NB/3,6 SP/4 SE/1

Consists of three units: Measurement (rulers and bar graphs), Time (clocks and ordering events), and Money (units of money). Each unit consists of several activities that vary in degree of structure. All require mouse. Clear graphics and speech (IBM speech attachment required). Can track progress or keep records if used with IBM network.

Extrateletactograph, The

Drawing and writing stories

◆◆◆◆◆◆◆ 73 FINAL RATING

◆◆◆◆◆◆ 67 User Friendliness

◆◆◆◆◆◆◆◆ 80 Educational Value

◆◆◆◆◆◆◆ 72 Instructional Design

DIL International
1986
$69.95
Ages 4-12
IBM, Apple II+ or IIe* (not IIc)
CP/1,4 LA/3

A drawing and writing program. Child touches graphic tablet with overlay (requires WonderWorker) to draw or to change colors. Text can be added to the picture. Work can be saved and printed. Includes supplementary materials.

EZ Logo

Problem solving, directionality

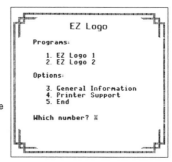

◆◆◆◆◆◆◆ 74 FINAL RATING

◆◆◆◆ 45 User Friendliness

◆◆◆◆◆◆◆◆◆ 94 Educational Value

◆◆◆◆◆◆◆◆ 89 Instructional Design

MECC
1985
$49.00
Ages 4-8
Apple (64K)
CP/1,3 SP/1,4,7,8 NB/1,3,5

Two levels on one disk. In level 1, child can draw using one-letter commands (e.g., F = Forward). Seventeen commands available. In level 2, child can create simple procedures and incorporate them into pictures. Five colors available. Work can be saved and printed. Manual includes many ideas and two keyboard sticker sets.

CL = Classification **CP** = Creative projects **LA** = Language **NA** = Not applicable **NB** = Number

Facemaker

Pattern matching, creative activity

◆◆◆◆◆ 54 FINAL RATING

◆◆◆◆ 41 User Friendliness

◆◆◆◆◆ 58 Educational Value

◆◆◆◆◆◆ 63 Instructional Design

Queue, Inc.
1982
$29.95
Ages 3-8
Apple, IBM*, C64, Atari
CP/2,3,4 TI/6

Children use spacebar and RETURN to select elements of a face: eyes, ears nose, mouth, hair. The face can then be made to wink, cry, etc., and a sequence activity can be done (like Simon Says). Simple reading required. See Facemaker Golden Edition.

Facemaker Golden Edition

Creativity, memory, and concentration

◆◆◆◆◆◆◆ 75 FINAL RATING

◆◆◆◆◆◆ 63 User Friendliness

◆◆◆◆◆◆◆◆ 86 Educational Value

◆◆◆◆◆◆◆ 79 Instructional Design

Queue, Inc.
1986
$39.95
Ages 3-8
Apple*, IBM (3.5")
SP/5 CP/3,4 LA/4,9 OT/1

Child uses spacebar to select features for a face (eyes, ears, nose, mouth, hair) as well as a body, hats, or glasses. Face can then be programmed to move or be used in a memory game. It can then be printed along with up to 1/2 page of text. Difficult for 3-year-olds to operate. A fun program.

Fact Track

Addition, subt., mult., div. basic facts

◆◆◆◆◆ 59 FINAL RATING

◆◆◆ 38 User Friendliness

◆◆◆◆◆◆◆◆ 83 Educational Value

◆◆◆◆◆◆ 64 Instructional Design

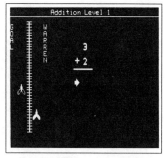

S.R.A.
1981
$40.00
Ages 6-up
Apple*, Atari, IBM, TRS 80
NB/9

Includes 390 problems. Difficulty levels range from finding "sums up to 5" to working with "divisors up to 9." A rather complex setup menu offers a variety of options, such as a "race against the clock" option and a "flashcard" option, which could be used by small groups.

OT = Other topics   **SE** = Seriation   **SP** = Spatial relations   **TI** = Time   * = Version reviewed

Farm, The

Creation of a "microworld"

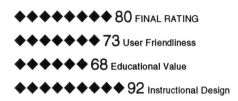

◆◆◆◆◆◆◆◆ 80 FINAL RATING

◆◆◆◆◆◆◆ 73 User Friendliness

◆◆◆◆◆◆ 68 Educational Value

◆◆◆◆◆◆◆◆◆ 92 Instructional Design

Mobius Corporation
1990
See KidWare 2
Ages 3-5
IBM
CP/1 SP/4,6

Child uses mouse to select people, animals, or farm objects and paste them into a farm scene. Contains 12 animals with sounds, 24 people representing three generations and various ethnic groups, and 9 farm objects. Resulting scenes can be printed or saved. Rather limited design (only one scene). While children initially like the graphics, they frequently become frustrated by the operation.

Firehouse Rescue

Maze navigation

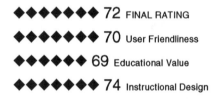

◆◆◆◆◆◆◆ 72 FINAL RATING

◆◆◆◆◆◆◆ 70 User Friendliness

◆◆◆◆◆◆ 69 Educational Value

◆◆◆◆◆◆◆ 74 Instructional Design

GameTek/IJE, Inc.
1988
$9.95
Ages 3-8
Apple, IBM*, C64
SP/4,7 TI/8

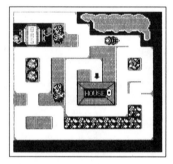

Child uses arrow keys or joystick (optional) to steer a Fisher-Price fire truck through a maze to rescue people from buildings. Contains seven levels of difficulty. Harder levels make use of multiscreen mazes, finding hidden keys, and racing against a clock to get to a burning building. Enjoyable activity but limited in educational value.

First "R": Kindergarten, The

Letter recognition; initial, ending sounds of words

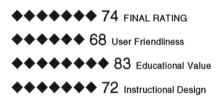

◆◆◆◆◆◆◆ 74 FINAL RATING

◆◆◆◆◆◆ 68 User Friendliness

◆◆◆◆◆◆◆◆ 83 Educational Value

◆◆◆◆◆◆◆ 72 Instructional Design

Milliken Publishing Co.
1987
$95.00
Ages 5-8
Apple
LA/4,5,6

Four activities—child types the first or last letter of a given word, selects letter to complete a word, selects a picture that goes with a partial word, or sees a partial word and picture and selects missing letter. Keeps records. Includes alphabet and tutorial disks, an alphabet book, and classroom materials.

CL = Classification   **CP** = Creative projects   **LA** = Language   **NA** = Not applicable   **NB** = Number

First Encounters

Computer literacy skills

◆◆◆ 32 FINAL RATING

◆◆◆◆ 41 User Friendliness

◆◆ 21 Educational Value

◆◆ 29 Instructional Design

Educational Activities, Inc.
1983
$98.00
Ages 4-6
Apple
OT/1

A "computer literacy" package designed to teach kindergarten children computer terms, computer operation, and writing of programs. Includes flashcards for memorizing terms, worksheets, keyboard models, workdisk with games. Reading required. Ratings apply only to programs.

First Letter Fun

Letter Recognition

◆◆◆◆◆◆◆◆ 82 FINAL RATING

◆◆◆◆◆◆ 67 User Friendliness

◆◆◆◆◆◆◆◆◆ 98 Educational Value

◆◆◆◆◆◆◆◆ 86 Instructional Design

MECC
1985
$59.00
Ages 3-6
Apple (64K)
LA/1,4,6

Four picture stories: Farm, Circus, Park, and Magic Show introduce all the letters except Q and X. Child sees an object from a story and must use the spacebar or arrow keys to select its initial letter. Teacher options allow selection of upper/lowercase display. Clear graphics. Good design.

First Letters and Words

Letters & words, dinosaurs

◆◆◆◆◆◆◆ 74 FINAL RATING

◆◆◆◆◆◆◆◆ 80 User Friendliness

◆◆◆◆◆◆◆◆ 80 Educational Value

◆◆◆◆◆◆ 62 Instructional Design

First Byte, Inc.
1987
$49.95
Ages 3-8
IIGS*, Mac, Amiga, Atari ST
LA/4,5,8 SP/5

Four games: (1) Introduces upper- and lower-case letters. (2) Shows a picture and says word when any letter is typed. (3) Says body parts as a child colors in a dinosaur. (4) Presents animal riddles for which child types the answer. Talks in a primitive voice. Options give teacher control.

OT = Other topics   SE = Seriation   SP = Spatial relations   TI = Time   * = Version reviewed

First Shapes

Five basic shapes

◆◆◆◆◆◆◆ 75 FINAL RATING

◆◆◆◆◆◆◆◆ 81 User Friendliness

◆◆◆◆◆◆◆◆ 88 Educational Value

◆◆◆◆◆◆ 64 Instructional Design

First Byte, Inc.
1987
$49.95
Ages 3-8
IIGS*, Mac, Amiga, Atari ST
CL/1 SP/8 SE/1 OT/1

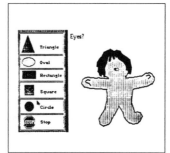

Four games: Child can (1) change the size of a shape by clicking the mouse, (2) design a toy out of shapes, (3) play Concentration by matching pairs of shapes, or (4) find a shape such as "the smallest circle" among three shapes presented. Gives design options. Toy designs can be printed and saved. Voice is difficult to understand.

First Verbs

Learning 40 common verbs

◆◆◆◆◆◆◆ 73 FINAL RATING

◆◆◆◆◆◆◆◆◆ 94 User Friendliness

◆◆◆◆◆◆ 61 Educational Value

◆◆◆◆◆◆ 66 Instructional Design

Laureate Learning Systems
1989
$225.00
Ages 4-up
IIGS
LA/5,8

Designed for children with language delays. Presents 40 verbs, such as "pet" or "wave." Children first hear and see the verb, then move on to matching the spoken verb (requires Echo speech synthesizer) with corresponding illustration. Adult setup required. Can be used with single switch or TouchWindow. Clear graphics and sound.

FirstWriter

Creative writing

◆◆◆◆◆◆◆ 76 FINAL RATING

◆◆◆◆◆ 59 User Friendliness

◆◆◆◆◆◆◆◆◆ 96 Educational Value

◆◆◆◆◆◆◆ 78 Instructional Design

Houghton Mifflin Co.
1988
$117.00
Ages 5-8
Apple
LA/1,3,4,5,6,9 CP/4

A large-letter word processor with features that include spoken instructions (Echo speech synthesizer optional), choice of five colors for text, a built-in dictionary, 125 pictures. Stories can be saved or printed in color. Words can be added to the dictionary. Print is somewhat blocky.

CL = Classification   **CP** = Creative projects   **LA** = Language   **NA** = Not applicable   **NB** = Number

Fish Dish, The

Short "i" sound and comprehension

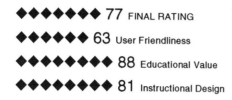 77 FINAL RATING

 63 User Friendliness

88 Educational Value

81 Instructional Design

Hartley Courseware, Inc.
1989
$49.95
Ages 3-6
Apple
LA/5,6,8

Contains 16 lessons on two disks. Each lesson consists of a short story (4 to 7 paragraphs) and comprehension questions. Child can hear sentences or words with an optional Echo or Ufonic synthesizer. Uses animated graphics to illustrate stories. Vocabulary builds on the short "i" sound, using C-V-C words from Dolch lists. Includes diagnostic record keeping.

Fish Scales

Measurement

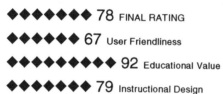 78 FINAL RATING

67 User Friendliness

92 Educational Value

79 Instructional Design

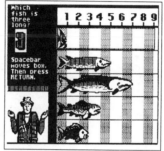

DLM
1985
$32.95
Ages 4-8
Apple
NB/1,3,4,6

Six games in which child uses spacebar, arrow keys, or RETURN to input answers, e.g., the height of a fish jump, the longest or shortest fish, and other measurement concepts. Games encourage using units of measurement. Menu requires reading.

Flodd, the Bad Guy

Letter and word recognition, reading stories

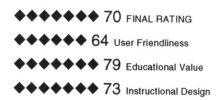 70 FINAL RATING

64 User Friendliness

79 Educational Value

73 Instructional Design

Tom Snyder Productions, Inc.
1988
$44.95
Ages 2-6
Apple*, IBM, Mac
LA/3,4,5

Child and adult read through a fairy-tale-like story, pressing any key to change the screen. Every five or six pages, a choice is offered, e.g., to go into a cave or not. Reading required for independent use, although clever graphics and sounds help to guide child through the story.

Fun Flyer

Eye-hand coordination, directional concepts

◆◆◆◆◆◆ 64 FINAL RATING

◆◆◆◆◆ 56 User Friendliness

◆◆◆◆◆◆ 65 Educational Value

◆◆◆◆◆◆◆ 70 Instructional Design

GameTek/IJE, Inc.
1990
$14.95
Ages 3-8
IBM (5.25"), CGA, 256K
SP/4 TI/3

Child uses joystick or arrow keys to steer a plane over a moving landscape. Points and fuel are earned by catching falling stars, snowflakes, kites, and balloons. Three levels of difficulty. Some adult assistance is required to get started. Simple, enjoyable game. Limited child-control.

Fun From A to Z

Alphabet skills practice

◆◆◆◆◆◆◆◆ 81 FINAL RATING

◆◆◆◆◆◆ 68 User Friendliness

◆◆◆◆◆◆◆◆◆ 92 Educational Value

◆◆◆◆◆◆◆◆ 85 Instructional Design

MECC
1985
$39.95
Ages 3-6
Apple (64K)
LA/4

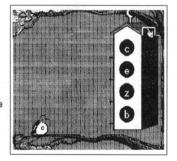

Child uses arrow keys to play three games: Birds—child matches letters. Dots— child completes a dot-to-dot picture by selecting next alphabet letter. Runners— child sees sequence (K,L,M,__,O) and must select missing letter. Management allows selection of upper/lower case. Well-designed.

Fun on the Farm

Coloring pictures

◆◆◆◆◆◆◆ 80 FINAL RATING

◆◆◆◆◆◆◆ 79 User Friendliness

◆◆◆◆◆◆◆ 73 Educational Value

◆◆◆◆◆◆◆◆ 84 Instructional Design

Merit Software
1986
$14.95
Ages 3-up
Apple* (128K), IBM, C64
CP/1,4 SP/4

A coloring program with 30 blank farm scenes. Child moves cursor with mouse, joystick, or arrow keys to fill in sections of a picture with 1 of 16 available colors. Prints in color. Mouse and color monitor recommended. Very easy to use. Prints picture with calendar.

CL = Classification　　　**CP** = Creative projects　　　**LA** = Language　　　**NA** = Not applicable　　　**NB** = Number

Fun With Colors

Color recognition

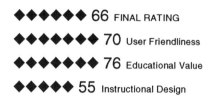 66 FINAL RATING

◆◆◆◆◆◆◆ 70 User Friendliness

◆◆◆◆◆◆◆ 76 Educational Value

◆◆◆◆◆ 55 Instructional Design

Access Unlimited
1989
$25.00
Ages 3-6
Apple
CL/1,2 SP/2,4 CP/4

For special education settings. Five simple games in which child uses spacebar and RETURN to match colored blocks, fill the screen with 1 of 16 colors, fill the screen with colored blocks, or draw a picture with the arrow keys. Child can also build with colored blocks, using the arrow keys. Color monitor required.

Fun With Directions

Perceptual and cognitive skills

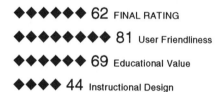 62 FINAL RATING

◆◆◆◆◆◆◆◆ 81 User Friendliness

◆◆◆◆◆◆ 69 Educational Value

◆◆◆◆ 44 Instructional Design

Mindscape, Inc.
1984
$61.00
Ages 3-6
Apple
SP/4 TI/6

Child selects a nodding (yes) or shaking (no) head to indicate if objects are in line, are facing same direction, or are in sequence, e.g., egg/chick/chicken. Allows for selection of difficulty level, performance feedback. No reading required.

Fun With Drawing

Drawing pictures

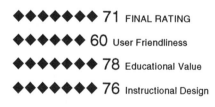 71 FINAL RATING

◆◆◆◆◆◆ 60 User Friendliness

◆◆◆◆◆◆◆ 78 Educational Value

◆◆◆◆◆◆◆ 76 Instructional Design

Wescott Software
1989
$20.00
Ages 3-up
IBM
CP/1 SP/4

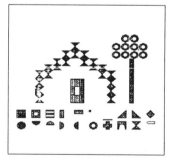

A drawing program. Child uses arrow keys to draw simple pictures made up of different shapes (15 colors, 19 shapes to choose from). Pictures can be saved or printed. Use of arrow keys (rather than mouse or joystick) makes drawing difficult.

Fun With Letters and Words

Letter recognition

◆◆◆◆◆◆ 76 FINAL RATING

◆◆◆◆◆◆ 73 User Friendliness

◆◆◆◆◆◆◆ 86 Educational Value

◆◆◆◆◆◆ 70 Instructional Design

Wescott Software
1987
$20.00
Ages 2-6
IBM
LA/4,5

Child can press any letter key to see a picture and word related to the letter, e.g., a bike for B. Six levels allow the addition of more words, with up to 147 possible. "Custom" words, such as a child's name, can be added. Will say each letter if used with a Covox Speech Adapter (optional).

Fun With Memory

Memory

◆◆◆◆◆◆ 77 FINAL RATING

◆◆◆◆◆ 65 User Friendliness

◆◆◆◆◆◆◆ 87 Educational Value

◆◆◆◆◆◆◆ 83 Instructional Design

Wescott Software
1987
$20.00
Ages 2-6
IBM
OT/1 LA/4,5 NB/4 CL/2

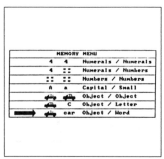

A seven-level Concentration game in which child uses the arrow keys, spacebar and ENTER to select a card. Child can match numerals, objects, or words. Options allow for control over the number of cards shown in a game. Can be played by one or two players.

Fun With Numbers

Numeral recognition, adding and subtracting

◆◆◆◆◆ 59 FINAL RATING

◆◆◆◆◆ 64 User Friendliness

◆◆◆◆◆◆ 78 Educational Value

◆◆◆ 46 Instructional Design

Wescott Software
1987
$20.00
Ages 3-7
IBM
NB/3,4,8

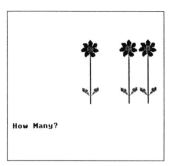

Six games provide experiences in counting by twos, adding with objects, or subtracting, all with sums less than 18. Nine skill levels determine the difficulty of the game. Adult options permit control over the difficulty level and pacing of the game. Rather dry presentation. Has speech capability with Echo or IBM speech adapters.

CL = Classification   **CP** = Creative projects   **LA** = Language   **NA** = Not applicable   **NB** = Number

Garden, The

Functional intelligence, social skills

◆◆◆◆◆◆ 62 FINAL RATING

◆◆◆◆◆◆◆ 76 User Friendliness

◆◆◆◆◆◆◆ 76 Educational Value

◆◆◆◆ 43 Instructional Design

DIL International
1986
$289.00
Ages 2-8
IBM, Apple*
CL/1,2 SP/7 TI/6 OT/1

Ten disks cover a range of topics, such as seasons, parts of a flower, pollination, and other thematic material. Child presses overlay on WonderWorker touch tablet (recommended) to select answers. Provides simple but limited activities.

Gertrude's Secrets

Classifying and seriating

◆◆◆◆◆◆◆◆ 84 FINAL RATING

◆◆◆◆◆◆◆ 78 User Friendliness

◆◆◆◆◆◆◆◆◆ 91 Educational Value

◆◆◆◆◆◆◆◆ 86 Instructional Design

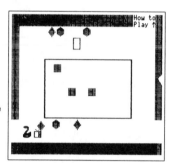

The Learning Company
1982
$59.95 (school edition)
Ages 4-10
Apple*, IBM*, C64 ($29.95)
CL/1,5 SP/4

Consists of seven attribute puzzles of varying difficulty. Child uses arrow keys or joystick to move through 25 rooms (screens). Children as young as age three can do easiest puzzle, but lose interest quickly. Content is best for ages five and up. School edition contains additional curriculum materials.

Getting Ready to Read and Add

Numerals, upper/lower-case letters

◆◆◆◆◆◆ 63 FINAL RATING

◆◆◆◆◆ 56 User Friendliness

◆◆◆◆◆◆◆ 77 Educational Value

◆◆◆◆◆◆◆◆ 80 Instructional Design

Sunburst Communications, Inc.
1984
$65.00
Ages 3-6
Apple, IBM*, Atari, C64*
LA/4 CL/2 NB/3,4

Six activities based on a matching format. Practice with shapes, letters, and numerals. Child presses any key when a match is shown for shapes, letters, and numerals. Options included for control of speed and number of problems.

Goofy's Railway Express

Noticing common shapes

◆◆◆◆◆◆ 62 FINAL RATING

◆◆◆◆◆◆◆◆ 83 User Friendliness

◆◆◆◆◆ 51 Educational Value

◆◆◆◆◆ 54 Instructional Design

Walt Disney Software
1990
$14.95
Ages 2-5
IBM, C64
SP/8 TI/4

One simple activity. As a train moves, basic shapes periodically appear above its smokestack. If the spacebar is pressed while a shape is shown, a shape-related object appears in the passing scenery (e.g., a yellow circle causes a round sun to shine). Engaging graphics. Very limited content. Poor design leaves little for children to do.

Grandma's House

Exploring and arranging

◆◆◆◆◆◆ 68 FINAL RATING

◆◆◆◆◆◆◆ 78 User Friendliness

◆◆◆◆◆ 57 Educational Value

◆◆◆◆◆◆ 65 Instructional Design

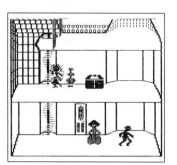

Queue, Inc.
1983
$24.95
Ages 4-8
Apple*, C64, Atari
SP/2

Child uses mouse or joystick (required) to move to and explore one of six different scenes. By pressing key, objects (e.g., a fish from the seashore) can be carried from scenes and collected in "Grandma's House." Easy to use but not strong in any content area.

Great Gonzo in WordRider, The

Fun with words, timing, and strategy

◆◆◆◆◆◆◆ 73 FINAL RATING

◆◆◆◆◆◆◆ 77 User Friendliness

◆◆◆◆◆◆◆ 70 Educational Value

◆◆◆◆◆◆◆ 71 Instructional Design

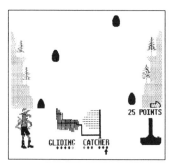

Joyce Hakansson Associates
1985
$19.95
Ages 6-up
Apple
TI/1,3,5 SP/2 LA/8

An adventure game in which child uses joystick (recommended) or arrow keys to move Gonzo through obstacles to earn points and rescue a chicken. On the way, Gonzo constructs machines that will get him through the dangers. An enjoyable program. Includes a Muppet storybook.

CL = Classification   **CP** = Creative projects   **LA** = Language   **NA** = Not applicable   **NB** = Number

Great Leap, A

Language experience

◆◆◆◆◆◆◆◆ 89 FINAL RATING

◆◆◆◆◆◆◆ 85 User Friendliness

◆◆◆◆◆◆◆◆ 94 Educational Value

◆◆◆◆◆◆◆◆ 91 Instructional Design

D. C. Heath & Company
1988
$75.00
Ages 5-10
Apple (128K)
LA/1,2,3,5,8,9 SP/4,7 CP/1,4

Children use mouse, Koala Pad, joystick, or arrow keys to select and move objects, words, or characters in a story. Children can also type their own words. Stories can be saved and printed in color. Package includes four copies of storybook. Colorful graphics, good child-control. Mouse recommended.

Hey Diddle

Rhyming words and phrases

◆◆◆◆ 47 FINAL RATING

◆◆◆◆ 46 User Friendliness

◆◆◆◆◆ 56 Educational Value

◆◆◆◆ 42 Instructional Design

Queue, Inc.
1983
$24.95
Ages 3-10
Apple*, IBM
LA/7,9

Three activities based on 30 classic nursery rhymes. The first two activities illustrate rhymes as they're being read by an adult. In the third, rhyming phrases are scrambled, and the child must put them in correct order. Joystick optional. Reading required. Not recommended.

Hobo's Luck

Counting and probability

◆◆◆◆◆ 54 FINAL RATING

◆◆◆◆◆ 54 User Friendliness

◆◆◆◆◆◆◆ 73 Educational Value

◆◆◆◆ 44 Instructional Design

Strawberry Hill Software
1985
$55.00
Ages 5-up
Apple*, C64
NB/1,3,4,6 SP/2

A computerized board game in which one to four players take turns rolling dice to earn jumps. The first one reaching the end of the course wins a bag of money. Includes 13 worksheet activities for practice in probability, counting, and statistical recording.

Hodge Podge

Letter recognition

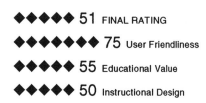

◆◆◆◆◆ 51 FINAL RATING

◆◆◆◆◆◆◆ 75 User Friendliness

◆◆◆◆◆ 55 Educational Value

◆◆◆◆◆ 50 Instructional Design

Artworx
1982
$14.95
Ages 1.5-6
Apple*, C64, IBM, Atari
LA/4

Child presses any key to get a response: a picture, a song, or both. Screen displays are blocky and not always appropriate for the letter pressed, e.g., P = Prism. Easy to use program, but its value is limited.

Holidays & Seasons

Coloring pictures

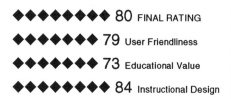

◆◆◆◆◆◆◆◆ 80 FINAL RATING

◆◆◆◆◆◆◆ 79 User Friendliness

◆◆◆◆◆◆◆ 73 Educational Value

◆◆◆◆◆◆◆◆ 84 Instructional Design

Merit Software
1988
$29.95
Ages 3-up
Apple* (128K), IBM, C64
CP/1,4 SP/4

A coloring program with 30 seasonal pictures on one disk. Child moves cursor with mouse, joystick, or arrow keys to fill in sections of a picture with 1 of 16 available colors. Prints in color. Mouse and color monitor recommended. Very easy to use. Prints picture with calendar, banner, or message.

Home Row

Keyboarding skills (touch-typing)

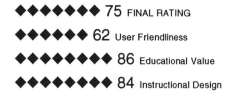

◆◆◆◆◆◆◆ 75 FINAL RATING

◆◆◆◆◆◆ 62 User Friendliness

◆◆◆◆◆◆◆◆ 86 Educational Value

◆◆◆◆◆◆◆ 84 Instructional Design

Hartley Courseware, Inc.
1987
$39.95
Ages 6-up
Apple
OT/3

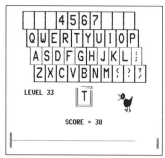

Has 39 levels of difficulty, ranging from work with two keys to work with the entire keyboard. Typist races against a moving line to score points, see graphics, and advance in levels. Custom lessons can be designed. Keeps up to 50 records. A well-designed program.

Hop To It!

Number lines, addition and subtraction

◆◆◆◆◆◆◆◆ 80 FINAL RATING

◆◆◆◆◆◆ 66 User Friendliness

◆◆◆◆◆◆◆◆◆ 92 Educational Value

◆◆◆◆◆◆◆◆ 84 Instructional Design

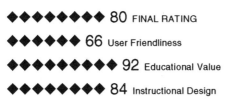

Press the SPACEBAR
and count to the
radish.

Sunburst Communications, Inc.
1990
$65.00
Ages 5-7
Apple
NB/3,7,8

Seven number line activities in which child uses spacebar, number keys, or arrows to move a marker (e.g., a rabbit) on a number line to collect items and complete an addition or subtraction number sentence. Teacher options allow control over many aspects of the presentation. Performance can be printed. Some reading required. Highly recommended for K–3 classrooms.

Human Being Machine, The

Recreation, body parts, sequencing, scanning

◆◆◆◆◆◆◆ 78 FINAL RATING

◆◆◆◆◆◆◆◆ 83 User Friendliness

◆◆◆◆◆◆◆ 79 Educational Value

◆◆◆◆◆◆◆ 71 Instructional Design

NOW A MOUTH...

R. J. Cooper & Associates
1990
$75.00 (Free preview copy)
Ages 3-up
Apple
SP/5 CP/2

Child uses keyboard, TouchWindow, or single switch to select the elements for a face or a body. Resulting products can be printed. Options allow for control over scanning speed or input device. Use of Echo speech synthesizer allows instructions to be spoken. Designed for children with limited motor abilities. Menu requires reading. An enjoyable program.

I Can Count

Counting up to 10

◆◆◆◆ 40 FINAL RATING

◆◆◆◆◆ 53 User Friendliness

◆◆◆◆ 45 Educational Value

◆◆ 26 Instructional Design

HOW MANY 🐕 ?
PRESS THE NUMBER.

Troll Associates
1987
$39.95
Ages 5-8
Apple
NB/2,3,4,8

Eight activities based around counting, matching numbers with sets, typing the number that comes next, finding a missing number in a sequence, recognizing zero, and concepts of greater or less than. Colorful graphics but poor design. Reading is required.

I Can Count the Petals of a Flower

Counting

◆◆◆◆◆ 56 FINAL RATING

◆◆◆◆◆◆ 69 User Friendliness

◆◆◆◆ 45 Educational Value

◆◆◆◆◆ 54 Instructional Design

Mobius Corporation
1990
See KidWare 2
Ages 3-5
IBM
NB/3

Children click the mouse button to see the petals counted on one of nine available flowers. One flower is offered for each number, giving children practice counting from one to nine. Scripted design and narrow range of challenge cause children to lose interest quickly. Poorly designed. Pictures are taken from the book of the same title.

I Can Remember

Memory skills

◆◆◆◆◆◆ 64 FINAL RATING

◆◆◆◆◆ 59 User Friendliness

◆◆◆◆◆◆◆ 71 Educational Value

◆◆◆◆◆◆ 63 Instructional Design

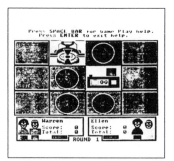

GameTek/IJE, Inc.
1988
$9.95
Ages 3 to 8
Apple, IBM*, C64
OT/1 SP/7

A concentration game. Child uses arrow keys and spacebar to find and match hidden Fisher-Price toys and earn points. Three levels of difficulty are available—a child can choose from a 6-, 8-, or 12-box grid. Can utilize joystick (optional). For one or two players. Color monitor recommended.

I Love You in the Sky, Butterfly

Language experience, thematic material

◆◆◆◆◆◆◆◆ 89 FINAL RATING

◆◆◆◆◆◆◆◆ 85 User Friendliness

◆◆◆◆◆◆◆◆◆ 94 Educational Value

◆◆◆◆◆◆◆◆ 91 Instructional Design

Hartley Courseware, Inc.
1990
$297.00 per unit
Ages 3-7
Apple*, IBM
LA/3,8,9 NB/3 SP/1,2,4 CP/1,4

Consists of nine units—animals, homes, families, patterns, feelings, self-concept, holidays, senses, and a teacher tool kit. Each unit contains two books, two audiotapes, two videotapes, five story disks, and a student disk. Software is easy to use and is similar in design to the Explore-a-Story series. (See "Rosie the Counting Rabbit.")

CL = Classification   **CP** = Creative projects   **LA** = Language   **NA** = Not applicable   **NB** = Number

IEP Generator Version 5.0

Generation of IEP forms

Not rated

```
IEP GENERATOR - MAIN MENU

<A>dd goals/objectives/activities to an existing file

<M>odify goal/objective/activity files

<D>elete goals/objectives/activities from the file

<L>ist entire goal/objective/activity file

<P>rint IEP

<F>ile Utilities (Compact or Expand Data Files)

<I>nstructions

<Q>uit this program

Select the letter corresponding to your choice
```

Ebsco Curriculum Materials
1984
$84.95
Ages na
Apple*, IBM
OT/4

A program teachers can use to create, store, and print children's Individual Educational Profile (IEP) forms. Stores 30 lists, each containing up to 100 goals, objectives, or activities from which IEP forms can be created. Formats are limited, and design could be smoother.

Inside Outside Opposites

Opposites

◆◆◆◆◆◆◆ 72 FINAL RATING

◆◆◆◆◆◆◆◆ 80 User Friendliness

◆◆◆◆◆◆◆◆ 84 Educational Value

◆◆◆◆◆◆ 62 Instructional Design

Queue, Inc.
1986
$29.95
Ages 3-7
Apple
SE/1 SP/4 LA/1

Contains 20 antonym pairs (in/out, high/low) that can be illustrated using the arrow keys. Pressing the spacebar brings up the next antonym pair. Easy to use. Similar to "Stickybear Opposites." Colorful graphics.

Inside Outside Shapes

Six shapes and corresponding words

◆◆◆◆◆◆◆ 76 FINAL RATING

◆◆◆◆◆◆◆ 70 User Friendliness

◆◆◆◆◆◆◆◆◆ 90 Educational Value

◆◆◆◆◆◆◆ 72 Instructional Design

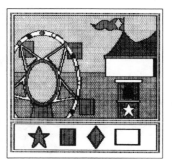

Queue, Inc.
1986
$29.95
Ages 3-7
Apple
SP/8 CL/1,2

Using arrow keys and spacebar, child must find a shape hidden in a picture. A correct response animates the picture and plays music. Pressing the spacebar brings up the next picture. Good graphics. Contains 18 pictures. Similar to "Stickybear Shapes."

Integrated Learning System

Math and reading K–9

◆◆◆◆◆◆◆ 79 FINAL RATING

◆◆◆◆◆◆◆ 71 User Friendliness

◆◆◆◆◆◆◆◆◆ 94 Educational Value

◆◆◆◆◆◆◆ 79 Instructional Design

Josten's Learning Corporation
1987
Starts at $16,800.00
Ages 5-up
IIGS, IBM*, Mac
LA/4-8 CL/1-6 NB/1-8 OT/1 CP/1

A networked computerized math and reading curriculum containing 1800 separate lessons stored on a laser disk which can be accessed by up to 40 stations at once. Employs the use of headphones, speech synthesis, and speech input. Keeps and prints records, and automatically adapts to each child. Good design, sound and graphics.

Introduction to Counting

Counting

◆◆◆◆◆◆ 66 FINAL RATING

◆◆◆◆◆◆ 60 User Friendliness

◆◆◆◆◆◆◆◆◆ 90 Educational Value

◆◆◆◆◆ 53 Instructional Design

Compton's New Media
1981
$39.95
Ages 4-7
Apple*, IBM, Atari
NB/3 CL/1 SE/1

A regimented sequence of eight counting activities. Begins with selecting a set to correspond with a given number and progresses all the way to subtraction. Management keeps score and controls presentation, which allows individualization. Requires adult setup with each use.

It's No Game

Personal safety skills

◆◆◆◆◆◆ 62 FINAL RATING

◆◆◆◆◆ 58 User Friendliness

◆◆◆◆◆◆ 67 Educational Value

◆◆◆◆◆◆ 61 Instructional Design

Teenagers like to go there.
Sometimes they do bad things.

Educational Activities, Inc.
1986
$49.95
Ages 5-11
Apple
LA/2,3

A simulation in which the child is put in a potentially dangerous situation and must make a choice. Each "wise decision" is rewarded with moves on a gameboard. Topics are trusting one's own feelings, saying no to bribes, telephone skills, dealing with strange adults, and asking for help. Reading required.

Jack and the Beanstalk

Word recognition, event sequence

◆◆◆◆◆◆ 69 FINAL RATING

◆◆◆◆◆◆◆ 70 User Friendliness

◆◆◆◆◆◆◆ 71 Educational Value

◆◆◆◆◆◆ 66 Instructional Design

Queue, Inc.
1985
$49.00
Ages 7-12
Apple
LA/5,8 TI/5

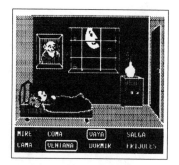

Children explore their own version of a traditional folk tale by playing the role of Jack, making decisions by selecting two-word commands, e.g., "trade cow." Reading required. Could be used as language experience with younger children. A Spanish version is available. Offered in a lab package (10 disks) for $147.00.

Jack and the Beanstalk

Letter and word recognition, reading stories

◆◆◆◆◆◆◆ 70 FINAL RATING

◆◆◆◆◆◆ 64 User Friendliness

◆◆◆◆◆◆◆ 79 Educational Value

◆◆◆◆◆◆◆ 73 Instructional Design

Tom Snyder Productions, Inc.
1988
$44.95
Ages 2-6
Apple*, IBM, Mac
LA/3,4,5

Child and adult read through a space-age version of Jack and the Beanstalk, pressing any key to change the page. Every five or six pages, a choice is offered, e.g., to continue climbing the beanstalk or not. Reading required for independent use, although graphics and sounds help guide child through the story.

Jen the Hen

Short "e" sound and reading comprehension

◆◆◆◆◆◆◆ 77 FINAL RATING

◆◆◆◆◆◆ 63 User Friendliness

◆◆◆◆◆◆◆◆ 88 Educational Value

◆◆◆◆◆◆◆ 81 Instructional Design

Hartley Courseware, Inc.
1989
$49.95
Ages 3-6
Apple
LA/5,6,8

Contains 18 lessons on two disks. Each lesson consists of a short story (four to seven paragraphs) and comprehension questions. Child can hear sentences or words with an optional Echo or Ufonic synthesizer. Makes use of animated graphics to illustrate stories. Vocabulary builds on the short "e" sound, using C-V-C words from Dolch lists. Includes diagnostic record keeping.

Joystick Trainer

Joystick skills for powered wheelchairs

◆◆◆◆◆◆ 78 FINAL RATING

◆◆◆◆◆◆ 67 User Friendliness

◆◆◆◆◆◆◆ 88 Educational Value

◆◆◆◆◆◆◆ 80 Instructional Design

R. J. Cooper & Associates
1989
$50.00
Ages 3-up
Apple
SP/3,7,9

Eight simple games designed to provide practice with a joystick. The games range in difficulty from seeing arrows move in the direction joystick is moved to moving through a six-room maze containing a treasure chest that holds the parts to a puzzle. A joystick is required. Call R. J. Cooper for a free demonstration disk.

Jr. Typer

Touch typing

◆◆◆◆ 41 FINAL RATING

◆◆◆ 33 User Friendliness

◆◆◆◆ 49 Educational Value

◆◆◆◆ 44 Instructional Design

Aquarius Instructional
1985
$45.00
Ages 5-up
Apple*, TRS 80
LA/4 OT/3

Presents a fixed series of typing problems. As a child types, graphics or words accumulate on the screen. Helpful graphic hands point out finger positions. Contains 54 combinations on two disks. Inflexible design allows little child-control.

Juggle's Butterfly

Spatial relationships

◆◆◆◆◆◆ 62 FINAL RATING

◆◆◆◆◆◆ 65 User Friendliness

◆◆◆◆◆◆◆ 74 Educational Value

◆◆◆◆◆ 54 Instructional Design

IBM Educational Systems
1982
$27.00
Ages 3-6
IBM, Apple*
SP/4

Location of keys on keyboard corresponds to spatial answers, e.g., above, right, below. However, pressing spacebar advances program to next segment, which children often unwittingly do. Contains three games, each of which contain three lessons on spatial concepts.

Jungle Safari

African plants and animals

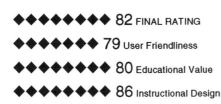

◆◆◆◆◆◆◆◆ 82 FINAL RATING

◆◆◆◆◆◆◆ 79 User Friendliness

◆◆◆◆◆◆◆◆ 80 Educational Value

◆◆◆◆◆◆◆◆ 86 Instructional Design

Orange Cherry Software
1991
$59.00
Ages 5-up
IIGS* (1 MB), IBM (with Covox)
SP/7 OT/6

Child uses mouse to gain access through a picture menu and explore four African habitats: plains, rain forest, river, and tall grass. Once in a habitat, child can move through various scenes to discover plants and animals. Clicking on a plant or animal prompts written paragraph of information. Contains over 80 animals and plants. Clear graphics and speech. Pictures of animals can be printed. Difficult for preschoolers.

Just Around the Block

Language experience

◆◆◆◆◆◆◆◆ 89 FINAL RATING

◆◆◆◆◆◆◆◆ 85 User Friendliness

◆◆◆◆◆◆◆◆◆ 94 Educational Value

◆◆◆◆◆◆◆◆◆ 91 Instructional Design

D. C. Heath & Company
1988
$75.00
Ages 5-10
Apple (128K)
LA/2,3,5,9 CP/4 SP/4,7

Children use mouse, Koala Pad, joystick, or arrow keys to select or move objects, backgrounds, words, or characters of a story. Children can also add their own words. Resulting stories can be saved and printed in color. Includes four copies of the storybook. Good design. Fun to use.

Katie's Farm

Exploring, talking about actions

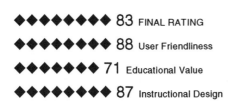

◆◆◆◆◆◆◆◆ 83 FINAL RATING

◆◆◆◆◆◆◆◆ 88 User Friendliness

◆◆◆◆◆◆ 71 Educational Value

◆◆◆◆◆◆◆◆ 87 Instructional Design

Lawrence Productions, Inc.
1990
$39.95
Ages 2-6
IIGS*, Mac, IBM (VGA or CGA),
    Mac II, Amiga
LA/1 TI/2,6 CL/1

Child uses a mouse (required) to operate a picture menu to explore a farm. For example, selecting the hen shows a girl checking a nest for eggs. Includes a cornfield, barn, old tree, corral, chicken coop, and a pond. Children respond well to this program, although it has limited content. It is very easy to operate and has clear graphics and recorded sounds. Similar to "McGee."

Kermit's Electronic Storymaker

Words and their meaning

◆◆◆◆◆◆◆ 77 FINAL RATING

◆◆◆◆◆◆ 67 User Friendliness

◆◆◆◆◆◆◆◆ 86 Educational Value

◆◆◆◆◆◆◆◆ 82 Instructional Design

Joyce Hakansson Associates
1984
$5.95
Ages 4-up
C64
LA/6,8,9 CP/4 TI/6

Child uses joystick to select the elements of a sentence, which are illustrated with clever animation and music. There are 14 different sentence forms, each on one screen. Resulting stories can be up to 14 pages long, and can be saved. Some reading required. Available in software stores only.

Keytalk

A beginning literacy activity

◆◆◆◆◆◆◆ 76 FINAL RATING

◆◆◆◆◆ 58 User Friendliness

◆◆◆◆◆◆◆◆ 88 Educational Value

◆◆◆◆◆◆◆◆ 84 Instructional Design

P.E.A.L. Software
1987
$99.00
Ages 3-8
Apple* (64K), IBM
LA/3,4,5,9 CP/4

A talking word processor that says in a robotic voice anything that is typed. Uses regular or Muppet keyboard. Says each letter, word, and sentence. Allows stories up to one page in 40-column text. Stories can be printed and saved. Includes on-screen word list. Pronunciation exceptions can be added.

Kid Works

Creative writing, drawing, creating printed material

◆◆◆◆◆◆◆◆◆ 90 FINAL RATING

◆◆◆◆◆◆◆◆ 83 User Friendliness

◆◆◆◆◆◆◆◆◆ 96 Educational Value

◆◆◆◆◆◆◆◆◆ 91 Instructional Design

Davidson and Associates, Inc.
1991
$49.95
Ages 4-10
IBM (640K, VGA, printer, mouse, hard drive)
LA/6,7,8,9 CP/1,4

A well-designed talking word processor that allows the creation of illustrated stories. Includes 245 built-in rebus icons, which can also be customized. Detailed illustrations can be created. Once story is complete, it can be played back (the computer illustrates and reads), printed, or saved. Two sizes of print. Teacher options allow customization. External speech device recommended (e.g., Echo II or Covox). Requires 2MB hard drive space.

CL = Classification   **CP** = Creative projects   **LA** = Language   **NA** = Not applicable   **NB** = Number

KidPix

Drawing, creation of visual effects

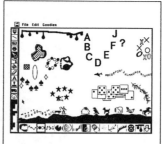

◆◆◆◆◆◆◆◆◆ 93 FINAL RATING

◆◆◆◆◆◆◆◆ 85 User Friendliness

◆◆◆◆◆◆◆◆◆ 98 Educational Value

◆◆◆◆◆◆◆◆◆ 96 Instructional Design

Broderbund Software
1991
$44.95
Ages 3-up
Mac* (color or B&W), IBM (VGA
    and hard drive)
CP/1,4 LA/3 SP/4,7 TI/2

A powerful, easy-to-use graphics creation program. Child uses mouse (required) to draw, dribble paint, stamp letters, erase, and create shapes and backgrounds. Includes 112 picture "stamps," 36 colors (16 for IBM), 13 fill shades, and a range of entertaining sound effects (sound device recommended for IBM). Can be customized for independent use by younger children. Pictures are saved or printed in color. Limited utility for writing. Highly recommended, fun program.

Kid's Stuff

Counting skills, letter recognition

◆◆◆◆◆◆◆ 76 FINAL RATING

◆◆◆◆◆◆ 64 User Friendliness

◆◆◆◆◆◆◆◆ 86 Educational Value

◆◆◆◆◆◆◆◆ 80 Instructional Design

Stone & Associates
1984
$39.95
Ages 3-8
IBM*, Apple, Atari ST
LA/4,5 SE/4,5

Offers three activities accessible by a picture menu. In the letter recognition activity, child types in letters of a word, which creates animation and sounds. An entertaining program that provides options for the child.

Kids at Work

Creation of graphics

◆◆◆◆◆◆ 69 FINAL RATING

◆◆◆◆◆ 53 User Friendliness

◆◆◆◆◆◆ 68 Educational Value

◆◆◆◆◆◆◆◆ 80 Instructional Design

Scholastic Software, Inc.
1984
$29.95
Ages 5-up
Apple
SP/4,7 CP/4

Child uses arrow keys to move a person around the screen to pick up objects and create city or country scenes. A total of 32 objects are available for each picture. Resulting pictures can be printed or saved. Children have trouble picking up objects. Rather limited potential. Not recommended.

Kids on Keys

Letter recognition

◆◆◆◆◆◆ 62 FINAL RATING

◆◆◆ 38 User Friendliness

◆◆◆◆◆ 63 Educational Value

◆◆◆◆◆◆ 79 Instructional Design

Queue, Inc.
1983
$29.95
Ages 4-9
Apple*, IBM
LA/4 CL/1 OT/3

Presents three games in which letters, pictures, or words rain down the screen. Child stops them and scores points by typing in the appropriate letter or word. Three levels of difficulty. Good keyboard practice, but requires skills that few three- or four-year-olds have.

KidsMath

Teaching and reinforcing basic math concepts

◆◆◆◆◆◆◆ 83 FINAL RATING

◆◆◆◆◆ 67 User Friendliness

◆◆◆◆◆◆◆◆ 97 Educational Value

◆◆◆◆◆◆◆ 88 Instructional Design

Great Wave Software
1989
$49.95
Ages 3-8
Mac (512K)
NB/1,3,4,5,6,8 TI/3,6 OT/1

Child uses mouse in eight counting and computing activities ranging from counting up to 9 to identifying fractions. Contains a fraction activity that combines a part-whole and a measurement approach. Management features make it easy to customize activities to each child. Some reading required.

KidsTime

Letters, numbers, matching, writing, music

◆◆◆◆◆◆◆ 82 FINAL RATING

◆◆◆◆◆◆◆ 80 User Friendliness

◆◆◆◆◆◆◆◆ 91 Educational Value

◆◆◆◆◆◆ 77 Instructional Design

Great Wave Software
1987
$49.95
Ages 3-8
Mac*, IIGS, IBM
LA/4,9 CP/2 CL/2 NB/3 OT/1
SE/1

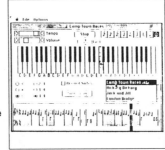

Five games in which child uses mouse to play a piano, record and play back melodies, match letters or pictures, use or create dot-to-dot pictures, find letters on the keyboard in upper or lower case, or write stories and have them read back using Mac's built-in speech. Nice range of activities. Good child-control.

CL = Classification   **CP** = Creative projects   **LA** = Language   **NA** = Not applicable   **NB** = Number

Kidsword

Large-type word processing

◆◆◆◆◆ 55 FINAL RATING

◆◆◆ 34 User Friendliness

◆◆◆◆◆◆◆ 73 Educational Value

◆◆◆◆◆◆ 63 Instructional Design

Kidsview Software, Inc.
1989
$49.95, $39.95 (Abbreviated
    versions available for IIGS,
    IBM)
Ages na
Apple*, C64
LA/9 CP/4

A word-processing program that displays large (20-letter-per-line) print on the screen. Includes such advanced features as cut and paste, insert or typeover modes, and word wrap. Text can be saved or printed. Complicated to use. Adult help is required to get started. See "Muppet Slate" or "Magic Slate" for other large-letter word processors.

KidTalk

Language experience

◆◆◆◆◆◆◆◆ 86 FINAL RATING

◆◆◆◆◆◆◆ 76 User Friendliness

◆◆◆◆◆◆◆◆◆ 95 Educational Value

◆◆◆◆◆◆◆◆ 88 Instructional Design

First Byte, Inc.
1988
$49.95
Ages 3-10
Mac*, IIGS*, Atari ST, Amiga
LA/3,4,5,6,8,9

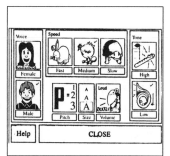

An easy-to-use word processor that will say what is typed. Makes features such as moving text, selecting sizes of type, changing sounds of words, and printing stories easy to use through clear picture menus. Uses built-in speech synthesizer.

KidWare 2 Learning Center

Variety of skills and experiences

See individual ratings of component programs

Mobius Corporation
1991
$1215.00 (1 station)
Ages 3-5
IBM
LA SP TI CP NB

Eleven programs networked together: Electronic Easel, The Farm, Fantastic Animals, Fun with Letters and Words, Mural Maker, I Can Count the Petals of a Flower, Electronic Builder, Music Maker, Word Processor for Kids, Facemaker, and Mixed-Up Mother Goose. Picture menus give access to each program. Management system keeps records for each child. Uses digitized speech. Price includes software and peripherals. For information on individual titles, see reviews elsewhere in this section.

OT = Other topics   SE = Seriation   SP = Spatial relations   TI = Time   * = Version reviewed

Kidwriter

Creating computer storybooks

◆◆◆◆◆◆◆ 73 FINAL RATING

◆◆◆◆ 48 User Friendliness

◆◆◆◆◆◆◆◆◆ 97 Educational Value

◆◆◆◆◆◆◆◆ 81 Instructional Design

Queue, Inc.
1984
$29.95
Ages 6-10
Apple*, IBM (3.5")
LA/9 CP/4

Child creates picture, selecting from 100 objects that can be moved and changed in size or color. Text can be typed on the lower third of the screen. Stories can be saved on disk and have several pages. Reading required. Good design.

Kieran

Letters, numbers, clocks,
upper/lower case

◆◆◆◆◆◆◆ 70 FINAL RATING

◆◆◆◆◆◆◆ 79 User Friendliness

◆◆◆◆◆◆◆ 79 Educational Value

◆◆◆◆◆ 57 Instructional Design

Ohm Software Company
1986
$39.95
Ages 3-6
Mac
LA/1 NB/3 TI/9 SP/2

An easy-to-use program with eight activities. Child uses mouse to choose a letter and see associated picture, to choose a number and see associated set, and to choose a clockface and hear the time. There is also an upper/lower case matching activity, a sliding square puzzle, a calculator, a typewriter, and a mystery picture. Uses Macintosh's internal speech.

Kinder Critters

Addresses, phone numbers and letter
recognition

◆◆◆◆◆◆◆ 70 FINAL RATING

◆◆◆◆◆◆ 61 User Friendliness

◆◆◆◆◆◆◆◆ 82 Educational Value

◆◆◆◆◆◆◆ 71 Instructional Design

Micrograms
1991
$29.95
Ages 5-6
Apple
LA/4,5 CL/2 OT/5

Two disks: (1) Child uses spacebar to match upper- or lower-case letters or three-letter words in simple multiple-choice format. (2) Child receives practice recognizing and typing own phone number and address. Data file can keep eight classes of 40 children each. Useful for kindergarten teachers.

Kinder Koncepts MATH

Number and math skills

◆◆◆◆◆ 57 FINAL RATING

◆◆◆◆ 46 User Friendliness

◆◆◆◆◆◆◆◆ 93 Educational Value

◆◆◆◆ 44 Instructional Design

Queue, Inc.
1985
$65.00
Ages 4-7
Apple
NB/1,2,3,4,5,6,7,8

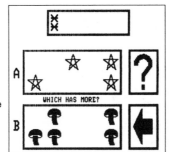

Fifteen well-designed math games cover various number concepts, e.g., estimating length, using units of measurement, counting, numeral recognition. All games follow same drill-and-practice format. Menu designed for adults, which limits child-control.

Kinder Koncepts Reading

Reading readiness

◆◆◆◆ 44 FINAL RATING

◆◆◆◆ 44 User Friendliness

◆◆◆◆◆ 56 Educational Value

◆◆◆ 37 Instructional Design

Queue, Inc.
1985
$65.00
Ages 4-8
Apple
LA/4 CL/1 OT/1

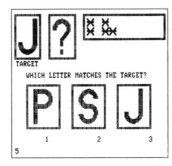

Fifteen activities on three disks each present 10 problems concerning a specific reading concept including matching letters and shapes, upper/lower case, alphabetical order, and memory. Keeps track of progress. Offers a wide range of content. Some reading required, especially for main menu.

Kindercomp

Matching, U/L-case practice, drawing

◆◆◆◆◆◆ 68 FINAL RATING

◆◆◆◆◆◆◆ 77 User Friendliness

◆◆◆◆◆◆◆ 72 Educational Value

◆◆◆◆◆◆◆◆ 83 Instructional Design

Queue, Inc.
1982
$29.95
Ages 3-8
Apple, IBM*
CP/1 CL/2 LA/4

Offers six games of varying difficulty, including a simple drawing (move cursor with arrow keys) and matching activity that increases in difficulty as child improves. Offers variety of content, which lengthens the life of the program. Menu requires reading.

OT = Other topics   **SE** = Seriation   **SP** = Spatial relations   **TI** = Time   * = Version reviewed

Kindercomp Golden Edition

Counting, letters, matching, and drawing

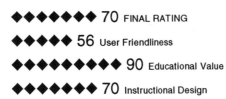 70 FINAL RATING

◆◆◆◆◆ 56 User Friendliness

◆◆◆◆◆◆◆◆◆ 90 Educational Value

◆◆◆◆◆◆◆ 70 Instructional Design

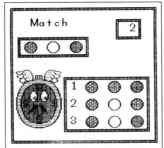

Queue, Inc.
1986
$39.95
Ages 3-7
Apple*, IBM (3.5")
NB/3 LA/4 CL/2 CP/1

Eight activities: Draw, Name, Match, Letters, Alphabet, Count, Sequence, and Add. Provides practice with the alphabet, upper/lower-case letters, counting (as high as 30), number sequence, counting by 2s, 3s, etc., and addition (sums up to 18). Offers good range in content and level of challenge.

Kindermath II

Math fundamentals

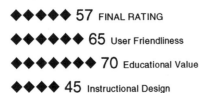 57 FINAL RATING

◆◆◆◆◆◆ 65 User Friendliness

◆◆◆◆◆◆◆ 70 Educational Value

◆◆◆◆ 45 Instructional Design

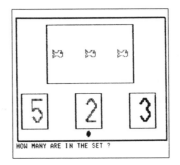

Houghton Mifflin Co.
1988
$276.00
Ages 4-7
Apple (64K)
NB/1,2,3,4,5,8 CL/2 SP/8

Ten disks cover 90 separate objectives, starting with "same" and "different" and ending with addition and subtraction problems with sums less than 10. Child uses joystick (required) to move cursor to correct answer. Keeps records. Requires adult setup and Echo speech synthesizer. Dry presentation.

Knowing Directions

Directions up, down, left, right

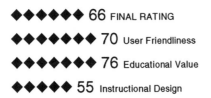 66 FINAL RATING

◆◆◆◆◆◆◆ 70 User Friendliness

◆◆◆◆◆◆◆ 76 Educational Value

◆◆◆◆◆ 55 Instructional Design

Access Unlimited
1988
$25.00
Ages 3-6
Apple
SP/4

Four activities on one disk: (1) Child indicates when two arrows point in the same direction, (2) child matches word (up, down, left, right) to arrow, (3) child indicates which arrow goes with a direction word, and (4) child moves a shape in a requested direction, using the arrow keys. Correct answers yield a burst of colors and a short tune, unrelated to concept.

CL = Classification **CP** = Creative projects **LA** = Language **NA** = Not applicable **NB** = Number

Knowing Numbers

Fundamental math skill practice

◆◆◆◆◆◆ 67 FINAL RATING

◆◆◆◆◆◆◆ 79 User Friendliness

◆◆◆◆◆◆◆ 77 Educational Value

◆◆◆◆◆ 53 Instructional Design

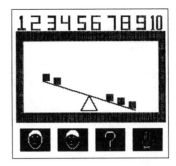

Mindscape, Inc.
1983
$61.00
Ages 3-6
Apple
NB/1,3,7

Presents counting, addition, and subtraction activities. Child uses nodding or shaking heads to decide (1) if a group matches a numeral, (2) which group has "more," and (3) if the sum of two groups equals a third. No reading. Some management.

Koala Pad Graphics Exhibitor

Drawing

◆◆◆◆◆◆◆ 76 FINAL RATING

◆◆◆◆◆◆◆◆ 85 User Friendliness

◆◆◆◆◆◆◆ 74 Educational Value

◆◆◆◆◆◆ 68 Instructional Design

Koala Technologies Corp.
1983
$139.50
Ages 5-up
Apple IIe*, IBM
CP/1,4 SP/7

This is the software that comes with the Koala Pad, which hooks into a joystick port. By moving finger or pointer across a pad surface, a child can draw lines, circles, or squares and fill or magnify shapes, using many available colors. Picture menu is usable but complex for young children. Price includes Koala Pad and program.

Language Experience Recorder Plus

Word processing

◆◆◆◆◆ 55 FINAL RATING

◆◆◆ 33 User Friendliness

◆◆◆◆◆◆◆ 75 Educational Value

◆◆◆◆◆◆ 63 Instructional Design

Teacher Support Software
1987
$99.95
Ages 5-up
Apple
LA/1,2,3,4,5,9 OT/4

A large-print (20-column) word processor. Stories can be saved, analyzed for readability level, printed, or read back through an Echo or Slotbuster speech synthesizer. Two small-print (40- and 80-column) versions are included. Adult help required to use menus.

OT = Other topics **SE** = Seriation **SP** = Spatial relations **TI** = Time * = Version reviewed

Learn About: Animals

Animals, environments, and creative writing

◆◆◆◆◆◆◆◆ 80 FINAL RATING

◆◆◆◆◆◆◆ 75 User Friendliness

◆◆◆◆◆◆◆◆◆ 94 Educational Value

◆◆◆◆◆◆◆ 74 Instructional Design

Wings for Learning
1989
$75.00
Ages 5-8
Apple (128K, 3.5" or 5.25")
CP/4 LA/8,9 SP/1,5 SE/1

Child uses a mouse (recommended), joystick, or Muppet Learning Keys to explore animal homes, babies, food, movements, or size. Includes activities that allow a child to write about habitats or to create and print animal masks. High degree of child-control. Work can be saved or printed. Startup with 5.25" disks requires disk change.

Learn About: Plants

Plants, environments, and creative writing

◆◆◆◆◆◆◆ 80 FINAL RATING

◆◆◆◆◆◆◆ 75 User Friendliness

◆◆◆◆◆◆◆◆◆ 94 Educational Value

◆◆◆◆◆◆◆ 74 Instructional Design

Wings for Learning
1990
$75.00
Ages 5-8
Apple (128K, 3.5" or 5.25")
CP/4 LA/8,9 SP/1,5 SE/1

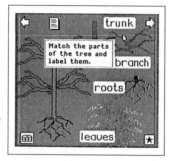

Child uses mouse (recommended), joystick, or Muppet Learning Keys to explore what plants are, where they live, their seeds, how we use them, and what they need to live. Additional activities allow child to write about plants or to create imaginary plants. High degree of child-control. Use of 5.25" disks requires disk change for startup.

Learn the Alphabet

Upper/lower case, alphabetical order

◆◆◆◆◆ 56 FINAL RATING

◆◆◆◆◆◆ 64 User Friendliness

◆◆◆◆ 49 Educational Value

◆◆◆◆◆ 54 Instructional Design

Queue, Inc.
1984
$24.95
Ages 4-8
Apple*, IBM, C64 (cartridge)
LA/4,5 CL/2 SP/4

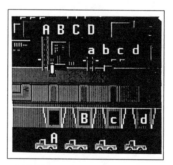

Child uses arrow keys or joystick to match letters to complete an alphabetical sequence or simple words. Eight levels, ranging from matching one letter to completing a word. Somewhat confusing graphics.

CL = Classification   **CP** = Creative projects   **LA** = Language   **NA** = Not applicable   **NB** = Number

Learn to Add

Matching numbers, addition, subtraction

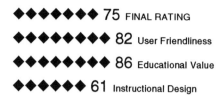 75 FINAL RATING

◆◆◆◆◆◆◆◆ 82 User Friendliness

◆◆◆◆◆◆◆◆ 86 Educational Value

◆◆◆◆◆◆ 61 Instructional Design

Queue, Inc.
1984
$24.95
Ages 3-7
Apple*, IBM
NB/1,3,4,7

Child uses joystick or arrow keys to match numbers to sets, match sets, or do simple addition or subtraction problems. Child is rewarded with rainbow. Four challenge levels (9 - 4 = 5 most difficult). Allows high level of child-control. IBM version comes on back of Apple disk.

Learning About Numbers

Counting, clocks, basic math facts

 78 FINAL RATING

◆◆◆◆◆ 56 User Friendliness

◆◆◆◆◆◆◆ 86 Educational Value

◆◆◆◆◆◆◆◆ 91 Instructional Design

How many?

C&C Software
1983
$50.00
Ages 3-6
Apple
NB/8 TI/9

Provides a variety of number experiences: Let's Count, Let's Tell Time, and Arithmetic Fun, all with varying difficulty levels. Many aspects of this program can be managed by an adult, due to a well-designed management system.

Learning Directions

Directions of up, down, left, right

◆◆◆◆◆◆ 62 FINAL RATING

◆◆◆◆◆◆◆ 71 User Friendliness

◆◆◆◆◆◆ 67 Educational Value

◆◆◆◆ 48 Instructional Design

Move Up

X

Access Unlimited
1988
$25.00
Ages 3-6
Apple
SP/4

For use in special education settings. Child progresses object towards a marker by pressing the spacebar or single switch. Also includes a nonstructured activity in which child uses the arrows to move many objects around the screen.

OT = Other topics   **SE** = Seriation   **SP** = Spatial relations   **TI** = Time   * = Version reviewed

Learning Letters

Matching letters

◆◆◆◆◆◆ 62 FINAL RATING

◆◆◆◆◆ 59 User Friendliness

◆◆◆◆◆◆◆ 76 Educational Value

◆◆◆◆◆ 55 Instructional Design

Access Unlimited
1988
$25.00
Ages 3-6
Apple
LA/4 OT/3

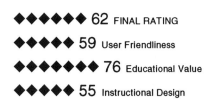

Three activities on one disk: Match the Letter—child sees two letters and uses spacebar and RETURN to indicate when they are the same. Press the Letter—child sees a letter and presses it on the keyboard. Typing Practice— child can "type" any letter with large upper-case, multicolored letters.

Learning Numbers

Counting from 1 to 5

◆◆◆◆◆ 63 FINAL RATING

◆◆◆◆◆◆◆ 71 User Friendliness

◆◆◆◆◆◆◆ 74 Educational Value

◆◆◆◆ 48 Instructional Design

Access Unlimited
1989
$25.00
Ages 3-6
Apple
NB/2,3,4

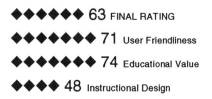

Three simple activities involving counting up to 5: Match Numbers—child uses spacebar to match two numerals. Match Sets—child sees a set and creates a matching one by pressing the spacebar. Match Sets to Numbers—child sees a set of 1 to 5 objects and selects matching number. Can be used with a single switch. Reinforcements not related to content.

Learning Shapes

Practice with four basic shapes

◆◆◆◆◆◆ 66 FINAL RATING

◆◆◆◆◆◆◆ 70 User Friendliness

◆◆◆◆◆◆◆ 76 Educational Value

◆◆◆◆◆ 55 Instructional Design

Access Unlimited
1988
$25.00
Ages 3-6
Apple
SP/8 CL/2 CP/1

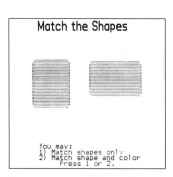

Four simple activities. Match the Shapes—child indicates when two shapes are the same. Name the Shape—child matches a shape with its name. Find the Shape—child selects a shape to match a given word. Draw a Picture—child uses arrows, spacebar, and RETURN to create structures from shapes. Color monitor recommended.

CL = Classification   **CP** = Creative projects   **LA** = Language   **NA** = Not applicable   **NB** = Number

Learning Sight Words

Matching and typing sight words

◆◆◆◆◆ 56 FINAL RATING

◆◆◆◆◆ 56 User Friendliness

◆◆◆◆◆◆◆ 75 Educational Value

◆◆◆◆ 45 Instructional Design

Access Unlimited
1988
$25.00
Ages 3-6
Apple
LA/5 CL/2

```
┌─────────────────────────────────┐
│  Match the Words                │
│                                 │
│            WOULD                │
│            THEIR                │
│                                 │
│                                 │
│     Press <Spacebar> or <Return>.   │
│  (Press Switch 1 or 2 if you prefer).│
│     Press <Esc> to return to Menu.  │
└─────────────────────────────────┘
```

Three simple activities. Match the Words—child matches two words. Spell the Word—child sees a word and must type it. Guess the Word—child sees a word spelled with cartoon letters and types it. Contains 220 sight words. Uses regular or alternate keyboards.

Learning the Alphabet

Alphabet skills

◆◆◆◆◆◆ 66 FINAL RATING

◆◆◆◆◆ 57 User Friendliness

◆◆◆◆◆◆ 72 Educational Value

◆◆◆◆◆◆ 70 Instructional Design

Access Unlimited
1988
$25.00
Ages 3-6
Apple
LA/4 CL/2

```
┌─────────────────────────────────┐
│      The Alphabet Song          │
│   A B C D E F G                 │
│   H I J K L M N                 │
│   O P                           │
└─────────────────────────────────┘
```

Contains three alphabet activities: The Alphabet Song—child can hear the alphabet song, one letter at a time, by pressing the spacebar. Practice the Alphabet—child sees a letter and must press the letter on the keyboard. Guess the Next Letter—child is shown part of the alphabet and must enter the next letter in sequence.

Learning the Alphabet

Matching letters, alphabetical order

◆◆◆◆◆ 50 FINAL RATING

◆◆◆◆ 49 User Friendliness

◆◆◆◆◆ 52 Educational Value

◆◆◆◆◆ 50 Instructional Design

MicroED, Inc.
1987
$29.95
Ages 3-6
Amiga (512K)
LA/4

Child is shown portion of the alphabet. By clicking the mouse, child selects matching letters, in order, from letters scattered on the screen. The computer says each letter and gives a feedback message in a fairly clear voice. Repetitive format causes children to lose interest.

OT = Other topics	SE = Seriation	SP = Spatial relations	TI = Time	* = Version reviewed

Let's Go to Hannah's House

Pre-literacy skills

◆◆◆◆ 48 FINAL RATING

◆◆◆◆ 49 User Friendliness

◆◆◆◆ 40 Educational Value

◆◆◆◆◆ 50 Instructional Design

Intellimation
1990
$39.95
Ages 3-5
Mac (hard disk, Hypercard)
LA/4 NB/4 CP/1

A computerized scrapbook for Hannah, the author's daughter. By clicking on one of 15 icons that appear in the main menu, a child can hear Hannah's family's voices and her favorite tunes, count the chimes of her clock, draw pictures, and so on. Content is of little meaning to most children. Consists of a large, 17-stack hypercard program. Not recommended.

Letter Games

Letter recognition

◆◆◆ 34 FINAL RATING

◆◆ 24 User Friendliness

◆◆◆◆ 40 Educational Value

◆◆◆◆ 49 Instructional Design

Island Software
1982
$25.00
Ages 3-6
Apple
LA/4 CL/2

Three drill games for letter discrimination. Upper/lower-case options are available. No branching. Has errors if used without light pen. Not recommended.

Letter Recognition

Location of letters on keyboard

◆◆◆◆ 48 FINAL RATING

◆◆◆◆ 40 User Friendliness

◆◆◆◆◆◆ 62 Educational Value

◆◆◆◆ 47 Instructional Design

Hartley Courseware, Inc.
1983
$29.95
Ages 5-7
Apple
LA/4

A single letter is presented for child to find on keyboard. Model keyboard appears as help is needed, showing letter location. Options include upper/lower-case and number words. Records are kept.

CL = Classification   **CP** = Creative projects   **LA** = Language   **NA** = Not applicable   **NB** = Number

Letters and First Words

Letters, initial consonants

◆◆◆◆◆◆ 68 FINAL RATING

◆◆◆◆◆ 55 User Friendliness

◆◆◆◆◆◆◆ 72 Educational Value

◆◆◆◆◆◆◆ 75 Instructional Design

C&C Software
1984
$60.00
Ages 3-6
Apple
LA/4,5,6

Three games: ABC, Letter Sounds, and Building Words. Management system allows for records for up to 50 children. Child makes selections by moving box cursor. Offers wide range of content and effective design features.

Letters and Words

Letter recognition, alphabet order

◆◆◆◆◆◆ 68 FINAL RATING

◆◆◆◆◆◆◆ 79 User Friendliness

◆◆◆◆◆◆ 68 Educational Value

◆◆◆◆◆ 60 Instructional Design

Mindscape, Inc.
1983
$61.00
Ages 3-6
Apple*, IBM
LA/4,5

Three games on letters and words. Child selects Y, N, ?, or ESCAPE for each problem. Provides drill on alphabet order by asking what letter fits into a missing series. Management features: selection of number of rounds, performance summary, selection of timing of cursor movement, and new word list.

Letters, Pictures & Words

Letter recognition

◆◆◆◆◆◆ 67 FINAL RATING

◆◆◆◆◆◆ 63 User Friendliness

◆◆◆◆◆ 61 Educational Value

◆◆◆◆◆◆ 74 Instructional Design

Queue, Inc.
1990
$39.95
Ages 3-6
Apple
LA/4,5

Four activities on two-sided disk: (1) A letter and scene are shown. Child must find letter on the keyboard to animate the scene. (2) An object in a scene is highlighted. Child selects beginning letter from four choices. (3) A letter is shown. Child moves pointer to a matching object. (4) A word is shown. Child moves pointer to the matching object. Uses cartoonist graphics. High in child-control. Limited in content.

OT = Other topics   SE = Seriation   SP = Spatial relations   TI = Time   * = Version reviewed

Lion's Workshop

Visual discrimination

◆◆◆◆ 49 FINAL RATING

◆◆◆◆ 49 User Friendliness

◆◆◆◆◆ 54 Educational Value

◆◆◆◆ 45 Instructional Design

Merit Software
1985
$24.95
Ages 4-8
Apple*, C64
CL/2

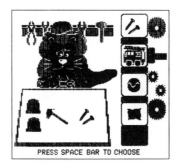

PRESS SPACE BAR TO CHOOSE

Two activities: (1) Child uses A and Z keys to move conveyer belt to select an object that goes with another (e.g., thread/needle). (2) Child selects missing piece of a given object. Limited content. Confusing graphics.

Little People Bowling Alley

Spatial relationships and addition practice

◆◆◆◆◆◆◆ 70 FINAL RATING

◆◆◆◆◆◆◆ 79 User Friendliness

◆◆◆◆◆◆◆ 71 Educational Value

◆◆◆◆◆◆ 68 Instructional Design

GameTek/IJE, Inc.
1988
$9.95
Ages 3-8
Apple, IBM*, C64
SP/4 TI/1 NB/7

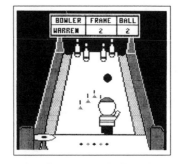

A bowling game. Child uses arrow keys (or joystick) to position a bowler and presses the spacebar to roll the ball and knock over up to six pins. Can be set for one or two players, or for child to add up own score (e.g., 33 + 6). More advanced level allows control over curve of the ball. Young children need help setting up options. Minor bugs in the IBM version.

Logic Blocks

Understanding geometry, patterns, and logic

◆◆◆◆◆◆◆◆ 86 FINAL RATING

◆◆◆◆◆◆◆◆ 83 User Friendliness

◆◆◆◆◆◆◆◆◆ 98 Educational Value

◆◆◆◆◆◆◆ 81 Instructional Design

The Learning Box
1991
$59.00
Ages 5-12
IIGS
SP/1,2,3,8,9,10 CL/1,2,3 SE/1-4
   CP/1

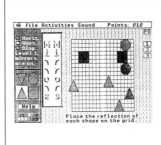

Four activities: (1) Layers—child copies colored block patterns. (2) Smokescreen—child uses attribute clues and memory to uncover a hidden block pattern. (3) Patterns—child finishes incomplete block patterns by following symmetrical design. (4) Mirrors—child creates a block pattern in reverse. Each activity contains an open-ended application that invites experimentation. An excellent addition to a K-3 math curriculum.

CL = Classification   **CP** = Creative projects   **LA** = Language   **NA** = Not applicable   **NB** = Number

Looney Tunes Print Kit

Creating printed materials

◆◆◆◆ 46 FINAL RATING

◆◆◆ 32 User Friendliness

◆◆◆◆◆◆ 60 Educational Value

◆◆◆◆◆ 50 Instructional Design

Hi Tech Expressions
1989
$11.95
Ages 3-up
Apple*, IBM, C64, Atari
CP/4 LA/9

A printing program featuring 60 Looney Tunes characters, 20 borders, and 7 typefaces in three sizes. Can make cards, banners, signs, stationery, or storybook. Design makes it difficult to use. Reading required.

Mad Match

Matching, visual discrimination

◆◆◆◆◆◆◆◆ 81 FINAL RATING

◆◆◆◆◆◆◆◆ 81 User Friendliness

◆◆◆◆◆◆◆◆ 87 Educational Value

◆◆◆◆◆◆◆ 78 Instructional Design

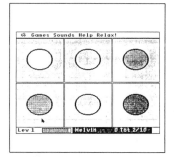

Baudville
1989
$39.95
Ages 4-up
IIGS
CL/1,2,5

A matching game in which child sees six objects and must select the two that are the same, using either the mouse or the number keypad. As matches are completed, the objects become more detailed, making the task more difficult. A score is kept, and progress can be tracked or adjusted. Good graphics, sound, and design. For one or two players.

Magic Crayon

Drawing with arrow keys

◆◆◆◆◆◆◆ 75 FINAL RATING

◆◆◆◆◆ 53 User Friendliness

◆◆◆◆◆◆ 67 Educational Value

◆◆◆◆◆◆◆◆ 95 Instructional Design

C&C Software
1983
$45.00
Ages 4-6
Apple
CP/1,3,4 SP/11

A simple drawing program in 16 colors and three difficulty levels. Good recordkeeping and management are available to the teacher or parent. Stickers are included to label the keys.

OT = Other topics   **SE** = Seriation   **SP** = Spatial relations   **TI** = Time   * = Version reviewed

Magic Melody Box

Creating music

◆◆◆◆◆ 59 FINAL RATING

◆◆◆◆ 45 User Friendliness

◆◆◆◆◆◆ 64 Educational Value

◆◆◆◆◆◆ 64 Instructional Design

W. Wes Horlacher's New Media
　Values Center
1988
$19.95
Ages 3-6
Atari
CP/2 SE/1

Child uses joystick to draw a melody line, to which the computer adds chords and replays. A three-octave major scale is available. A basic cartridge is required. Some reading required.

Magic Slate

Word processing

◆◆◆◆◆◆◆◆ 81 FINAL RATING

◆◆◆◆◆◆◆ 70 User Friendliness

◆◆◆◆◆◆◆◆◆ 92 Educational Value

◆◆◆◆◆◆◆◆ 85 Instructional Design

Sunburst Communications, Inc.
1984
$99.95
Ages 7-up
Apple
LA/4,9 CP/4 OT/3,4

Easy-to-use word processor with large (20-column) text and picture menu. Effective for experience stories for preschool level. Stories can be saved, printed, and edited. Graphics printer desirable.

Magic String, The

Reading skills

◆◆◆◆ 46 FINAL RATING

◆◆◆◆◆ 52 User Friendliness

◆◆◆◆ 46 Educational Value

◆◆◆◆ 41 Instructional Design

Troll Associates
1985
$39.95
Ages 5-6
Apple
LA/11

Three activities: (1) Shows six words. Using spacebar, child arranges words in alphabetical order. (2) Child selects word that doesn't belong, e.g., "swan, duck, fail." (3) Child arranges letters to make words. Menus require reading, limiting child-control.

CL = Classification　　　**CP** = Creative projects　　　**LA** = Language　　　**NA** = Not applicable　　　**NB** = Number

Make-A-Book

Creation of books

◆◆◆◆◆◆ 67 FINAL RATING

◆◆◆ 37 User Friendliness

◆◆◆◆◆◆◆◆ 86 Educational Value

◆◆◆◆◆◆◆◆ 83 Instructional Design

Teacher Support Software
1991
$59.95
Ages 5-11
IBM
LA/9 CP/4

A talking word processing program with printing routines that allow creation of five sizes of books on standard printing paper. Pull-down menus include help screens and printing and speech options. Includes 14 large-sized fonts, although only one can be used per file. Mouse optional, but recommended. Supports a variety of printers. Works with DoubleTalk PC, Echo, Covox, or Sound Blaster speech cards. Setup required.

Mask Parade

Creative design

◆◆◆◆◆◆◆ 77 FINAL RATING

◆◆◆◆◆◆◆ 75 User Friendliness

◆◆◆◆◆◆◆◆ 86 Educational Value

◆◆◆◆◆◆ 69 Instructional Design

Queue, Inc.
1984
$39.95
Ages 4-12
Apple*, IBM
CP/1,4 SP/5,7

Child can design and print masks and other cutouts. The design part requires choosing the components of the mask (eyes, nose, etc.). Easy to print, once printer is set up. Pictures can be saved on disk. No reading required. Will not print on the IIGS.

Match Maker (Beginning)

Matching objects

◆◆◆◆◆◆◆ 77 FINAL RATING

◆◆◆◆◆◆◆◆ 81 User Friendliness

◆◆◆◆◆◆◆◆ 80 Educational Value

◆◆◆◆◆◆◆ 70 Instructional Design

Wescott Software
1991
$20.00
Ages 3-6
IBM
CL/2 OT/1

A version of concentration in which the child uses the arrow keys or a mouse to turn over cards and make matches. Includes 10 sets of pictures that vary in difficulty level (e.g., numerals, colors, safety signs, upper- and lower-case letters, finger spell signs). Options allow for number of cards (from 4 to 30), selection of one or two players, and presentation of cards.

OT = Other topics   SE = Seriation   SP = Spatial relations   TI = Time   * = Version reviewed

Match-On-A-Mac

Matching letters, shapes, numbers, words; mouse practice

◆◆◆◆◆◆◆ 79 FINAL RATING

◆◆◆◆◆◆◆◆ 82 User Friendliness

◆◆◆◆◆◆◆◆ 83 Educational Value

◆◆◆◆◆◆◆ 75 Instructional Design

Teach Yourself by Computer
1986
$39.95
Ages 3-7
Mac
CL/2 NB/1,3,4 LA/4,5 SP/8

A multiple-choice program in which child matches shapes, upper/lower-case letters, short words, the letters b and d, quantities, and numbers with quantities. Also has a game for practicing mouse use. Keeps records. Has a "lesson plan" feature whereby adult can determine the activities that appear. Easy to use.

Math and Me

Shapes, patterns, numbers, and addition

◆◆◆◆◆◆◆ 78 FINAL RATING

◆◆◆◆◆◆◆◆ 80 User Friendliness

◆◆◆◆◆◆◆◆◆ 94 Educational Value

◆◆◆◆◆◆ 67 Instructional Design

Davidson and Associates, Inc.
1987
$39.95
Ages 3-6
Apple* (128K), IBM, IIGS
   ($49.95)
NB/1,3,4,7 CL/2 SE/4

Twelve activities covering shape matching, number recognition, patterns, numerical order, and addition with objects or numbers. In each activity, child uses mouse (optional) or arrow keys to select one of four boxes in a multiple-choice format. Good design and graphics. Good range of content. Talking version for the IIGS gives verbal feedback.

Math Blaster Plus

Basic math facts practice

◆◆◆◆◆◆◆◆ 85 FINAL RATING

◆◆◆◆◆◆◆◆ 84 User Friendliness

◆◆◆◆◆◆◆◆ 88 Educational Value

◆◆◆◆◆◆◆◆ 83 Instructional Design

Davidson and Associates, Inc.
1991
$59.95
Ages 6-12
Mac* 1 MB (2MB for color), IBM
   (CGA, VGA)
NB/9 TI/3

Four activities provide practice with math problems involving basic addition, subtraction, multiplication, division, and percentages. Activities mix math facts with arcade-style games. Features include choice of problem display, record keeping, customization of problems, and creation of printed math work-sheets. Excellent use of sound and graphics. Mouse and printer recommended, but not required. Very well designed. Fun to use.

CL = Classification   **CP** = Creative projects   **LA** = Language   **NA** = Not applicable   **NB** = Number

Math Concepts Level P

Math concepts and symbols

◆◆◆◆◆◆◆ 73 FINAL RATING

◆◆◆◆◆ 43 User Friendliness

◆◆◆◆◆◆◆◆ 88 Educational Value

◆◆◆◆◆◆◆◆ 86 Instructional Design

IBM Educational Systems
1987
$76.00
Ages 4-5
IBM
NB/1,3,4,6,7,8 CL/2 SE/3 SP/8

The first in IBM's Math Concepts series, this program offers 4 units and 18 lessons that range from comparing sizes (child uses arrows to select largest picture) to identifying shapes. Child first types in password for custom lesson. Keeps records. Offers many setup and teacher options. Wide range of content. Some reading required.

Math Magic

Math facts (add, sub., mult., div.)

◆◆◆◆◆ 53 FINAL RATING

◆◆◆◆◆ 53 User Friendliness

◆◆◆◆◆◆ 67 Educational Value

◆◆◆◆ 43 Instructional Design

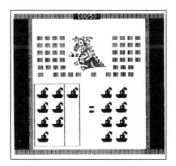

MindPlay
1984
$49.99
Ages 4-9
Apple*, IBM
NB/3

A math game in which player deflects bouncing ball to break down a wall while periodically answering math problems to score points. Design options include paddle size, level and number of problems, and speed of ball.

Math Maze

Basic math facts

◆◆◆◆◆ 52 FINAL RATING

◆◆◆◆ 47 User Friendliness

◆◆◆◆◆◆ 62 Educational Value

◆◆◆◆◆ 50 Instructional Design

Compton's New Media
1983
$51.00
Ages 6-10
Apple*, IBM, Atari ($19.95), C64
NB/9

Child moves fly through 1 of 40 simple mazes (can design own) to the correct answer, using a basic fact concerning addition, subtraction, division, or multiplication. Available option turns spider loose in maze. A well-designed activity for basic math practice.

OT = Other topics **SE** = Seriation **SP** = Spatial relations **TI** = Time * = Version reviewed

Math Rabbit

Counting, matching sets, addition, subtraction

◆◆◆◆◆◆ 78 FINAL RATING

◆◆◆◆◆◆ 67 User Friendliness

◆◆◆◆◆◆◆◆ 92 Educational Value

◆◆◆◆◆◆◆ 79 Instructional Design

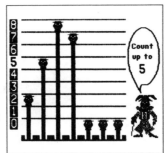

The Learning Company
1986
$39.95
Ages 5-7
Apple*, IBM
NB/1,3,4,8 OT/1

Enjoyable activities. Child uses arrow keys, spacebar, and RE-TURN to count using a number line and musical scale; to match numerals; to match a set of objects or a math problem to a given number; to solve math problems; to create number patterns; and to match sets of objects, numbers, and math problems. Four levels of play.

Math Sequences

Number readiness

◆◆◆◆◆◆ 69 FINAL RATING

◆◆◆◆◆◆ 62 User Friendliness

◆◆◆◆◆◆◆ 74 Educational Value

◆◆◆◆◆◆ 69 Instructional Design

Milliken Publishing Co.
1985
$60.00
Ages 5-6
Apple
NB/3,8

First of a 17-disk sequence spanning grades K-10 ($495 for all). Uses a flexible, powerful password system that can control content and keep records for up to 100 children. Children start by using number keys to count objects and can work up to numerical order, e.g., (6,__,8).

Mathematics Level A

Whole numbers, addition, subtraction

◆◆◆◆◆◆ 69 FINAL RATING

◆◆◆ 39 User Friendliness

◆◆◆◆◆◆◆ 85 Educational Value

◆◆◆◆◆◆◆ 83 Instructional Design

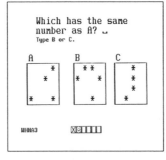

S.R.A.
1988
$150.00
Ages 6-7
Apple* (128K), IBM
NB/1,3,4,5,7,9

A six-disk computer-managed math program for grades 1 and 2. Contains 39 lessons on whole numbers, 26 lessons on addition, and 17 lessons on subtraction. Each contains 10 problems. A teacher can design a custom "lesson disk" for keeping track of each child's progress. Allows creation of worksheets. Good management. Rather dry presentation and complex setup routine.

CL = Classification   **CP** = Creative projects   **LA** = Language   **NA** = Not applicable   **NB** = Number

Mathosaurus Level K

Beginning number concepts

◆◆◆◆◆◆ 72 FINAL RATING

◆◆◆◆◆◆◆ 76 User Friendliness

◆◆◆◆◆◆◆◆ 83 Educational Value

◆◆◆◆◆◆ 62 Instructional Design

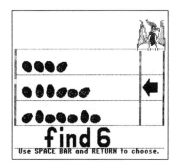

Micrograms, Inc.
1989
$24.95
Age 5
Apple
NB/1,2,3,4,5 CL/2

Contains six multiple-choice number activities in which child uses spacebar and RETURN to match numbers and sets, create a matching set, make a set to match a number, or identify a set that has more or less. Provides a range of easy-to-use activities involving numbers up to 10. No management. One disk can be used to load several computers.

McGee

Independent exploration

◆◆◆◆◆◆◆ 78 FINAL RATING

◆◆◆◆◆◆◆◆ 81 User Friendliness

◆◆◆◆◆◆◆ 76 Educational Value

◆◆◆◆◆◆◆ 76 Instructional Design

Lawrence Productions, Inc.
1989
$39.95
Ages 2-4
IIGS (3.5"), IBM (VGA or CGA),
    Mac, Amiga
SP/6,7 CL/2

Child uses a picture menu to help a boy (McGee) explore and play in a seven-room house. There are things to do in each room, e.g., bouncing a ball. Very easy to use. Clever design. A good program for first-time computer users.

McGee at the Fun Fair

Exploring, talking about actions

◆◆◆◆◆◆◆◆ 83 FINAL RATING

◆◆◆◆◆◆◆◆ 88 User Friendliness

◆◆◆◆◆◆◆ 71 Educational Value

◆◆◆◆◆◆◆◆ 87 Instructional Design

Lawrence Productions, Inc.
1991
$39.95
Ages 2-6
IIGS*, Mac, IBM (VGA or CGA),
    Mac II, Amiga
LA/1 TI/2,6 CL/1

Child uses a mouse (required) to operate a picture menu and explore a street fair. For example, selecting a clown prompts a balloon demonstration. Includes 13 animated sequences (e.g., a hot dog vender, a playground, a one-man band). Young children respond well to this program. Very easy to operate. Clear graphics and recorded sounds. Limited content. Similar to "McGee."

Measure Works

Practice with measurements

◆◆◆◆◆◆◆◆ 80 FINAL RATING

◆◆◆◆◆◆ 68 User Friendliness

◆◆◆◆◆◆◆◆◆ 97 Educational Value

◆◆◆◆◆◆◆◆ 81 Instructional Design

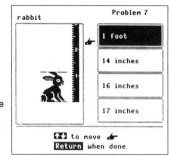

MECC
1989
$59.00
Ages 6-12
Apple (128K, 3.5" or 5.25")
NB/3,4,5,6 SP/4 CP/1

Contains five activities providing practice recognizing linear sizes; drawing objects of various perimeters and areas; and selecting units for measuring volume, weight, and length. Can be set for English or metric units or for use with various grade levels. Contains minor content inaccuracies. Design is good for use in classrooms.

Memory Building Blocks

Visual and auditory memory skills

◆◆◆◆◆◆◆◆ 83 FINAL RATING

◆◆◆◆◆◆◆◆ 83 User Friendliness

◆◆◆◆◆◆◆◆ 85 Educational Value

◆◆◆◆◆◆◆◆ 80 Instructional Design

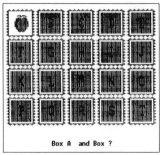

Sunburst Communications, Inc.
1986
$65.00
Ages 5-adult
Apple
OT/1 CL/2

Five Concentration-type games on one disk: Pictures, Words, Letters, Shapes, and Tunes. An easy-to-use management system allows use of own words or control over game difficulty. Minimal reading required. Operates with regular keyboard, Muppet keyboard, or TouchWindow.

Memory Lane 2.0

Matching, sequencing, memory skills

◆◆◆◆◆◆ 68 FINAL RATING

◆◆◆◆◆◆ 60 User Friendliness

◆◆◆◆◆◆◆ 73 Educational Value

◆◆◆◆◆◆ 68 Instructional Design

Stone & Associates
1990
$39.95
Ages 2-6
IBM* (VGA or CGA), Atari ST
LA/5 OT/1

Consists of five activities. In the first three, child matches object with object, object with related object, or object with word. In the final two activities, child can choose from an 18-card concentration game or an ordering activity in which three objects are shown individually, prompting the child to select the correct order from three possibilities. Poor design requires that the child must find a keyboard letter to enter each answer. Good graphics.

CL = Classification   **CP** = Creative projects   **LA** = Language   **NA** = Not applicable   **NB** = Number

Mickey & Minnie's Fun Time Print Kit

Creating printed products

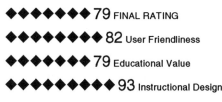

◆◆◆◆◆◆◆ 79 FINAL RATING

◆◆◆◆◆◆◆◆ 82 User Friendliness

◆◆◆◆◆◆◆ 79 Educational Value

◆◆◆◆◆◆◆◆◆ 93 Instructional Design

Walt Disney Computer Software
1991
$19.95
Ages 5-up
IBM (CGA, VGA)
CP/3,4 LA/8

A printing program that allows the creation of greeting cards, posters, banners, invitations, letterhead, and placemats. Includes 6 typefaces in three sizes, 20 borders, and 40 Disney-related clip art items. Menus can be used with a mouse (optional) and require reading ability. Page formatting capability is limited. Products can be previewed, saved, or printed in color. Uses copy protection puzzle.

Mickey's 123's

Counting from 1 to 9

◆◆◆◆◆◆ 74 FINAL RATING

◆◆◆◆◆◆ 68 User Friendliness

◆◆◆◆◆◆◆ 84 Educational Value

◆◆◆◆◆◆ 73 Instructional Design

Walt Disney Computer Software
1990
$49.95
Ages 2-5
IBM
NB/3

Child helps Mickey Mouse prepare for a surprise party by pressing number keys to determine how many guests to invite, how many party items to buy, how many wheels for Mickey's car, and so on. Children like the clear graphics and recorded sounds. Clumsy copy-protection system requires adult setup with each use. Requires The Sound Source ($34.95) for high-quality sound.

Mickey's ABC's

Recognizing upper- or lower-case letters

◆◆◆◆◆◆◆ 78 FINAL RATING

◆◆◆◆◆◆◆ 77 User Friendliness

◆◆◆◆◆◆◆◆ 82 Educational Value

◆◆◆◆◆◆◆ 76 Instructional Design

Walt Disney Computer Software
1990
$49.95
Ages 2-5
IBM
LA/4

Child presses any letter key to see a letter-related routine, e.g., the letter "L" causes Mickey Mouse to turn off a light. Contains 80 different animated responses. Children like the animation and sounds, though they find the routines to be unresponsive at times. Clumsy copy-protection system requires adult setup with each use. Requires The Sound Source ($34.95) for high quality sound.

OT = Other topics   SE = Seriation   SP = Spatial relations   TI = Time   * = Version reviewed

Mickey's Colors & Shapes

Colors and shapes

◆◆◆◆◆◆◆ 72 FINAL RATING

◆◆◆◆◆◆ 69 User Friendliness

◆◆◆◆◆◆◆◆ 87 Educational Value

◆◆◆◆◆◆ 63 Instructional Design

Walt Disney Computer Software
1990
$49.95
Ages 2-5
IBM (VGA, Sound Source
    recommended)
CL/1,2 SP/8

Three activities: (1) Child selects objects for Mickey to juggle by pressing a color or shape on a vinyl keyboard overlay (included). (2) Child selects shapes and colors to be added to a scene that can be printed. (3) Child finds hidden animal by identifying the color and shape of an object animal is hiding behind. Fun context to experiment. Good graphics and sound. Uses clumsy copy protection puzzle.

Mickey's Crossword Puzzle Maker

Reading, problem solving

◆◆◆◆◆◆◆ 76 FINAL RATING

◆◆◆◆◆◆ 62 User Friendliness

◆◆◆◆◆◆◆◆ 87 Educational Value

◆◆◆◆◆◆◆◆ 81 Instructional Design

Walt Disney Computer Software
1990
$14.95
Ages 5-8
IBM, Apple*
LA/5,9

Allows the solving and creation of crossword puzzles that can be played on screen or paper via printer. Includes a variety of puzzles ranging in difficulty from 4 to 20 words. Children can solve puzzles by competing either with another player or with the computer. Uses both picture and word clues. Apple version requires frequent disk swapping. Requires adult help to get started. Supports mouse and color printer (optional). A good value. Uses copy protection puzzle.

Mickey's Jigsaw Puzzles

Spatial problem solving

◆◆◆◆◆◆◆◆ 85 FINAL RATING

◆◆◆◆◆◆◆◆ 85 User Friendliness

◆◆◆◆◆◆◆◆◆ 91 Educational Value

◆◆◆◆◆◆◆◆ 81 Instructional Design

Walt Disney Computer Software
1991
$49.95
Ages 5-up
IBM (VGA)
SP/2,7,8

Fifteen jigsaw puzzles with a variety of options. Child uses mouse (recommended) or joystick to drag puzzle pieces into place. When complete, puzzle can be animated or printed for coloring. Puzzles range from 4 to 64 pieces. Outlines, "peek" option, and optional timer included. Supports a variety of sound devices. Excellent design puts children in control.

CL = Classification   **CP** = Creative projects   **LA** = Language   **NA** = Not applicable   **NB** = Number

Mickey's Magic Reader

Reading for enjoyment

◆◆◆◆◆◆◆ 75 FINAL RATING

◆◆◆◆◆◆◆ 70 User Friendliness

◆◆◆◆◆◆◆◆ 83 Educational Value

◆◆◆◆◆◆◆ 72 Instructional Design

Sunburst Communications, Inc.
1989
$65.00
Ages 5-up
Apple
LA/5,6

Three activities in which child uses arrow keys and RETURN to (1) select one of three words to solve a riddle, (2) help Mickey Mouse bake cookies, or (3) help Goofy, Minnie, or Donald dress, by selecting clothing items. Each answer is rewarded by appropriate animation. Can be used with TouchWindow. Some reading required. Color monitor required. Limited content.

Mickey's Runaway Zoo Fun With Numbers

Counting from 1 to 9

◆◆◆◆◆◆ 60 FINAL RATING

◆◆◆◆◆ 55 User Friendliness

◆◆◆◆◆◆ 71 Educational Value

◆◆◆◆◆◆◆ 70 Instructional Design

Walt Disney Computer Software
1990
$14.95
Ages 2-5
IBM*, C64
NB/3

One simple counting activity. Five partially hidden numerals are scattered on the screen. By pressing one of the hidden numerals, child causes a corresponding number of animals to move into a zoo wagon one at a time, which promotes counting. Contains 18 animals on four screens. Good graphics. No design options. Limited range of content. Uses copy protection puzzle.

Micro-LADS

Covers 46 fundamental syntactic rules

He is in the wagon.

◆◆◆◆◆◆◆ 75 FINAL RATING

◆◆◆◆◆◆◆◆ 85 User Friendliness

◆◆◆◆◆◆ 65 Educational Value

◆◆◆◆◆◆◆ 75 Instructional Design

Laureate Learning Systems
1984
$750.00
Ages 2-up (special education)
Apple
LA/1,8

Seven disks covering grammatical constructions. Child hears sentence, e.g., "The dogs walk," and must pick correct picture (using spacebar). Keeps complete records. Adult must set up a lesson. Designed for learning disabled children. Requires an Echo speech synthesizer. Available in French.

Microzine Jr. (Sept/Oct. '88)

Habitats, making masks, programming

◆◆◆◆◆◆◆◆ 81 FINAL RATING

◆◆◆◆◆◆◆ 73 User Friendliness

◆◆◆◆◆◆◆◆ 87 Educational Value

◆◆◆◆◆◆◆◆ 84 Instructional Design

Scholastic Software, Inc.
1988
$169.00 ($10 shipping)
Ages 6-9
Apple
CP/3,4 OT/1 CL/1 SP/5

A subscription series (five issues per year). Disks can be copied. This issue has five activities: Mask Maker—child makes masks which can be printed. Safari—child's decisions help animals survive. Eye Spy—a "which doesn't belong" activity. B.E.R.T.— child plays a question-and-answer game. Good design. Reading required.

Milk Bottles

Comparing amounts

◆◆◆ 39 FINAL RATING

◆◆◆ 30 User Friendliness

◆◆◆◆ 41 Educational Value

◆◆◆◆ 45 Instructional Design

Island Software
1982
$25.00
Ages 3-6
Apple
NB/1

Four numbered areas with differing amounts of white represent milk in bottles. Child types number of cylinder or touches bottle with light pen to answer question that is written below, e.g., "Which is full?" Not recommended.

Milliken Storyteller, The

Early reading skills

◆◆◆◆◆◆◆◆ 82 FINAL RATING

◆◆◆◆◆◆◆◆ 80 User Friendliness

◆◆◆◆◆◆◆◆ 87 Educational Value

◆◆◆◆◆◆◆◆ 80 Instructional Design

Milliken Publishing Co.
1989
$49.95
Ages 4-7
IIGS*, IBM (requires Covox for
    speech), Mac
LA/5,10 CP/1

Three stories: The Ugly Duckling, Henny Penny, and Little Red Riding Hood, consisting of 21 to 23 screens (pages). The text is read in a clear voice; child clicks the mouse to see next screen. Questions are asked, e.g., "Point to the acorn." Two of the screens can be colored with the mouse. Options allow for control over questions and speech. Clear graphics.

| **CL** = Classification | **CP** = Creative projects | **LA** = Language | **NA** = Not applicable | **NB** = Number |

Mixed-Up Mother Goose

Nursery rhymes, using maps, memory practice

◆◆◆◆◆◆◆◆ 80 FINAL RATING

◆◆◆◆◆◆◆◆ 85 User Friendliness

◆◆◆◆◆◆◆ 73 Educational Value

◆◆◆◆◆◆◆◆ 80 Instructional Design

Sierra On-Line
1987
$39.95
Ages 4-up
Apple*, IBM*, Mac, IIGS,
   Atari ST
SP/3,4,6,7 OT/1 CL/2

Child uses arrow keys, mouse, or joystick to move a person in a village in search of items related to nursery rhymes. For example, finding a pail and taking it to Jack and Jill causes them to perform their rhyme with music and animation. Contains 18 rhymes. Games can be saved and continued later. Good level of child-control. Enjoyable and cleverly designed. CD-ROM version available.

Money Works

Money skills

◆◆◆◆◆◆◆ 76 FINAL RATING

◆◆◆◆◆ 55 User Friendliness

◆◆◆◆◆◆◆◆◆ 91 Educational Value

◆◆◆◆◆◆◆◆ 88 Instructional Design

MECC
1987
$59.00
Ages 6-8
Apple (128K)
NB/1,3

Four activities on one disk. Child uses arrows keys, ESCAPE, and RETURN to decide how much money is in a safe, count out an amount with a change machine, or make and print currency. Offers many teacher options. Correlates with many textbooks. Good child-control. The best money program we've seen.

Monkey Math

Basic math facts, numerical order

◆◆◆◆ 49 FINAL RATING

◆◆◆ 38 User Friendliness

◆◆◆◆◆ 53 Educational Value

◆◆◆◆ 43 Instructional Design

Artworx
1983
$19.95
Ages 4-10
Apple*, C64, Atari
NB/4

Provides drill and practice with math facts. Monkey knocks out correct answers on an assembly line to earn bananas and beat the clock. Practice with basic math facts (four operations) available at three levels.

OT = Other topics   **SE** = Seriation   **SP** = Spatial relations   **TI** = Time   * = Version reviewed

Monsters & Make-Believe

Creative writing, matching, spatial relations

◆◆◆◆◆◆◆ 71 FINAL RATING

◆◆◆◆◆ 59 User Friendliness

◆◆◆◆◆◆◆ 74 Educational Value

◆◆◆◆◆◆◆◆ 81 Instructional Design

Queue, Inc.
1987
$39.95 ($99.95 for lab pack)
Ages 6-up
Apple*, Mac, IBM
CP/1 SP/4,5,7 LA/9

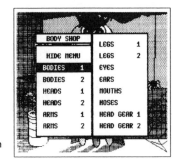

Using single-word menus to select background, head, body, arms, legs, mouth, nose, and hair, child uses spacebar and RETURN to build a monster. Half page of small print (40-column) can be created as well. Stories and monsters can be saved or printed.

Monsters & Make-Believe Plus

A graphics program with text-writing feature

◆◆◆◆◆◆ 69 FINAL RATING

◆◆◆◆ 46 User Friendliness

◆◆◆◆◆◆◆◆ 83 Educational Value

◆◆◆◆◆◆◆◆ 81 Instructional Design

Queue, Inc.
1989
$49.95 ($99.95 for lab pack)
Ages 5-up
Apple (128K)
CP/4 LA/3,6,9 SP/2,5

Child selects from a variety of clip art (arms, bodies, heads, props, etc.) to create monster scenes that can be saved or printed in color. Words can be added and spoken on Echo synthesizer (optional). Our five-year-olds liked the graphics but needed help to use the program. Graphics can be used with the older children's program "SuperPrint!" Available in Spanish.

Moptown Parade

Classification and seriation

◆◆◆◆◆ 55 FINAL RATING

◆◆◆◆◆ 51 User Friendliness

◆◆◆◆◆◆◆◆ 81 Educational Value

◆◆◆◆ 45 Instructional Design

The Learning Company
1981
$59.95 (school edition)
Ages 6-10
Apple*, IBM*, C64
CL/1,2,4 SE/4

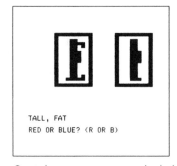

Contains seven progressively harder attribute games. Effective in focusing child's attention on attributes and the logic of sets. Strong in content. However, requires reading for independent use. Color monitor required. School edition includes back-up disk, teacher's guide, blackline masters, and activity ideas.

CL = Classification   **CP** = Creative projects   **LA** = Language   **NA** = Not applicable   **NB** = Number

Mosaic Magic

Spatial problem solving

◆◆◆◆◆◆◆ 79 FINAL RATING

◆◆◆◆◆◆◆ 71 User Friendliness

◆◆◆◆◆◆◆◆◆ 92 Educational Value

◆◆◆◆◆◆◆ 76 Instructional Design

KinderMagic Software
1989
$35.00
Ages 4-11
IBM (CGA, VGA)
SP/2,7,8,9

Child completes a mosaic-like picture that is presented with some pieces missing. Through use of a model or symmetry clues, a piece is first constructed by selecting the color, shape, and orientation. It is then moved into the picture. Contains 120 pictures that provide a nice range of challenge. Child also can create own pictures. Some menus require reading. No printing options. An excellent activity for encouraging simple geometric thinking.

Mount Murdoch

Adventure game and word processor

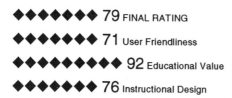

◆◆◆◆ 45 FINAL RATING

◆◆◆◆ 40 User Friendliness

◆◆◆ 34 Educational Value

◆◆◆◆◆ 53 Instructional Design

Kidsview Software, Inc.
1987
$49.95 ($39.95 for C64)
Ages 5-up
Apple*, IBM, C64
LA/10

An adventure game where child types simple commands (e.g., look, help, up) to get to Mount Murdoch. Uses large letters (19 across the screen). Permits the creation of custom games. Reading required.

Mr. and Mrs. Potato Head

Creative projects, imagination, memory skills

◆◆◆◆◆◆◆ 71 FINAL RATING

◆◆◆◆◆ 58 User Friendliness

◆◆◆◆◆◆◆◆ 84 Educational Value

◆◆◆◆◆◆◆ 73 Instructional Design

Queue, Inc.
1985
$29.95
Ages 3-8
Apple
SP/1,2,5 CP/3,4 OT/1

Child uses arrow keys or joystick to animate an existing potato character. Also can create own potato character. A Simon-Says memory game is included on the back of the disk. Attractive graphics. Minimal reading required, e.g., "press return." Color monitor recommended. No printing capacity.

OT = Other topics　　　**SE** = Seriation　　　**SP** = Spatial relations　　　**TI** = Time　　　* = Version reviewed

Muppet Slate

Language experiences

◆◆◆◆◆◆◆◆ 88 FINAL RATING

◆◆◆◆◆◆◆ 73 User Friendliness

◆◆◆◆◆◆◆◆◆ 93 Educational Value

◆◆◆◆◆◆◆◆◆ 98 Instructional Design

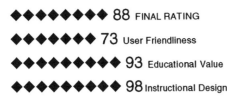

Sunburst Communications, Inc.
1988
$75.00
Ages 5-7
Apple
LA/9 OT/4

A large-letter word processor with 126 pictures that can be added to the story. Stories can be saved and printed with 10 borders. Not good for long stories. Options allow teacher control. Can be used with Muppet Learning Keys.

Muppet Word Book

Letters and words

◆◆◆◆◆◆◆ 82 FINAL RATING

◆◆◆◆◆◆◆ 85 User Friendliness

◆◆◆◆◆◆◆◆ 92 Educational Value

◆◆◆◆◆◆ 73 Instructional Design

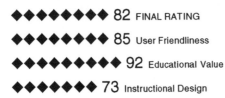

Sunburst Communications, Inc.
1986
$65.00
Ages 3-6
Apple
LA/4,6 CL/1,2

Six games on one disk provide practice with letters, upper/lower-case matching, beginning consonants, and word endings. The final activity is a simple word processor using large letters that can be printed. Can be used with a mouse, TouchWindow, Muppet Learning Keys, or regular keyboard.

Muppets On Stage

Counting skills, letter recognition

◆◆◆◆◆◆◆◆ 81 FINAL RATING

◆◆◆◆◆◆◆ 73 User Friendliness

◆◆◆◆◆◆◆ 77 Educational Value

◆◆◆◆◆◆ 69 Instructional Design

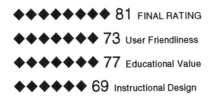

Sunburst Communications, Inc.
1984
$65.00
Ages 3-6
Apple*, IBM, C64
LA/4 NB/4

Three games: Discovery, Letters, and Numbers. Provides experience with letters, colors, numerals, and number. Well-designed. Is effective in giving child-control. This is the program that comes with the Muppet Learning Keys, although it can be used with a regular keyboard.

Muppetville

Classifying, memory skills

◆◆◆◆◆◆◆◆ 87 FINAL RATING

◆◆◆◆◆◆◆◆◆ 94 User Friendliness

◆◆◆◆◆◆◆◆◆ 95 Educational Value

◆◆◆◆◆◆◆ 75 Instructional Design

Sunburst Communications, Inc.
1986
$65.00
Ages 4-6
Apple
CL/2 NB/3,4 OT/1

Six activities on one disk, starring the Muppets. Menu design allows child-control. Supports TouchWindow (used for review), Muppet Learning Keys, mouse, or keyboard. Gives practice with shapes, colors, and numbers. Options allow for several difficulty settings.

Mural Maker

Creating printed products

◆◆◆◆◆ 58 FINAL RATING

◆◆◆◆◆◆ 64 User Friendliness

◆◆◆ 35 Educational Value

◆◆◆◆◆◆ 69 Instructional Design

Mobius Corporation
1990
See KidWare 2
Ages 3-5
IBM
CP/4

Child touches large arrows on a PowerPad overlay to select from 215 objects that can be displayed and printed in four sizes. Names of pictures can be spoken. Our children and teachers found it difficult to recognize the pictures, particularly the larger ones. Not recommended.

Music

Seriation of pitch

◆◆◆◆◆ 59 FINAL RATING

◆◆◆◆◆◆ 63 User Friendliness

◆◆◆◆◆◆◆ 70 Educational Value

◆◆◆◆◆ 51 Instructional Design

Lawrence Hall of Science
1984
$34.95
Ages 4-6
Apple
CP/2 SE/1,4

Make Music, Note Sandwich, and Play a Tune give experience with an eight-tone C-scale, associating notes with numbers and colored bars of correlated lengths. Limited in content. Design is effective in giving child-control.

OT = Other topics   **SE** = Seriation   **SP** = Spatial relations   **TI** = Time   * = Version reviewed

Music Maker

Creation of music

◆◆◆◆◆ 65 FINAL RATING

◆◆◆◆◆◆ 74 User Friendliness

◆◆◆◆◆ 55 Educational Value

◆◆◆◆◆ 62 Instructional Design

Mobius Corporation
1990
See KidWare 2
Ages 3-5
IBM
CP/2 SE/1

Child presses one octave (eight-block) scale on a PowerPad template (required) to hear a note, creating musical notes on the screen. Resulting music can be printed, played, or stored on disk. Limited design.

My ABC's

Letter and numeral recognition

◆◆◆◆◆◆ 63 FINAL RATING

◆◆◆◆◆◆ 67 User Friendliness

◆◆◆◆◆◆◆◆ 91 Educational Value

◆◆◆◆ 45 Instructional Design

Paperback Software
1984
$24.95
Ages 3-7
IBM
LA/4 NB/3 OT/1

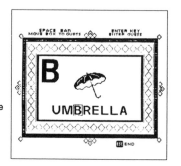

Five activities: First Letter, Match Letters, Dancing Letters (any key pressed makes pictures dance on the screen), Counting Objects, and a multilevel game of Concentration. Good child-control and graphics. A good all-purpose program for IBM PC owners.

My Grand Piano

Learning notes and playing familiar songs

◆◆◆◆◆◆◆ 79 FINAL RATING

◆◆◆◆◆◆ 61 User Friendliness

◆◆◆◆◆◆◆◆ 91 Educational Value

◆◆◆◆◆◆◆ 87 Instructional Design

GameTek/IJE, Inc.
1988
$9.95
Ages 3-8
C64*, Apple, IBM
CP/2 SE/1

A musical octave can be played using the bottom row of computer keys. One feature shows notes on a staff line as they are played and automatically plays them back. Includes a 33-song library from which selections can be played by following flashing keys. Some reading. Initial adult help will be required.

My House Language Activities of Daily Living

Practice with names of common objects

◆◆◆◆◆◆◆ 77 FINAL RATING

◆◆◆◆◆◆◆◆ 90 User Friendliness

◆◆◆◆◆◆ 61 Educational Value

◆◆◆◆◆◆◆ 79 Instructional Design

Laureate Learning Systems
1991
$175.00
Ages 3-up
Apple* (Echo synthesizer
    required), IIGS
LA/5

Four activities based on 114 household objects and their functions: (1) Discover Names—select object to hear its name. (2) Discover Functions—select object to hear its function. (3) Identify Names—find a specific object. (4) Identify Function—child finds object based on its function. Can be used with single switch, TouchWindow, or regular keyboard. Includes many setup options.

My Letters, Numbers, and Words

Letter recognition

◆◆◆◆ 46 FINAL RATING

◆◆◆ 35 User Friendliness

◆◆◆◆◆◆◆ 79 Educational Value

◆◆◆ 38 Instructional Design

Spell object shown.   (key ESC to stop)

Stone & Associates
1983
$39.95
Ages 2-6
IBM*, Apple, Atari ST
LA/5

Practice with words, the numbers 1-10, key location, and letters, all reinforced through well-designed graphics and sounds. Design requires adult to start and stop the program, however. This program has later version called "Kid's Stuff" with better design features.

My Puzzles and Alphabet

Letter recognition, spatial relations

◆◆◆◆ 49 FINAL RATING

◆◆◆◆ 47 User Friendliness

◆◆◆◆◆ 50 Educational Value

◆◆◆◆ 49 Instructional Design

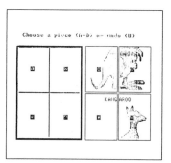

Choose a piece (A-D) or undo (U)

Micro Power & Light Company
1986
$29.95
Ages 3-8
IBM
LA/4,5 SP/2

Three activities dealing with letter recognition and a fourth on solving puzzles: (1) Child sees each letter animated in short routine. (2) Child presses any letter to see the associated animation. (3) Child must spell a word (e.g., kangaroo) to see the animation. (4) Child constructs puzzles of from 2-6 pieces to see animation. Menus require reading. Feedback can be confusing.

| OT = Other topics | SE = Seriation | SP = Spatial relations | TI = Time | * = Version reviewed |

My Words

Language experience

◆◆◆◆◆◆◆ 78 FINAL RATING

◆◆◆◆◆◆ 60 User Friendliness

◆◆◆◆◆◆◆◆◆ 92 Educational Value

◆◆◆◆◆◆◆◆ 89 Instructional Design

Hartley Courseware, Inc.
1987
$69.95
Ages 5-8
Apple (64K)
LA/2,3,4,5,9 CP/4

A talking word processor that keeps a list of every word used in a story. Lists can be stored, printed, and used again for other writing activities. While words are typed, they are also spoken in robotic voice (Echo speech synthesizer required). A mouse is recommended. Uses small (40-column) print.

New Talking Stickybear Alphabet, The

Letter recognition

◆◆◆◆◆◆ 64 FINAL RATING

◆◆◆◆ 46 User Friendliness

◆◆◆◆◆◆◆ 73 Educational Value

◆◆◆◆◆◆◆ 74 Instructional Design

Optimum Resource, Inc.
1988
$49.95
Ages 3-6
IIGS (512K, 3.5"), IBM with
   Covox or Echo
LA/4,5

Three activities come on two disks: Alphabet—press any letter key to hear the letter and see an animated letter-related scene. There are 52 scenes available. Letter Hunt—hear letter and find it to see a picture. Fast Letters—press any letter key to hear the name. Clear graphics and speech. IBM version requires Covox or Echo.

New Talking Stickybear Opposites, The

Opposites, e.g. "near/far"

◆◆◆◆◆◆◆ 73 FINAL RATING

◆◆◆◆◆◆◆ 75 User Friendliness

◆◆◆◆◆◆◆ 79 Educational Value

◆◆◆◆◆◆ 68 Instructional Design

Optimum Resource, Inc.
1986
$39.95
Ages 3-6
Apple*, Atari, C64
SP/4 SE/1

Contains 21 antonym pairs that are changed using the arrow keys. Spacebar changes the scene. Colorful graphics and animation. Similar in design to "Inside Outside Opposites" and "City Country Opposites." Employs speech if used with an Echo speech synthesizer. Easy to use.

CL = Classification   **CP** = Creative projects   **LA** = Language   **NA** = Not applicable   **NB** = Number

New Talking Stickybear Shapes, The

Identification of five common shapes

◆◆◆◆◆◆◆ 75 FINAL RATING

◆◆◆◆◆◆◆ 70 User Friendliness

◆◆◆◆◆◆◆◆ 92 Educational Value

◆◆◆◆◆◆◆ 74 Instructional Design

Optimum Resource, Inc.
1989
$49.95
Ages 3-6
IIGS (3.5"), IBM with Covox or
    Echo
SP/8

Three activities. Pick It—shows succession of 10 pictures, each one missing a shape, and child uses arrows or mouse to select shape to complete each picture. Name It—a voice says, e.g., "Find the rectangle," and child selects it from five given shapes. Find It—a voice says, "Find the circle," and child uses arrows to highlight circle in a given scene. Clever graphics and sounds. Somewhat limited content. IBM version requires Covox or Echo.

Not Too Messy, Not Too Neat

Language experience

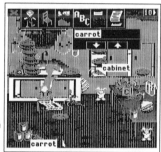

◆◆◆◆◆◆◆◆ 89 FINAL RATING

◆◆◆◆◆◆◆◆ 85 User Friendliness

◆◆◆◆◆◆◆◆◆ 94 Educational Value

◆◆◆◆◆◆◆◆◆ 91 Instructional Design

D. C. Heath & Company
1988
$75.00
Ages 5-10
Apple
LA/2,3,5,9 CP/4 SP/4,7

Children use mouse, Koala Pad, joystick, or arrow keys to select or move objects, backgrounds, words, or characters of a story. They can also add their own words. Resulting stories can be saved and printed in color. Includes four copies of the storybook. Good design. Fun to use.

Notable Phantom, The

Musical notation, pitch recognition

◆◆◆◆◆◆ 66 FINAL RATING

◆◆◆◆◆◆ 68 User Friendliness

◆◆◆◆◆◆◆ 80 Educational Value

◆◆◆◆◆ 56 Instructional Design

Compton's New Media
1984
$9.95
Ages 5-10
Apple*, IBM, C64
SE/1 CP/2

Uses a plastic overlay to simulate a full 1 1/2 octave keyboard for use with three activities. Effective in teaching note names and for playing and recording songs in a game context. Main menu is confusing. May require adult help to start younger child.

OT = Other topics   **SE** = Seriation   **SP** = Spatial relations   **TI** = Time   * = Version reviewed

Now You See It, Now You Don't

Memory skills

◆◆◆◆◆◆◆ 79 FINAL RATING

◆◆◆◆◆◆◆ 72 User Friendliness

◆◆◆◆◆◆◆◆◆ 91 Educational Value

◆◆◆◆◆◆◆ 77 Instructional Design

Sunburst Communications, Inc.
1987
$75.00
Ages 8-11
Apple
OT/1 CL/2,4,5 SP/4,8

Child uses keyboard, TouchWindow, or Muppet keyboard to select answers. On disk 1, child is shown a set of objects to memorize, and then must identify one of the objects. On disk 2, child sees picture with, then without, one or more of its objects, and must identify what's missing. Some reading required.

Number Farm

Counting skills

◆◆◆◆◆◆◆ 78 FINAL RATING

◆◆◆◆◆◆ 67 User Friendliness

◆◆◆◆◆◆◆◆◆ 92 Educational Value

◆◆◆◆◆◆◆ 79 Instructional Design

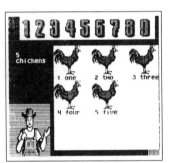

DLM
1984
$32.95
Ages 3-6
Apple*, C64, IBM
NB/3,4,5,8

Six entertaining games present multiple counting experiences. Feedback is effective. One game presents counting in a unique way by having child count sounds. Provides good number practice.

Number Sea Hunt

Counting, adding, number order, subtraction

◆◆◆◆◆◆ 66 FINAL RATING

◆◆◆◆◆◆◆ 74 User Friendliness

◆◆◆◆◆◆ 68 Educational Value

◆◆◆◆◆ 55 Instructional Design

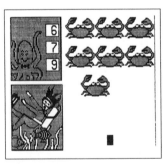

Gamco Industries, Inc.
1985
$49.95
Ages 3-6
Apple*, TRS 80, C64
NB/2

Contains four multiple-choice activities using numbers up to 10. Activities include counting to 10, filling a partial number line, and adding and subtracting with object clues. Rather dry presentation. Good management features allow setting up lessons and keeping records for up to 200 children.

NumberMaze

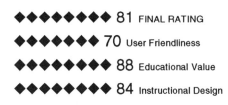

Practice with basic math facts

◆◆◆◆◆◆◆◆ 81 FINAL RATING

◆◆◆◆◆◆◆ 70 User Friendliness

◆◆◆◆◆◆◆◆ 88 Educational Value

◆◆◆◆◆◆◆◆ 84 Instructional Design

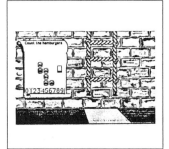

Great Wave Software
1988
$49.95
Ages 5-12
Mac (512K)
NB/3,8 SP/4

Child uses a mouse to navigate through a simple maze, answering math problems to remove roadblocks. Challenge levels (48 in all) range from counting objects to multiplication and division computation. Password system keeps records for each child. Good for classroom use. Allows for individualized presentation. Good program.

Numbers

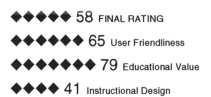

Numerical disc., counting

◆◆◆◆◆ 58 FINAL RATING

◆◆◆◆◆◆ 65 User Friendliness

◆◆◆◆◆◆◆ 79 Educational Value

◆◆◆◆ 41 Instructional Design

Lawrence Hall of Science
1984
$34.95
Ages 4-6
Apple
NB/3,4,8

Provides two activities: Balloons—lets the child pop balloons in relation to a number on the keyboard, using spacebar and RETURN. Secret Numbers—reveals parts of numerals for the child to identify. Well-designed. Best for kindergarten.

Observation and Classification

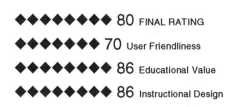

Classification skills

◆◆◆◆◆◆◆◆ 80 FINAL RATING

◆◆◆◆◆◆◆ 70 User Friendliness

◆◆◆◆◆◆◆◆ 86 Educational Value

◆◆◆◆◆◆◆◆ 86 Instructional Design

Hartley Courseware, Inc.
1985
$35.95
Ages 3-5
Apple
CL/1,2,4

Three activities. Child selects which object is different from others, which is the same size as one shown, or which belongs to the same class as a group shown, e.g., "all animals." Teacher options allow control over sound, movement of cursor, and number of plays per game. Child selects own difficulty level.

Odd One Out

Matching/discrimination

◆◆◆◆◆◆◆ 74 FINAL RATING

◆◆◆◆◆ 58 User Friendliness

◆◆◆◆◆◆◆◆ 84 Educational Value

◆◆◆◆◆◆◆◆ 83 Instructional Design

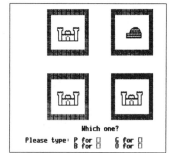

Sunburst Communications, Inc.
1983
$65.00
Ages 3-10
Apple*, C64
CL/1,2,4

Consists of five games based on format of selecting one of four boxes that doesn't belong. Child presses first letter of the color of the box containing the odd shape, e.g., "B" for blue. Content accessible to teacher.

Ollie and Seymour

Pedestrian safety, readiness skills

◆◆◆◆◆◆◆ 77 FINAL RATING

◆◆◆◆◆◆◆◆ 85 User Friendliness

◆◆◆◆◆◆◆ 75 Educational Value

◆◆◆◆◆◆ 71 Instructional Design

Hartley Courseware, Inc.
1984
$49.95
Ages 3-up
Apple
CL/2 SP/4,6,8 TI/1 OT/1

A unique simulation in which child uses arrow keys to move "Ollie" around a park and through the streets, where he can practice safe street crossings, obeying traffic signals, or games. Games involve shape and color matching, Concentration with traffic signs, and stacking and counting blocks.

Ollie Begins It

Matching beginning sounds and letters

◆◆◆◆◆◆ 64 FINAL RATING

◆◆◆◆◆ 55 User Friendliness

◆◆◆◆◆◆◆ 77 Educational Value

◆◆◆◆◆◆ 62 Instructional Design

S.R.A.
1985
$49.95
Ages 3-up
Apple
LA/6

A multiple-choice-style program in which child matches letters with objects (e.g., "D" with dog) using arrow keys and RETURN. Structured lessons have four steps: demonstration, practice, testing, and worksheets (included). A simple record-keeping system shows which letters have been matched. Menu requires reading. No escape from activities.

CL = Classification   **CP** = Creative projects   **LA** = Language   **NA** = Not applicable   **NB** = Number

Ollie Compares It

Avoiding common letter reversals

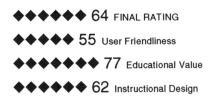 64 FINAL RATING

◆◆◆◆◆ 55 User Friendliness

◆◆◆◆◆◆◆ 77 Educational Value

◆◆◆◆◆◆ 62 Instructional Design

S.R.A.
1985
$49.95
Ages 3-up
Apple
LA/4,6 CL/2

A multiple-choice-style program in which child matches two letters or two three- or four-letter words, using arrow keys and RETURN. Structured lessons have four steps: demonstration, practice, testing, and worksheets (included). A simple record-keeping system shows which problems have been successfully completed. Menu requires reading. No escape from activities.

Ollie Finds It !

Matching shapes, letters, and words

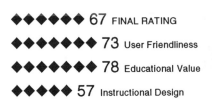 67 FINAL RATING

◆◆◆◆◆◆◆ 73 User Friendliness

◆◆◆◆◆◆◆ 78 Educational Value

◆◆◆◆◆ 57 Instructional Design

S.R.A.
1985
$49.95
Ages 3-6
Apple
CL/2

Shows child an object, a shape, a letter, or a word. Child uses arrow keys and RETURN to select a match from three choices. There are four steps to each lesson: demonstration, practice, testing, and worksheets (included). Keeps success/failure records. Rather dry presentation. No escape from activities.

Ollie Hears and Remembers

Auditory memory skills

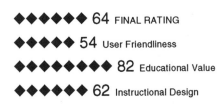 64 FINAL RATING

◆◆◆◆◆ 54 User Friendliness

◆◆◆◆◆◆◆◆ 82 Educational Value

◆◆◆◆◆◆ 62 Instructional Design

S.R.A.
1985
$49.95
Ages 3-up
Apple
CL/2 OT/1

Child hears one to three objects (or letters) named and then uses arrows and RETURN to select a corresponding sequence of pictures (or letters) on the screen. Adult can select criteria for success. Records if a child passes or fails. Contains 30 pictures. Uses a clear voice. Echo synthesizer is required. Dry presentation. No escape from activities.

OT = Other topics   **SE** = Seriation   **SP** = Spatial relations   **TI** = Time   * = Version reviewed

Ollie Hears and Sequences

Auditory memory skills

◆◆◆◆◆◆ 64 FINAL RATING

◆◆◆◆◆ 54 User Friendliness

◆◆◆◆◆◆◆ 82 Educational Value

◆◆◆◆◆◆ 62 Instructional Design

S.R.A.
1985
$49.95
Ages 3-up
Apple
CL/2 OT/1

Two or three objects or letters are named (e.g., pear and light-bulb), and child uses arrows and RETURN to select the corre-sponding pictures in correct order. Adult can select criteria for success. Records if a child passes or fails. Contains 30 pictures. Uses a clear voice. Echo speech synthesizer is required. Little child-control.

Ollie Letters It

Matching upper- and lower-case letters

◆◆◆◆◆◆ 64 FINAL RATING

◆◆◆◆◆ 55 User Friendliness

◆◆◆◆◆◆◆ 77 Educational Value

◆◆◆◆◆◆ 62 Instructional Design

S.R.A.
1985
$49.95
Ages 3-up
Apple
LA/4 CL/2

A multiple-choice-style program in which child sees a letter and must find its upper- or lower-case match using arrow keys and RETURN. Structured lessons have four steps: demonstration, practice, testing, and worksheets (included). A simple record-keeping system shows which letters have been successfully matched. Menu requires reading.

Ollie Matches It

Matching beginning and ending letters

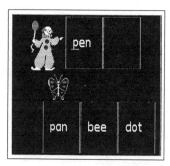

◆◆◆◆◆◆ 64 FINAL RATING

◆◆◆◆◆ 55 User Friendliness

◆◆◆◆◆◆◆ 77 Educational Value

◆◆◆◆◆◆ 62 Instructional Design

S.R.A.
1985
$49.95
Ages 3-up
Apple
LA/4 CL/2

A multiple-choice-style program in which child matches two short words that start or end with the same letter or letters, using the arrow keys and RETURN. Structured lessons have four steps: demonstration, practice, testing, and worksheets (included). A simple record-keeping system shows which letters have been successfully matched. Menu requires reading.

Ollie Numbers It

Numeral/set association

◆◆◆◆◆◆ 64 FINAL RATING

◆◆◆◆◆ 55 User Friendliness

◆◆◆◆◆◆◆ 77 Educational Value

◆◆◆◆◆◆ 62 Instructional Design

S.R.A.
1985
$49.95
Ages 3-up
Apple
NB/4 CL/2

A multiple-choice-style program in which child matches numbers less than 10 with sets, using arrow keys and RETURN. Structured lessons have four steps: demonstration, practice, testing, and worksheets (included). A simple record-keeping system shows which letters have been matched. Menu requires reading.

Ollie Remembers It

Visual memory

◆◆◆◆◆◆ 66 FINAL RATING

◆◆◆◆◆◆ 68 User Friendliness

◆◆◆◆◆◆◆ 78 Educational Value

◆◆◆◆◆ 57 Instructional Design

S.R.A.
1985
$49.95
Ages 3-6
Apple
OT/1 CL/2

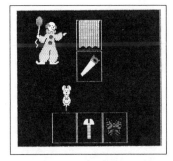

Shows child up to three objects or letters for 1-10 seconds, then covers them up. Child must use the arrows to select those same objects from another set. Keeps success/failure records. Dry presentation. Adult can set difficulty level. Includes demonstration, practice, and test modes. No escape from activities.

Ollie Remembers Numbers !

Visual memory

◆◆◆◆◆◆ 66 FINAL RATING

◆◆◆◆◆◆ 68 User Friendliness

◆◆◆◆◆◆◆ 78 Educational Value

◆◆◆◆◆ 57 Instructional Design

S.R.A.
1985
$49.95
Ages 3-6
Apple
OT/1 CL/2

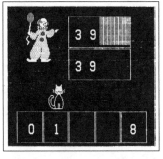

Shows child three to five numbers for up to 10 seconds, then covers them up. Child must use the arrows to select those same numbers from another set shown on screen. Keeps success/failure records. Dry presentation. Adult can set difficulty level. Design allows no escape from activities.

Ollie Sequences It !

Visual memory

◆◆◆◆◆◆ 66 FINAL RATING

◆◆◆◆◆◆ 68 User Friendliness

◆◆◆◆◆◆◆ 78 Educational Value

◆◆◆◆◆ 57 Instructional Design

S.R.A.
1985
$49.95
Ages 3-6
Apple
OT/1 CL/2

Shows child two or three objects (or letters) for up to 10 seconds, then covers them up. Child uses the arrows to select those same objects (or letters) from another set, in the order they were first presented. Keeps success/failure records. Dry presentation. Adult can set difficulty level. Menu requires reading. Allows no escape from activities.

Once Upon a Time . . .

Language experience, creation of storybooks

◆◆◆◆◆ 59 FINAL RATING

◆◆ 29 User Friendliness

◆◆◆◆◆◆ 62 Educational Value

◆◆◆◆◆◆◆◆ 85 Instructional Design

Compu-Teach
1987
$39.95
Ages 6-12
IBM* (256K), Apple (128K), Mac
LA/1,3,4,5,8,9

Consists of three sets of about 30 objects from the farm, safari, or main street. Child creates picture by typing the names of objects and moving them with the arrow keys. Pictures can be printed or saved. Reading required. Includes colored pencil set. Design could be improved. Two additional volumes are available. Volume I deals with underwater, dinosaurs, and animals; Volume II covers medieval times, Wild West, and outer space.

One Banana More

Reading readiness, counting

◆◆◆ 34 FINAL RATING

◆◆◆ 37 User Friendliness

◆◆◆◆ 42 Educational Value

◆◆ 26 Instructional Design

Data Command
1984
$39.95
Ages 5-6
Apple
CL/2 NB/1 LA/4,5

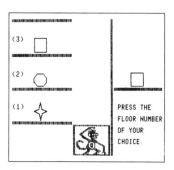

Six multiple-choice activities in which a child sees an object and presses the numeral of a matching shape, letter, size, word, number, or set, depending on the level selected. Bananas are rewards. No escape. Menu requires reading.

CL = Classification   **CP** = Creative projects   **LA** = Language   **NA** = Not applicable   **NB** = Number

Paint With Words

Word recognition

◆◆◆◆◆◆◆ 73 FINAL RATING

◆◆◆◆◆◆ 63 User Friendliness

◆◆◆◆◆◆◆◆◆ 91 Educational Value

◆◆◆◆◆◆ 69 Instructional Design

MECC
1986
$39.95
Ages 3-7
Apple (64K)
LA/5 CP/1,4

Using mouse, joystick, or keyboard, child creates a scene by moving one of eight words to a spot on the screen, where it becomes a picture that is a part of the scene. Scenes can be printed, saved, or changed. Twelve word-sets can be created from 124 words. Ufonic speech synthesizer (optional) will say words.

Parquetry and Pictures

Visual perception, parts and wholes, directions

◆◆◆◆◆◆◆ 76 FINAL RATING

◆◆◆◆◆◆◆ 79 User Friendliness

◆◆◆◆◆◆◆◆ 87 Educational Value

◆◆◆◆◆◆ 68 Instructional Design

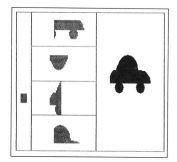

Hartley Courseware, Inc.
1989
$39.95
Ages 3-6
Apple
SP/1,2,6,8 CL/2

Contains three activities. The first two provide a multiple-choice format whereby a child selects a puzzle piece to fill in a picture (e.g., a car outline) or a geometric shape. In the third, scenes are created by using the arrow keys to move and place objects. Easy-to-use menus allow child to select own difficulty level.

Path-Tactics

Counting, basic math facts

◆◆◆◆◆◆ 69 FINAL RATING

◆◆◆◆◆ 50 User Friendliness

◆◆◆◆◆◆◆◆◆ 91 Educational Value

◆◆◆◆◆◆◆ 72 Instructional Design

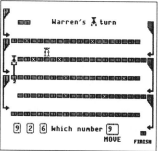

MECC
1986
$59.00
Ages 5-11
Apple*, IBM, C64
NB/3,5,6

A strategy game in which child does a math problem to decide how many steps a robot must move to get to a finish point in the least amount of steps. Levels range from counting to division (e.g., 63 / ___ = 7). Teacher options allow control over presentation of content. Child can play against partner or computer. Enjoyable program.

OT = Other topics   SE = Seriation   SP = Spatial relations   TI = Time   * = Version reviewed

Pattern Blocks 2.1

Visual imagery, symmetry

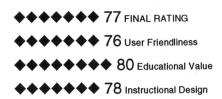 77 FINAL RATING

◆◆◆◆◆◆ 76 User Friendliness

◆◆◆◆◆◆◆ 80 Educational Value

◆◆◆◆◆◆ 78 Instructional Design

Chariot Software Group
1985
Shareware
Ages 4-up
Mac
SP/4,7,8,9 CP/1,4

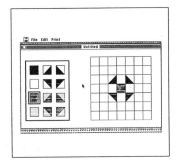

Consists of 12 blocks on one side of the screen and an empty grid on the other. By using the mouse, a child can easily drag blocks over and paste them in the grid. A "block editor" allows the creation of custom blocks. Work can be saved or printed. A rather limited program makes it easy for children to be successful.

Patterns

Pattern recognition: shapes, sounds, movements

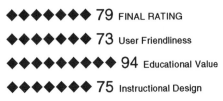 79 FINAL RATING

◆◆◆◆◆◆ 73 User Friendliness

◆◆◆◆◆◆◆◆ 94 Educational Value

◆◆◆◆◆◆◆ 75 Instructional Design

MECC
1988
$39.95
Ages 5-6
Apple
CL/1,2 SE/1,2 CP/1

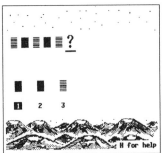

Three activities that give practice with static, sound, or animated patterns. A fourth activity allows the creation of pattern designs. Teacher options allow modification of content. Good design, child-control, and range of content.

Patterns and Sequences

Matching/discrimination

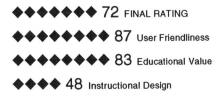 72 FINAL RATING

◆◆◆◆◆◆◆ 87 User Friendliness

◆◆◆◆◆◆◆ 83 Educational Value

◆◆◆◆ 48 Instructional Design

Hartley Courseware, Inc.
1984
$35.95
Ages 3-6
Apple
CL/1 SE/1

Contains four clearly designed activities that provide large objects, positive feedback, and multiple skill levels. No reading required.

CL = Classification   **CP** = Creative projects   **LA** = Language   **NA** = Not applicable   **NB** = Number

Peanuts Maze Marathon

Problem solving (mazes)

◆◆◆◆ 46 FINAL RATING

◆◆◆◆ 45 User Friendliness

◆◆◆◆◆ 50 Educational Value

◆◆◆◆ 46 Instructional Design

Queue, Inc.
1984
$29.95
Ages 4-8
Apple*, IBM
TI/4 SP/4

Peanuts cartoons animate themselves after the completion of simple maze. Use with the keyboard is not smooth; a joystick is recommended. Time is kept for each maze.

Peanuts Picture Puzzlers

Problem solving (puzzles)

◆◆◆◆◆ 59 FINAL RATING

◆◆◆◆ 44 User Friendliness

◆◆◆◆◆ 51 Educational Value

◆◆◆◆◆◆◆ 74 Instructional Design

Queue, Inc.
1984
$29.95
Ages 4-8
Apple*, IBM
SP/1

Presents a picture to the child, then makes a puzzle by dividing it into sections. After the child puts all the pieces into the puzzle, the picture becomes animated. Entertaining program. Could be difficult for 4-year-olds to operate, however.

Perception, Inc.

Problem solving and thinking skills

◆◆◆◆◆◆◆ 71 FINAL RATING

◆◆◆◆◆◆ 63 User Friendliness

◆◆◆◆◆◆◆ 71 Educational Value

◆◆◆◆◆◆◆ 77 Instructional Design

IRI Group
1989
$185.00
Ages 5-8
Apple
CL/3,4,5,6 SE/2

Child uses mouse, arrow keys, or joystick to steer a robot around a nine-room factory to play three activities: Assembly Line—child makes a part that satisfies four "attribute" criteria. Quality Control—child sees part and sorts it by attribute. Packaging—child fills in grid by matching attributes. Three difficulty levels.

OT = Other topics   **SE** = Seriation   **SP** = Spatial relations   **TI** = Time   * = Version reviewed

Perfect Fit

Spatial relationships and picture recognition

◆◆◆◆◆◆◆ 70 FINAL RATING

◆◆◆◆◆◆ 61 User Friendliness

◆◆◆◆◆◆◆◆ 83 Educational Value

◆◆◆◆◆◆◆ 71 Instructional Design

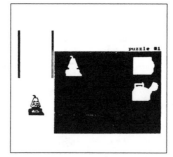

GameTek/IJE, Inc.
1988
$9.95
Ages 3-8
Apple, IBM*, C64
SP/1,4,8 CL/2

A puzzle game in which child uses arrows or joystick (optional) to move a puzzle piece onto a board containing three to five silhouettes of letters, numbers, and Fisher-Price toys (30 available). Can be set for play against a clock. For one or two players. Harder levels require flipping puzzle pieces. Some adult help required to get started.

Peter's Growing Patterns

Pattern recognition

◆◆◆◆◆◆◆ 73 FINAL RATING

◆◆◆◆◆◆ 69 User Friendliness

◆◆◆◆◆◆◆◆◆ 91 Educational Value

◆◆◆◆◆◆ 64 Instructional Design

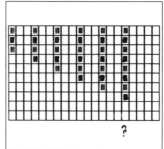

Strawberry Hill Software
1985
$19.00
Ages 5-up
Apple
SE/1,2,3,4 CL/6 SP/9 NB/5
    CP/4

Six activities that range in difficulty and present visual and numerical patterns. Child uses joystick or keyboard to select or construct the next member of a given sequence. Teacher's edition ($55.00) includes many classroom activities. "U-Design-It" feature allows creation of new pattern problems.

Phonics Plus

Letter/word relationships

◆◆◆◆◆◆◆ 78 FINAL RATING

◆◆◆◆◆◆ 65 User Friendliness

◆◆◆◆◆◆◆◆◆ 92 Educational Value

◆◆◆◆◆◆◆ 80 Instructional Design

Stone & Associates
1988
$39.95
Ages 4-8
IBM
LA/4,5,6

Six activities in which child sees picture and types the starting, middle, or ending letter; selects a word to match picture; selects vowel to match word; or creates words by typing the starting letters of a series of pictures. Also includes a word-search game and a crossword puzzle using simple words. Enjoyable activities. Picture menus allow child-control.

CL = Classification   **CP** = Creative projects   **LA** = Language   **NA** = Not applicable   **NB** = Number

Phonics Prime Time: Initial Consonants

Initial consonant phonics skills

◆◆◆◆◆◆◆◆ 83 FINAL RATING

◆◆◆◆◆◆◆ 70 User Friendliness

◆◆◆◆◆◆◆◆◆ 92 Educational Value

◆◆◆◆◆◆◆◆ 87 Instructional Design

MECC
1986
$59.00
Ages 5-6
Apple
LA/4,5,6

Two activities on one disk. Frog Frolics—child uses spacebar to select a picture that goes with a given letter (e.g., G = Girl). Puppet Show—child sees a picture and a sentence with a blank and selects a picture to complete sentence. Contains 193 pictures. Allows for customized lessons. Keeps records for 75. Good for classroom use.

Picture Chompers

Classification practice

◆◆◆◆◆◆◆ 79 FINAL RATING

◆◆◆◆◆◆ 67 User Friendliness

◆◆◆◆◆◆◆◆◆ 91 Educational Value

◆◆◆◆◆◆◆◆ 81 Instructional Design

MECC
1990
$49.00
Ages 5-6
Apple*
CL/1,2,3,6

Child uses arrows or joystick to move a set of "chompers" around a 4 by 4 grid filled with pictures of items. The object is to select items that share an attribute such as size, color, shape, design, class, or use. Timer and scoring options are available. There are three difficulty levels. Minimal reading required. An enjoyable activity.

Picture Parade

Ordering of events

◆◆◆◆◆◆ 63 FINAL RATING

◆◆◆ 39 User Friendliness

◆◆◆◆◆◆◆◆ 87 Educational Value

◆◆◆◆◆◆◆ 70 Instructional Design

Hartley Courseware, Inc.
1988
$39.95
Ages 5-7
Apple
TI/6

Child sees two to six pictures that form an ordered sequence but are placed out of order, e.g., the steps involved in a boy diving into the water. Child puts pictures in correct order by placing a number under each box. Contains 48 sets of picture sequences, some difficult to interpret. Menu requires reading. Keeps records for up to 48 children.

Picture Perfect

Draw, color, and write

◆◆◆◆◆◆◆ 79 FINAL RATING

◆◆◆◆◆◆◆◆ 82 User Friendliness

◆◆◆◆◆◆◆ 77 Educational Value

◆◆◆◆◆◆◆ 75 Instructional Design

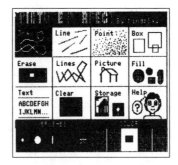

MindPlay
1984
$49.99
Ages 4-up
Apple*, IBM
CP/1 LA/3

Child uses joystick or mouse to draw points, lines, or boxes and to write text. Features include a 72-picture library, five color selections, and drawing tool options. Drawing requires going between two screens, which is difficult for young children. Pictures can be saved and printed.

Pictures, Letters, and Sounds

Letter recognition

◆◆◆◆◆◆◆ 78 FINAL RATING

◆◆◆◆◆◆ 63 User Friendliness

◆◆◆◆◆◆◆◆◆ 91 Educational Value

◆◆◆◆◆◆◆◆ 82 Instructional Design

Hartley Courseware, Inc.
1986
$35.95
Ages 5-6
Apple
LA/4,5

Five games offer a range of activity. Child can type using picture symbols for letters (e.g., Saw = S), pop balloons, or position X's or O's in a game of tic-tac-toe. Design allows child-control.

Playroom, The

Letters, numbers, and time

◆◆◆◆◆◆◆◆◆ 91 FINAL RATING

◆◆◆◆◆◆◆◆ 85 User Friendliness

◆◆◆◆◆◆◆◆◆ 95 Educational Value

◆◆◆◆◆◆◆◆◆ 94 Instructional Design

Broderbund Software
1989
$49.95
Ages 3-6
IBM, Mac* (color version now
    available), Apple
LA/4,5 NB/2,3,8 TI/6,9 SP/2
    CP/4

Child uses mouse (recommended) or keyboard to explore a room full of objects. Six of the objects trigger activities, including ones on counting, clocks, combining parts, letters, upper/lower-case, and words. Promotes child-control by making it easy for child to enter or exit a range of activities. Easy to use. Incorporates some speech. Apple version requires frequent disk changes. Uses copy protection puzzle. Highly recommended.

CL = Classification   **CP** = Creative projects   **LA** = Language   **NA** = Not applicable   **NB** = Number

Playwrite

Writing scripts

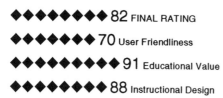

82 FINAL RATING

70 User Friendliness

91 Educational Value

88 Instructional Design

Sunburst Communications, Inc.
1990
$75.00
Ages 6-11
IIGS (1 MB)
LA/3,8,9

A script-writing program featuring two talking puppets. A child types in the puppet dialog and uses pop-up menus to incorporate one of eight special effects (e.g., canned laughter, a drum roll, a curtain rising). Stage sets and costumes can be changed. Scripts can be saved, printed, and played back. Uses IIGS's internal speech capacity. Fun program. Limited features.

Preschool Disk 1

Letter, counting, alphabetical order

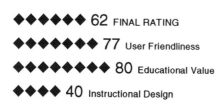

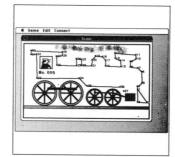

62 FINAL RATING

77 User Friendliness

80 Educational Value

40 Instructional Design

Nordic Software, Inc.
1986
$39.95
Ages 3-7
Mac (512K)
LA/4 NB/3,8 CP/1

Three games: Alphaworks—child sees picture, hears the picture name and starting letter, and must press the letter key. Counting—shows up to 10 objects and number line. Child clicks the mouse on the number shown. Connect the Dots—child uses mouse to connect dots, using numbers or letters. Possible to create own puzzles. Gives verbal feedback.

Preschool Disk 2

Matching, counting, adding, memory skills

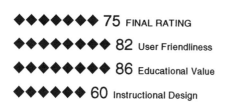

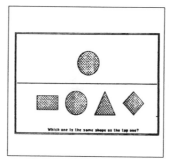

75 FINAL RATING

82 User Friendliness

86 Educational Value

60 Instructional Design

Nordic Software, Inc.
1986
$39.95
Ages 3-7
Mac (512K)
CL/2 NB/3,7 OT/1

Four games: Shape Works—child clicks mouse to match shape shown. Can print worksheets. Bar Math—child counts two sets to get a total. A voice helps count. Tic-tac-toe—child plays against computer or another person. Concentration—a memory game with a 30- to 88-box grid. Many setup options available.

OT = Other topics   SE = Seriation   SP = Spatial relations   TI = Time   * = Version reviewed

Preschool IQ Builder I

Concepts of same and different

◆◆◆ 38 FINAL RATING

◆◆◆ 35 User Friendliness

◆◆◆◆◆ 51 Educational Value

◆◆◆ 33 Instructional Design

Queue, Inc.
1982
$34.95
Ages 3-6
Apple*
CL/2 LA/4

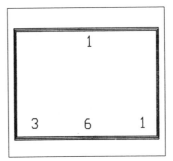

Contains seven lessons in which the child presses the S or L key to indicate if the two objects on the screen are the same or different. Lessons range from colors (color monitor required) to letters. Provides little range of challenge or child-control.

Preschool IQ Builder II

Matching, shapes, numbers, letters

◆◆◆◆ 43 FINAL RATING

◆◆◆◆ 41 User Friendliness

◆◆◆◆ 48 Educational Value

◆◆◆◆ 42 Instructional Design

Queue, Inc.
1984
$34.95
Ages 3-6
Apple*
CL/2 LA/5

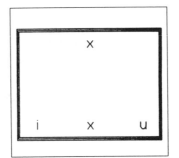

Contains six lessons, all with same format showing model object at top of screen. To receive smile face, child uses spacebar and arrow keys to move model object to a mate at the screen bottom. Records are kept.

Preschool Pack

Letters, numbers, and shapes

◆◆◆◆◆◆◆ 79 FINAL RATING

◆◆◆◆◆◆ 61 User Friendliness

◆◆◆◆◆◆◆◆◆ 91 Educational Value

◆◆◆◆◆◆◆◆ 87 Instructional Design

Nordic Software, Inc.
1989
$69.95
Ages 3-6
Mac (1 MB, hard disk
    recommended)
CL/2 NB/3 LA/4,6 OT/1

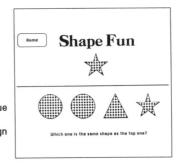

Four activities on two disks: ShapeWorks—child uses mouse to match shapes, letters, or numerals. AlphaWorks—child matches pictures with letters. Counting—child counts 1 to 20 objects. Block Math—child adds with sets of blocks. Also contains 20 dot-to-dot puzzles and a Concentration game. Clear graphics. Uses digitized speech.

CL = Classification   **CP** = Creative projects   **LA** = Language   **NA** = Not applicable   **NB** = Number

Primary Editor Plus

Word processing, drawing,
making banners

◆◆◆◆◆◆◆ 74 FINAL RATING

◆◆◆◆◆◆ 60 User Friendliness

◆◆◆◆◆◆◆◆ 83 Educational Value

◆◆◆◆◆◆◆◆ 81 Instructional Design

IBM Educational Systems
1988
$91.00
Ages 5-up
IBM PS/2
LA/9 CP/1,4 OT/4

Three programs: Picture Editor allows a child to draw in color, using arrows or mouse. Banner Maker prints banners in three different sizes of type. Primary Editor is a 40- or 80-column word processor with spell checker, eight screen colors, block move, copy and others. Menus and stories can be read aloud using the PS/2's built-in speech synthesizer.

Princess and the Pea, The

Creative writing

◆◆◆◆◆◆ 62 FINAL RATING

◆◆◆◆◆◆◆ 77 User Friendliness

◆◆◆◆◆◆◆◆ 80 Educational Value

◆◆◆◆ 40 Instructional Design

William K. Bradford Publishing
1989
$75.00
Ages 5-up
Apple* (3.5" or 5.25"), Mac LC
LA/3,8,9 NB/3 SP/1,2,4,7 CP/1,4

Contains three parts: Story Teller—child reads through a story. Story Maker—child creates own story or scenes, using animated objects or own text. Activities—contains story-starters, a house-building activity, a crown-making activity, and a puppet kit. Mouse recommended. Good design, graphics. No sound. Can print in color with an Imagewriter II. Some reading required.

Print Power

Creating printed materials

◆◆◆◆ 46 FINAL RATING

◆◆◆ 32 User Friendliness

◆◆◆◆◆◆ 60 Educational Value

◆◆◆◆◆ 50 Instructional Design

Hi Tech Expressions
1989
$12.70
Ages 6-up
Apple (128K)
CP/4 LA/9

A printing program featuring 60 graphics, 20 borders, and seven type faces in three sizes. Can make cards, banners, signs, or stationery. Design makes it difficult to use. Reading required. Young children require assistance. Similar in design to "Sesame Street Print Kit."

Print Shop, The

Creation of printed materials

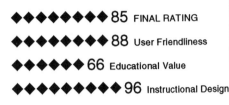

◆◆◆◆◆◆◆◆ 85 FINAL RATING

◆◆◆◆◆◆◆ 88 User Friendliness

◆◆◆◆◆◆ 66 Educational Value

◆◆◆◆◆◆◆◆ 96 Instructional Design

Broderbund Software
1987
$54.95
Age na
Apple*, Mac, IBM, C64, Atari,
    IIGS*
CP/1,4

An easy-to-use printing program that includes 120 graphic elements. Good for teacher use. Allows the creation of greeting cards, signs, letterheads, or banners. Includes 6 envelopes and 20 sheets of colored paper. Four Print Shop Graphics Libraries can be purchased separately for $24.95. Prints in color.

Professor Al's Sequencing Lab

Sequencing pictures and sentences into temporal order

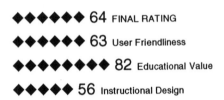

◆◆◆◆◆◆ 64 FINAL RATING

◆◆◆◆◆◆ 63 User Friendliness

◆◆◆◆◆◆◆ 82 Educational Value

◆◆◆◆◆ 56 Instructional Design

Micrograms, Inc.
1990
$39.95
Ages 5-12
Apple
TI/6

Consists of two disks. Disk A contains 20 picture sets, each of which includes four pictures in scrambled order. A child uses the spacebar and RETURN to number the correct sequence. Menu requires reading. Disk B contains 40 short stories. Story is shown, and then child is shown selected sentences and must put them in correct order. Can be somewhat confusing at first.

Puss in Boot

Spatial concepts

◆◆◆ 34 FINAL RATING

◆◆◆ 33 User Friendliness

◆◆◆ 33 Educational Value

◆◆◆ 35 Instructional Design

Island Software
1982
$25.00
Ages 3-6
Apple
SP/4

Gives practice with 14 "positional concepts," such as below, above, in, out. Some concepts not presented accurately in a two-dimensional presentation. Limited content. Poorly designed. Not recommended.

CL = Classification   **CP** = Creative projects   **LA** = Language   **NA** = Not applicable   **NB** = Number

Puzzle Master

Problem solving (puzzles)

◆◆◆◆◆◆ 79 FINAL RATING

◆◆◆◆◆◆ 72 User Friendliness

◆◆◆◆◆◆◆◆ 91 Educational Value

◆◆◆◆◆◆ 77 Instructional Design

Queue, Inc.
1984
$34.95
Ages 4-up
Apple*
SP/1,2 CP/1,4

Child uses joystick or arrow keys either to select 1 of 30 pictures or to create own, which can be scrambled and reassembled using icons. Offers hints if needed. Puzzles can be saved on disk. Child can select puzzles of varying difficulty (2-800 pieces). No reading required.

Puzzle Storybook, The

Writing, creating pictures, matching shapes, solving puzzles

◆◆◆◆◆ 66 FINAL RATING

◆◆◆◆◆ 64 User Friendliness

◆◆◆◆◆◆ 70 Educational Value

◆◆◆◆◆ 63 Instructional Design

First Byte, Inc.
1988
$39.95
Ages 3-8
IBM*, IIGS, Mac, Amiga
LA/3 CP/4 CL/2 SP/8

Child uses mouse (optional) to create simple pictures by selecting backgrounds and other elements. Pictures can be saved, printed, used to illustrate a story, or turned into one of two kinds of puzzles. Stories make use of a simple talking word processor that will say whatever is typed. Speech is not clear but can be improved with an external speech device. Children have some trouble getting started with this program.

Quarter Mile, The

Math fact practice, numeral and letter matching

◆◆◆◆◆◆◆ 79 FINAL RATING

◆◆◆◆◆ 56 User Friendliness

◆◆◆◆◆◆◆ 84 Educational Value

◆◆◆◆◆◆◆◆ 93 Instructional Design

Barnum Software
1987
$45.00
Ages 5-up
Apple
NB/4

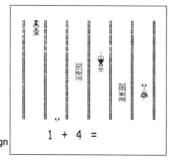

Child "races" against five other dragsters by entering correct responses to a math or letter problem. The child's own best scores are represented by the competing dragsters, so children can race against their own performance. Content ranges widely, from numeral and letter recognition to algebra. Scores can be saved. Requires some reading.

OT = Other topics   **SE** = Seriation   **SP** = Spatial relations   **TI** = Time   * = Version reviewed

Rabbit Scanner, The

Eye tracking, matching

◆◆◆◆◆ 67 FINAL RATING

◆◆◆◆◆ 58 User Friendliness

◆◆◆◆◆◆◆ 83 Educational Value

◆◆◆◆◆ 64 Instructional Design

E.C.S.
1986
$29.95
Ages 2-5
Apple
TI/1,3 CL/2

A simple program designed to provide practice scanning. Child watches a rabbit move across the screen and presses spacebar when the rabbit is over a carrot. Level of challenge can be adjusted by changing distractors, speed of rabbit, starting position. Requires adult setup.

Race the Clock

Memory

◆◆◆◆◆ 69 FINAL RATING

◆◆◆◆◆ 57 User Friendliness

◆◆◆◆◆◆ 72 Educational Value

◆◆◆◆◆◆ 77 Instructional Design

MindPlay
1984
$39.99
Ages 5-12
Apple*, IBM
LA/5 OT/1

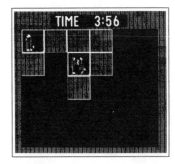

Concentration game with animated pictures. Child is given an amount of time to use joystick, mouse, paddles, or arrow keys to match pairs: picture/picture, picture/word, or word/word. Flexible design allows control of difficulty.

Rainbow Painter

Drawing

◆◆◆◆◆◆◆ 80 FINAL RATING

◆◆◆◆◆◆◆ 80 User Friendliness

◆◆◆◆◆◆ 73 Educational Value

◆◆◆◆◆◆◆ 86 Instructional Design

Queue, Inc.
1984
$34.95
Ages 4-12
Apple*
CP/1 SP/9

Presents an electronic coloring book in which the colors can be selected and filled in. Menus are easy to use. A free-draw option contains "mirror drawing" activity. Offers range of activities that child can control.

Read, Write, & Publish 1

Word processing and story illustrating

◆◆◆◆◆◆◆ 81 FINAL RATING

◆◆◆◆◆◆ 66 User Friendliness

◆◆◆◆◆◆◆◆◆ 97 Educational Value

◆◆◆◆◆◆◆ 87 Instructional Design

D. C. Heath & Company
1988
$99.00
Ages 6-up
Apple* (128K), IBM
LA/1,2,3,4,5,9 CP/1,4 SP/1,4

Child uses keyboard or mouse to select and move objects, words, or characters and then write about them. Three two-sided disks contain eight story topics with pull-down menus that contain word files and over 35 theme-related objects each. Stories and pictures can be saved or printed in color. Story disks can be copied. Mouse recommended. Available in Spanish.

Read-a-Logo

Use of commercial logos to practice reading skills

◆◆◆◆◆◆ 70 FINAL RATING

◆◆◆◆◆◆ 65 User Friendliness

◆◆◆◆◆◆◆◆ 88 Educational Value

◆◆◆◆◆◆ 60 Instructional Design

Teacher Support Software
1987
$149.95
Ages 4-up
Apple (network version available)
LA/3,4,5,6,9

Child first types name and personal information, such as family names, pets, etc., and then plays one of six activities that incorporate 24 popular logos, such as McDonald's, Coke, and Pizza Hut, with the child's personalized words. Reading required, although text can be spoken with a Slotbuster speech synthesizer. Includes many support materials.

Reader Rabbit

Basic reading skills/comprehension

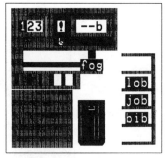

◆◆◆◆◆◆◆ 71 FINAL RATING

◆◆◆◆◆ 59 User Friendliness

◆◆◆◆◆◆◆◆ 87 Educational Value

◆◆◆◆◆◆◆ 71 Instructional Design

The Learning Company
1984
$39.95
Ages 5-7
Apple*, IBM, C64, Mac,
   IIGS ($59.95)
LA/4,5 OT/1

Four activities in which child uses spacebar, joystick, or paddles to match letters of C-V-C words, unscramble letters to create words, create word ladders, or play one of seven levels of Concentration. Uses over 200 lower-case three-letter words. Apple IIGS version says words.

Readiness Fun

Cause and effect, scanning

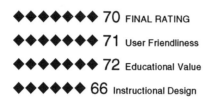 70 FINAL RATING

◆◆◆◆◆◆◆ 71 User Friendliness

◆◆◆◆◆◆◆ 72 Educational Value

◆◆◆◆◆◆ 66 Instructional Design

Access Unlimited
1989
$25.00
Ages 2.5-6
Apple
TI/1,2

Designed for special education settings. Two activities: Cause and Effect Clown—child sees a large face, presses any key to see an expression, e.g., a wink or a frown. Fun With Scanning—child sees two objects, one still and the other moving, and presses any key when they are next to each other.

Reading and Me

Matching, classifying, recognizing letters & words

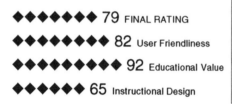 79 FINAL RATING

◆◆◆◆◆◆◆◆ 82 User Friendliness

◆◆◆◆◆◆◆◆◆ 92 Educational Value

◆◆◆◆◆◆ 65 Instructional Design

Davidson and Associates, Inc.
1987
$49.95
Ages 4-7
Apple* (128K), IBM, IIGS
   ($49.95)
CL/2,4 LA/4,5,6,7

Twelve activities include matching shapes, letter recognition, upper/lower case, alphabetical order, rhyming words, picture/word matching and completing a sentence. In each, child uses mouse or arrow keys to select one of four boxes in a multiple-choice format. Good design. Talking version for IIGS gives spoken feedback.

Reading Comprehension: Level 1

Reading comprehension skills

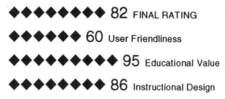 82 FINAL RATING

◆◆◆◆◆◆ 60 User Friendliness

◆◆◆◆◆◆◆◆◆ 95 Educational Value

◆◆◆◆◆◆◆◆ 86 Instructional Design

Houghton Mifflin Co.
1988
$174.00
Ages 6-7
Apple (64K)
LA/5,6,8

Child uses spacebar, arrow keys, and RETURN to page through a story in which comprehension questions are asked through an Echo speech synthesizer (required). Uses clear voice. To assist reading, child can select and listen to any word in the story. Sixteen stories come on eight disks. Keeps records. Good design.

CL = Classification   **CP** = Creative projects   **LA** = Language   **NA** = Not applicable   **NB** = Number

Reading Fun: Beginning Consonants

Beginning consonants

◆◆◆◆ 56 FINAL RATING

◆◆◆◆◆ 55 User Friendliness

◆◆◆◆◆◆◆ 74 Educational Value

◆◆◆ 44 Instructional Design

Troll Associates
1985
$39.95
Ages 5-6
Apple
LA/4,6

Child uses spacebar and RETURN to identify objects that start with the same sound, start with different sounds, or start with a given letter. Offers little child-control. Allows teacher to select letters, set the difficulty level, and set the number of problems.

Reading Fun: Final Consonants

Final consonants

◆◆◆◆ 56 FINAL RATING

◆◆◆◆◆ 55 User Friendliness

◆◆◆◆◆◆◆ 74 Educational Value

◆◆◆ 44 Instructional Design

Troll Associates
1989
$39.95
Ages 5-6
Apple
LA/4,6

Child uses spacebar and RETURN to identify objects that start with the same sound, start with different sounds, or start with a given letter. Offers little child-control. Allows teacher to select letters, set the difficulty level, and set the number of problems.

Reading Fun: Vowel Sounds

Long and short vowel sounds

◆◆◆ 46 FINAL RATING

◆◆◆ 46 User Friendliness

◆◆◆◆ 59 Educational Value

◆◆◆ 40 Instructional Design

Troll Associates
1990
$39.95
Ages 6-7
Apple
LA/6,7

Two activities: Crazy Crayons—child sees a word (e.g., axe) and uses the spacebar and the number keys to select and color in pictures that start with that letter. Brush Ups—child sees two words (e.g., drum and cup) and indicates (Y or N) if the words have the same vowel sound. Rigid design limits child-control. Not recommended.

OT = Other topics   **SE** = Seriation   **SP** = Spatial relations   **TI** = Time   * = Version reviewed

Reading Helpers

Reading skills

◆◆◆◆◆◆ 69 FINAL RATING

◆◆◆◆◆ 53 User Friendliness

◆◆◆◆◆◆◆◆ 88 Educational Value

◆◆◆◆◆◆◆ 70 Instructional Design

Houghton Mifflin Co.
1986
$135.00
Ages 5-6
Apple (64K)
LA/1,4,6,8 CL/2

Five disks. Child presses any key to make selections in 11 games based around decoding and encoding, sight vocabulary, letter recognition, memory, thinking skills, matching, words in context, and alphabetical order of words. Content best for grade 1 and above. Initial adult help required.

Reading 1

Letters, letter sounds, and words

◆◆◆◆◆◆◆ 79 FINAL RATING

◆◆◆◆◆◆◆ 70 User Friendliness

◆◆◆◆◆◆◆◆◆ 94 Educational Value

◆◆◆◆◆◆◆ 76 Instructional Design

Queue, Inc.
1985
$39.95
Ages 3-6
Apple*, C64
LA/4,5,6 TI/6

Child uses arrows keys or joystick to move Peter Rabbit to his home. On the way, Peter matches letters, sounds, and vowels. Contains four levels. Clear graphics, enjoyable activities. In some games, words are "spoken," but voice is hard to understand (extra synthesizer not required).

Reading Machine, The

Various language skills

◆◆◆◆◆◆ 65 FINAL RATING

◆◆◆◆◆ 56 User Friendliness

◆◆◆◆◆◆ 69 Educational Value

◆◆◆◆◆◆ 67 Instructional Design

SouthWest EdPsych Services
1982
$59.95
Ages 5-8
Apple
LA/4

Separate activities (28) that range from matching letters to phonics practice (cassette interface available). Good management options allow teacher to set up lessons, diagnose progress, or keep records for up to 60 children. Blocky graphics.

CL = Classification   **CP** = Creative projects   **LA** = Language   **NA** = Not applicable   **NB** = Number

Reading Starters

Reading skills

◆◆◆◆◆◆ 63 FINAL RATING

◆◆◆◆◆ 51 User Friendliness

◆◆◆◆◆◆◆◆ 84 Educational Value

◆◆◆◆◆◆◆ 70 Instructional Design

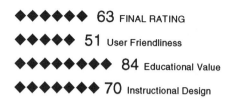

Houghton Mifflin Co.
1986
$135.00
Ages 5-6
Apple (64K)
LA/4,5,6,7,8 CL/2 SP/4

Child use six animals' names, Deb, Jip, Sam, Ben, Meg, and Tim, to play games based on encoding and decoding, sight vocabulary, letter recognition, memory, matching, alphabetizing, and positional words. Eighteen games on five disks offer a broad range in content. Keeps score. Initial adult help required.

ReadingMaze

Basic language skills

◆◆◆◆◆◆◆ 74 FINAL RATING

◆◆◆◆◆◆◆ 73 User Friendliness

◆◆◆◆◆◆◆ 76 Educational Value

◆◆◆◆◆◆◆ 74 Instructional Design

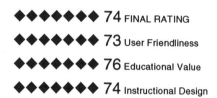

Great Wave Software
1991
$49.95
Ages 3-7
Mac
LA/4,5,6,10 SP/4,6

Child uses mouse or arrow keys to move through a maze in search of hidden objects. To pick up an object, child must answer a series of language skill questions. Child moves to a more difficult level after mastering current one. Matching pictures, letters/pictures, and words/pictures, following instructions (e.g., "Put the rake over the barn"), and unscrambling sentences are covered in 460 levels. Rather dry presentation. Tracks progress for up to 50 students.

Representational Play

Early language acquisition

◆◆◆◆◆◆◆ 71 FINAL RATING

◆◆◆◆◆◆ 62 User Friendliness

◆◆◆◆◆◆ 69 Educational Value

◆◆◆◆◆◆◆◆ 84 Instructional Design

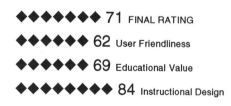

P.E.A.L. Software
1985
$150.00
Ages 2-5
Apple (64K)
LA/1,5 SP/7

Two overlays for the Muppet Learning Keys (required). Child first plays with real toys, then presses their pictures on the overlay to hear the associated words in a robotic voice. Requires Echo speech synthesizer. Covers 24 words. Adult setup required.

OT = Other topics   **SE** = Seriation   **SP** = Spatial relations   **TI** = Time   * = Version reviewed

Robot Writer Plus

A graphics program with text-writing feature

◆◆◆◆◆◆ 69 FINAL RATING

◆◆◆◆ 46 User Friendliness

◆◆◆◆◆◆◆◆ 83 Educational Value

◆◆◆◆◆◆◆◆ 81 Instructional Design

Queue, Inc.
1990
$49.95
Ages 6-13
Apple*, IBM
CP/4 LA/3,6,9 SP/2,5

Child selects from a variety of clip art (e.g., arms, bodies, heads, props) to create robot scenes that can be saved or printed in color. Words can be added and spoken on Echo synthesizer (optional). Our five-year-olds liked the graphics but needed help to use the program. Pages can be printed in seven sizes.

Rosie the Counting Rabbit

Language experience

◆◆◆◆◆◆◆ 89 FINAL RATING

◆◆◆◆◆◆◆ 85 User Friendliness

◆◆◆◆◆◆◆◆◆ 94 Educational Value

◆◆◆◆◆◆◆◆ 91 Instructional Design

D. C. Heath & Company
1988
$75.00
Ages 5-10
Apple (128K), Mac LC
LA/2,3,5,9 NB/3 CP/4 SP/4,7

Children use mouse, Koala Pad, joystick, or arrow keys to select or move objects, backgrounds, words, or characters of a story. Children can also add their own words. Resulting stories can be saved and printed in color. Includes four copies of the storybook. Good design. Fun to use. Mac LC version includes word processor.

Rumpelstiltskin

Reading comprehension

◆◆◆◆ 43 FINAL RATING

◆◆◆◆◆ 51 User Friendliness

◆◆◆◆ 48 Educational Value

◆◆◆ 35 Instructional Design

Troll Associates
1987
$39.95
Ages 5-8
Apple
LA/10 SP/4

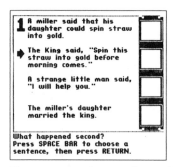

Three games: Sequencing—child puts eight sentences from "Rumpelstiltskin" in 1-2-3 order. Tic-tac-toe—child answers T/F question to win a square. Following Directions—child moves a marker in a scene, according to written directions, then creates a pattern. Best for ages 6 and up. Includes book.

CL = Classification   **CP** = Creative projects   **LA** = Language   **NA** = Not applicable   **NB** = Number

Run Rabbit Run

Scanning, directionality, and attention

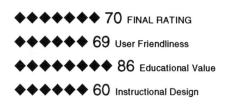 70 FINAL RATING

◆◆◆◆◆◆ 69 User Friendliness

◆◆◆◆◆◆◆ 86 Educational Value

◆◆◆◆◆◆ 60 Instructional Design

E.C.S.
1988
$39.95
Ages 4-8
Apple
TI/1,3,5

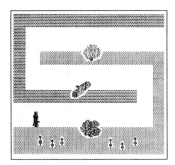

Child practices visual skills and timing by helping a rabbit through an obstacle course. Correct timing is required to jump over obstacles. Teacher options permit control of rabbit's speed, length of course, and number of obstacles. Can be used with joystick, paddle switches, or keyboard.

Same and Different

Matching

◆◆◆◆◆◆ 64 FINAL RATING

◆◆◆◆◆◆◆ 71 User Friendliness

◆◆◆◆◆◆◆ 76 Educational Value

◆◆◆◆ 48 Instructional Design

Access Unlimited
1989
$25.00
Ages 3-6
Apple
CL/2

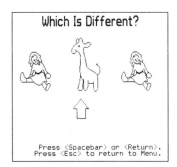

Two straightforward activities: Which Is the Same?—child sees two objects and indicates when they match. Which Is Different?—child sees three objects, one of which is different from the other two, and uses an arrow to select the one that is different. Child uses spacebar and RETURN to enter answers. Program can be set on scan mode for use with single switch.

Same or Different

Visual discrimination, matching

◆◆◆◆◆ 55 FINAL RATING

◆◆◆◆ 45 User Friendliness

◆◆◆◆◆◆ 68 Educational Value

◆◆◆◆◆ 54 Instructional Design

Merit Software
1985
$24.95
Ages 4-8
Apple*, C64
CL/1,2

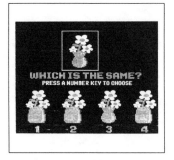

Child presses a number key to select which of four numbered objects is different from the others in some way or which of four objects matches one shown. Menus require reading. Offers a narrow range in content. Keeps score.

OT = Other topics   SE = Seriation   SP = Spatial relations   TI = Time   * = Version reviewed

Scanning Fun

Visual scanning

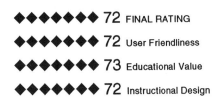 72 FINAL RATING

 72 User Friendliness

73 Educational Value

72 Instructional Design

Access Unlimited
1989
$25.00
Ages 3-6
Apple
TI/1,2

Designed for special education settings. Four activities in which child uses a regular (or alternate) keyboard, or single switch, to indicate when a moving object is next to another. Very easy to use. Somewhat distracting reinforcements. Options allow for adjusting scanning speed. Color monitor advised.

School Bus Driver

Coordination, judgment, and recall of details

73 FINAL RATING

77 User Friendliness

61 Educational Value

77 Instructional Design

Gametek/IJE, Inc.
1988
$9.95
Ages 3-8
IBM*, Apple, C64
SP/4,6 TI/4,8 NB/3

Child uses arrow keys or joystick (optional) to move a bus through a 15-screen country neighborhood to pick up six children scattered at six bus stops and drop them off at the school. There are four levels of play. Harder levels include road blocks and a timer to work against. Easy to use. No reading required. Limited in content.

School Mom

Basic skills practice

54 FINAL RATING

45 User Friendliness

73 Educational Value

49 Instructional Design

Software Excitement!
1991
Shareware
Ages 4-16
IBM (CGA)
LA/4 TI/9 CP/1,2 NB/4

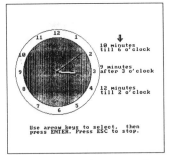

A range of activities covering six subjects. Music—a hard-to-use activity in which child uses letter keys to create notes on a staff line. Art—five simple drawing programs. Spelling—five drill activities from upper/lower-case letters to spelling lists (can be customized). English—tutorials and drill on parts of speech. Time—analog clock drill. Math—set/numeral matching, base ten, and an enjoyable math facts game.

Sentence Master Level 1

Reading skills, vocabulary development

◆◆◆◆◆◆◆ 75 FINAL RATING

◆◆◆◆◆◆◆ 79 User Friendliness

◆◆◆◆◆◆◆ 73 Educational Value

◆◆◆◆◆◆ 74 Instructional Design

Laureate Learning Systems
1990
$475.00 per level
Ages 5-8
Apple (Echo synthesizer required)
LA/5,6,8

Eight stories with three activities in each. First, a story can be read (Echo synthesizer required) and illustrated. Second, children read with assistance from the synthesizer, if necessary. The third part includes a drill on the words found in the story. Story vocabulary is carefully sequenced according to difficulty, making content rather dry. Allows control over presentation.

Sesame Street Astro-Grover

Counting, adding, and subtracting

◆◆◆◆ 41 FINAL RATING

◆◆◆◆ 45 User Friendliness

◆◆◆◆ 44 Educational Value

◆◆◆ 36 Instructional Design

Hi Tech Expressions
1984
$9.95
Ages 3-6
Apple, IBM, C64*
NB/3,4

Consists of five games that provide practice counting, adding, and subtracting objects in an "outer space" context. Lively graphics and sounds not related to content. Includes keyboard overlay. Apple version compatible with Muppet Learning Keys.

Sesame Street Big Bird's Special Delivery

Object recognition

◆◆◆ 31 FINAL RATING

◆◆◆◆ 43 User Friendliness

◆◆◆ 34 Educational Value

◆◆ 21 Instructional Design

Hi Tech Expressions
1984
$9.95
Ages 3-6
C64*, IBM, Apple
CL/2

Consists of a multiple-choice format in which child uses arrow keys to match one of four pictures according to form (easiest), class, and function (hardest). Menu requires reading.

OT = Other topics   **SE** = Seriation   **SP** = Spatial relations   **TI** = Time   * = Version reviewed

Sesame Street Crayon: Letters for You

Coloring pictures

◆◆◆◆◆◆◆ 80 FINAL RATING

◆◆◆◆◆◆◆ 79 User Friendliness

◆◆◆◆◆◆◆ 73 Educational Value

◆◆◆◆◆◆◆◆ 84 Instructional Design

Merit Software
1987
$14.95
Ages 3-up
Apple* (128K), IBM, C64, Amiga
CP/1,4 SP/4

A coloring program with 30 blank Muppets scenes. Child moves cursor with mouse, joystick, or arrow keys to fill in sections of a picture with 1 of 16 available colors. Prints in color. Mouse and color monitor recommended. Very easy to use. Prints picture with calendar.

Sesame Street Crayon: Numbers Count

Coloring pictures

◆◆◆◆◆◆◆ 80 FINAL RATING

◆◆◆◆◆◆◆ 79 User Friendliness

◆◆◆◆◆◆◆ 73 Educational Value

◆◆◆◆◆◆◆◆ 84 Instructional Design

Merit Software
1987
$14.95
Ages 3-up
Apple* (128K), IBM, C64, Amiga
CP/1,4 SP/4

A coloring program with 30 number pictures. Child moves cursor with mouse, joystick, or arrow keys to fill in sections of a picture with 1 of 16 available colors. Prints in color. Mouse and color monitor recommended. Very easy to use. Prints picture with calendar.

Sesame Street Crayon: Opposites Attract

Coloring pictures

◆◆◆◆◆◆◆ 80 FINAL RATING

◆◆◆◆◆◆◆ 79 User Friendliness

◆◆◆◆◆◆◆ 73 Educational Value

◆◆◆◆◆◆◆◆ 84 Instructional Design

Merit Software
1987
$14.95
Ages 3-up
Apple* (128K), IBM, C64, Amiga
CP/1,4 SP/4

A coloring program with 30 number pictures. Child moves cursor with mouse, joystick, or arrow keys to fill in sections of a picture with 1 of 16 available colors. Prints in color. Mouse and color monitor recommended. Very easy to use. Prints picture with calendar.

CL = Classification   **CP** = Creative projects   **LA** = Language   **NA** = Not applicable   **NB** = Number

Sesame Street Ernie's Big Splash

Planning, predicting, problem solving

◆◆◆◆◆ 59 FINAL RATING

◆◆◆◆◆ 51 User Friendliness

◆◆◆◆◆◆ 63 Educational Value

◆◆◆◆◆◆ 60 Instructional Design

Hi Tech Expressions
1985
$9.95
Ages 4-6
C64*, IBM
SP/4,7

Using function keys, child builds path that transports Rubber Duckie from his soap dish to Ernie's bathtub. The path is made by choosing squares that will move Duckie to Ernie. Three levels. Program takes three minutes to load from disk. Limited content.

Sesame Street Ernie's Magic Shapes

Visual discrimination practice

◆◆◆◆ 45 FINAL RATING

◆◆◆◆ 43 User Friendliness

◆◆◆◆◆◆ 61 Educational Value

◆◆◆ 37 Instructional Design

Hi Tech Expressions
1984
$9.95
Ages 3-6
C64*, Atari, IBM, Apple
CL/1,2

In all of the six shape- and color-matching games, child uses two arrow keys to decide if a shape or color matches one shown. Features Ernie, who nods feedback and brings new shapes. Provides little interaction or variety. Color monitor required.

Sesame Street First Writer

Writing & printing words, sentences, and stories

◆◆◆◆◆◆◆◆ 81 FINAL RATING

◆◆◆◆◆◆ 65 User Friendliness

◆◆◆◆◆◆◆◆ 81 Educational Value

◆◆◆◆◆◆◆◆ 89 Instructional Design

Hi Tech Expressions
1989
$14.95
Ages 4-up
Apple* (128K), IBM
LA/4,5,9 CP/4 OT/4

A word-processing program that allows the creation of text in two sizes (large and small) and three colors (white, green, and blue). Includes a 36 on-screen word list that can be customized. Does not have features, such as word wrap, that could be confusing to a child. Text can be saved or printed.

| **OT** = Other topics | **SE** = Seriation | **SP** = Spatial relations | **TI** = Time | * = Version reviewed |

Sesame Street Grover's Animal Adventures

Classifying animals

◆◆◆◆◆◆◆ 76 FINAL RATING

◆◆◆◆◆◆◆ 75 User Friendliness

◆◆◆◆◆◆◆ 73 Educational Value

◆◆◆◆◆◆◆ 79 Instructional Design

Hi Tech Expressions
1985
$9.95
Ages 4-6
C64*, IBM
CL/2

Child uses joystick to move Grover to one of four environments. Pressing joystick button adds animals or objects. Each environment is divided into land, sky, and water areas. Child must place animal in appropriate area.

Sesame Street Learning Library 1

Matching, counting, adding, subtracting

Not rated

Hi Tech Expressions
1985
$24.95
Ages 3-6
Apple, IBM, Nintendo
NB/3,4 CL/1,2

A combination of three separate programs—Sesame Street: Astro Grover, Ernie's Magic Shapes, and Big Bird's Special Delivery. Includes a 12-page teacher guide. See reviews of individual Sesame Street programs.

Sesame Street Learning Library 2

Problem solving, classifying animals

Not rated

Hi Tech Expressions
1985
$24.95
Ages 3-6
IBM, Nintendo
CL/2 SP/4,6,7

A combination of three separate programs—Sesame Street: Ernie's Big Splash, Grover's Animal Adventures, and Pals Around Town. Includes a 12-page teacher guide. See reviews of individual Sesame Street programs.

CL = Classification   **CP** = Creative projects   **LA** = Language   **NA** = Not applicable   **NB** = Number

Sesame Street Letter-Go-Round

Letter matching

◆◆◆◆◆ 56 FINAL RATING

◆◆◆◆◆◆ 61 User Friendliness

◆◆◆◆◆◆◆ 71 Educational Value

◆◆◆◆ 43 Instructional Design

Hi Tech Expressions
1984
$9.95
Ages 3-7
C64*, IBM, Atari, Apple
LA/4,5 TI/1,3

Child presses spacebar to stop and start ferris wheel, to match upper/lower-case letters, or to spell three-letter words. Good graphics and sounds. Menu requires reading. Includes keyboard overlay.

Sesame Street Pals Around Town

Community exploration

◆◆◆◆◆◆◆ 73 FINAL RATING

◆◆◆◆◆◆◆ 76 User Friendliness

◆◆◆◆◆◆◆ 73 Educational Value

◆◆◆◆◆◆ 69 Instructional Design

Hi Tech Expressions
1985
$9.95
Ages 4-6
C64*, IBM
SP/4,6,7

Child uses joystick (required) and function keys to explore and add objects to one of five scenes, e.g., a playground, a schoolroom, Sesame Street, Bert and Ernie's house, and downtown. Good graphics and sound. Disk version takes about three minutes to load. Color monitor recommended.

Sesame Street Print Kit

Creating printed materials

◆◆◆◆ 46 FINAL RATING

◆◆◆ 32 User Friendliness

◆◆◆◆◆◆ 60 Educational Value

◆◆◆◆◆ 50 Instructional Design

Hi Tech Expressions
1988
$14.95
Ages 3-up
Apple*, IBM, C64, Atari
CP/4 LA/9

A printing program featuring 60 Sesame Street characters, 20 borders, and 7 typefaces in 3 sizes. Can make cards, banners, signs, stationery, or storybook. Design makes it difficult to use. Reading required. Young children will require assistance.

Shape & Color Rodeo

Recognizing shapes and colors

◆◆◆◆◆◆◆ 73 FINAL RATING

◆◆◆◆◆◆ 62 User Friendliness

◆◆◆◆◆◆◆◆ 92 Educational Value

◆◆◆◆◆◆◆ 72 Instructional Design

DLM
1984
$32.95
Ages 4-8
Apple*, IBM, C64
CL/1

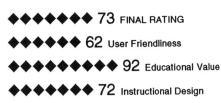

Six activities. Child uses spacebar and RETURN to select matching shapes or colors or to find hidden shapes in a rodeo picture. Lively graphics and sounds. Menu requires reading. For one or two players.

Shape Starship

Matching attributes of shape and size

◆◆◆◆◆◆ 65 FINAL RATING

◆◆◆◆◆◆◆ 79 User Friendliness

◆◆◆◆◆◆ 69 Educational Value

◆◆◆◆◆ 51 Instructional Design

Gamco Industries, Inc.
1986
$49.95
Ages 3-6
Apple*, C64, TRS 80
CL/1,2,3 SE/4

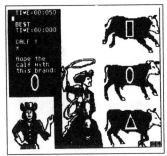

Child uses spacebar to move pointer in four multiple-choice-style activities in which child (1) matches objects of same shape and size but different color, (2) matches objects of same color and shape but different size, (3) decides what shape goes next in a series, or (4) matches object with a similar shape. Repetitive format. Good management options can keep up to 200 individual records.

Shapes & Patterns

Visual disc., cognitive skills

◆◆◆◆◆◆ 66 FINAL RATING

◆◆◆◆◆◆◆◆ 80 User Friendliness

◆◆◆◆◆◆◆ 72 Educational Value

◆◆◆◆◆ 52 Instructional Design

Mindscape, Inc.
1984
$61.00
Ages 3-6
Apple
CL/1,2 SE/2

Child uses nodding heads to decide (1) if shapes shown are the same, (2) if there is a common shape among several objects, or (3) if pattern is correct. Easy-to-use format. Utilities provide feedback on last-played round and some selection of difficulty level.

CL = Classification **CP** = Creative projects **LA** = Language **NA** = Not applicable **NB** = Number

Shutterbug's Patterns

Sequencing, pattern recognition

◆◆◆ 36 FINAL RATING

◆◆◆◆◆ 56 User Friendliness

◆◆◆ 32 Educational Value

◆◆◆ 36 Instructional Design

Merit Software
1985
$24.95
Ages 4-8
Apple*, C64
CL/2

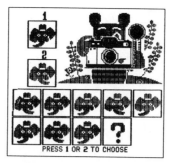

PRESS 1 OR 2 TO CHOOSE

Child sees a series of eight pictures and must select the ninth and tenth of the series. Graphics are distracting. Content is limited.

Shutterbug's Pictures

Memory skills, reading readiness

◆◆◆◆◆◆ 61 FINAL RATING

◆◆◆◆◆◆ 69 User Friendliness

◆◆◆◆◆◆◆ 72 Educational Value

◆◆◆◆◆ 51 Instructional Design

Merit Software
1985
$24.95
Ages 4-8
Apple*, C64
OT/1

One game in which child sees picture, then is flashed the same picture with one element missing. Child uses the number keys to select the missing object. No branching.

Sight Word Spelling

Letter, word, and numeral recognition

◆◆◆ 39 FINAL RATING

◆◆◆ 30 User Friendliness

◆◆◆◆◆ 55 Educational Value

◆◆◆ 36 Instructional Design

E.C.S.
1987
$39.95
Ages 6-7
Apple
LA/4,5 NB/4 OT/1

DOG

Designed for first- and second-grade special education students, this program presents 10 words or numbers on the screen, one at a time, and pronounces them (Echo speech synthesizer required). The child must type what is shown. Poor design. Keeps records. Custom word lists can be created and stored.

OT = Other topics   SE = Seriation   SP = Spatial relations   TI = Time   * = Version reviewed

Silly Letters & Numbers

Letter and numeral recognition

◆◆◆◆◆◆◆ 70 FINAL RATING

◆◆◆◆◆◆◆ 70 User Friendliness

◆◆◆◆◆◆◆◆ 84 Educational Value

◆◆◆◆◆◆ 60 Instructional Design

Access Unlimited
1988
$25.00
Ages 3-6
Apple
LA/4 NB/4 CL/2 OT/3

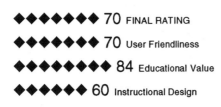

Five simple activities that use large, cartoon-style letters or numerals. Child uses keyboard to match letters or numerals, fill the screen with silly numerals, find a given letter on the keyboard, or freely type with a choice of two large, customized typefaces. Can be used with regular or alternate keyboards.

Simon Says

Chaining memory exercise

◆◆◆◆◆◆◆◆ 80 FINAL RATING

◆◆◆◆◆◆◆◆ 83 User Friendliness

◆◆◆◆◆◆◆◆◆ 91 Educational Value

◆◆◆◆◆◆◆ 72 Instructional Design

Sunburst Communications, Inc.
1987
$65.00
Ages 6-11
Apple*, C64
OT/1 SE/4

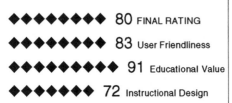

Child must re-create sequences of colors, numbers, or letters, which get longer with each correct answer. Options allow child to create the original sequence, select the speed with which it is flashed, or select the letters used. Uses regular keyboard, Muppet keyboard, or TouchWindow. Can be played by one to four players.

Simple Addition

Addition with sums less than nine

◆◆◆◆◆◆ 69 FINAL RATING

◆◆◆◆◆◆◆ 71 User Friendliness

◆◆◆◆◆◆◆ 79 Educational Value

◆◆◆◆◆◆ 60 Instructional Design

Access Unlimited
1988
$25.00
Ages 3-6
Apple
NB/3,4,7

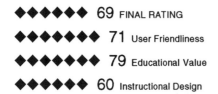

Two straightforward addition activities. Adding Dinosaurs—child first counts two sets, then adds them together. Dragon Addition—child sees addition equation and enters answer. Incorrect answers prompt the appearance of a set that a child can count for help. Easy to use though limited in content.

CL = Classification   **CP** = Creative projects   **LA** = Language   **NA** = Not applicable   **NB** = Number

Simple Cause and Effect

Cause and effect

◆◆◆◆◆◆◆ 73 FINAL RATING

◆◆◆◆◆◆◆ 78 User Friendliness

◆◆◆◆◆◆ 63 Educational Value

◆◆◆◆◆◆◆ 74 Instructional Design

Access Unlimited
1989
$25.00
Ages 3-6
Apple
TI/1,2

```
Cause & Effect Menu

 1) Screens
 2) Robot
 3) Boxes
 4) Sketch
 5) Patterns
 6) Shapes


   Press O for Options.
  Press I for Instructions.
 Press a number 1-6 to Play.
```

Six simple activities in which a child presses the spacebar or a single switch to create colors on the screen, build a robot one part at a time, fill the screen with colored boxes, randomly draw a design, create a colored pattern, or move a shape across the screen. Easy to use. Color monitor recommended.

Size and Logic

Size discrimination, patterns

◆◆◆◆◆◆◆ 77 FINAL RATING

◆◆◆◆◆◆ 69 User Friendliness

◆◆◆◆◆◆◆◆ 91 Educational Value

◆◆◆◆◆◆◆ 75 Instructional Design

Hartley Courseware, Inc.
1984
$35.95
Ages 3-6
Apple
SE/1,2,4 CL/1

Four games in which child uses spacebar and RETURN to match objects by size, select the object that comes next in a series, or create a matching set. Three levels to each game. Child can use picture menu to select own difficulty level. Clear graphics.

Sleepy Brown Cow, The

Language experience

◆◆◆◆◆◆◆◆ 89 FINAL RATING

◆◆◆◆◆◆◆◆ 85 User Friendliness

◆◆◆◆◆◆◆◆◆ 94 Educational Value

◆◆◆◆◆◆◆◆ 91 Instructional Design

D. C. Heath & Company
1988
$75.00
Ages 5-10
Apple
LA/2,3,5,9 CP/4 SP/4,7

Children use mouse, Koala Pad, joystick, or arrow keys to select or move objects, backgrounds, words, or characters of a story. They can also add their own words. Resulting stories can be saved and printed in color. Good design. Fun to use.

OT = Other topics   **SE** = Seriation   **SP** = Spatial relations   **TI** = Time   * = Version reviewed

SocPix

Classification (class membership)

◆◆◆◆◆◆ 61 FINAL RATING

◆◆◆◆◆◆◆ 80 User Friendliness

◆◆◆◆◆ 57 Educational Value

◆◆◆◆ 47 Instructional Design

American Guidance Service
1985
$49.95
Ages 3-7
Apple
CL/2,4

Three activities on one disk. Child uses arrow keys and spacebar to decide whether pictures belong to a given category. Includes 175 pictures in 7 categories. A separate record-keeping program ($19.95) keeps records for 40 children.

Sound Ideas: Consonants

Consonant sounds

◆◆◆◆◆◆◆◆ 80 FINAL RATING

◆◆◆◆◆◆◆ 79 User Friendliness

◆◆◆◆◆◆◆◆ 88 Educational Value

◆◆◆◆◆◆◆ 76 Instructional Design

Houghton Mifflin Co.
1986
$165.00
Ages 5-6
Apple (64K)
LA/4,5,6

Seven disks present the "th," "sh," and "ch" and 17 consonants. There are four levels. Child matches a sound (said by synthesizer) with a picture, a letter, or a word by using spacebar and RETURN to select a box in a multiple-choice format. Includes workbook and other materials. Requires Echo speech synthesizer.

Sound Ideas: Vowels

Five vowel sounds (long, short) and y

◆◆◆◆◆◆◆◆ 80 FINAL RATING

◆◆◆◆◆◆◆ 79 User Friendliness

◆◆◆◆◆◆◆◆ 88 Educational Value

◆◆◆◆◆◆◆ 76 Instructional Design

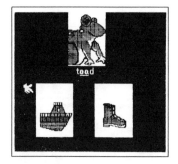

Houghton Mifflin Co.
1986
$165.00
Ages 5-6
Apple (64K)
LA/4,5,6

Five disks. Child uses spacebar and RETURN to select one of three objects with the same vowel sound as a picture. Uses spoken and pictorial examples to illustrate letter/sound correspondence. Includes workbook and other support materials. Requires Echo speech synthesizer.

Sound Ideas: Word Attack

Consonant blends, clusters and digraphs

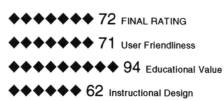

◆◆◆◆◆◆◆ 72 FINAL RATING

◆◆◆◆◆◆◆ 71 User Friendliness

◆◆◆◆◆◆◆◆◆ 94 Educational Value

◆◆◆◆◆◆ 62 Instructional Design

Houghton Mifflin Co.
1987
$174.00
Ages 5-6
Apple (64K)
LA/4,5,6

Six disks. Each disk has three parts: a tutorial, a practice session, and a story. Successful completion of each part is required to get to the next level. Practice session gives child a choice of three games to play. Story puts phonics in sentence context. Workbook and support materials included. Provides verbal feedback. Requires Echo speech synthesizer.

Space Waste Race

Letter/numeral recognition

◆◆◆◆ 49 FINAL RATING

◆◆◆◆ 44 User Friendliness

◆◆◆◆◆ 57 Educational Value

◆◆◆◆ 47 Instructional Design

Sunburst Communications, Inc.
1984
$65.00
Ages 3-7
Apple*, Atari, TRS 80
LA/8 NB/3,4 SP/4

Consists of an animated musical storybook with theme-related drill-and-practice activities on counting, letter/numeral recognition, and spatial concepts. Reading required.

Spaceship Lost

Spatial relationships

◆◆◆◆ 45 FINAL RATING

◆◆ 28 User Friendliness

◆◆◆◆◆◆ 63 Educational Value

◆◆◆◆ 49 Instructional Design

Educational Activities, Inc.
1984
$59.95
Ages 4-6
Apple
SP/3

Child moves captain through simple maze by typing first letter of direction term. Reading required. Two levels of difficulty: one with captain taking child's perspective each time, and one with child taking captain's perspective. Simple design of graphics limits the program.

Spatial Concepts

24 spatial concepts, e.g., top, left, below

◆◆◆◆◆◆ 61 FINAL RATING

◆◆◆ 37 User Friendliness

◆◆◆◆◆◆◆ 88 Educational Value

◆◆◆◆◆◆ 67 Instructional Design

S.R.A.
1984
$249.00
Ages 3-6
Apple
SP/4 LA/5

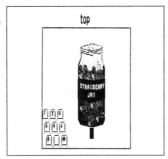

A six-disk program with clear graphics and speech (Echo speech synthesizer required). For each concept, such as "top," child sees an object and presses spacebar when a scanning cursor is in the top position; indicates (by Y or N) whether or not a cursor is in the top position; or types the word "top." Requires teacher setup. Keeps data and scores for 30 children.

Spell-A-Word

Spelling

◆◆◆◆◆ 53 FINAL RATING

◆◆◆ 32 User Friendliness

◆◆◆◆◆◆◆ 75 Educational Value

◆◆◆◆◆ 59 Instructional Design

Access Unlimited
1988
$69.00
Ages 5-13
Apple
LA/4,6,8

A talking, large-print spelling program that keeps individual records and spelling lists for more than one child. A word is first shown and then pronounced by Echo speech synthesizer (recommended), then typed by child. A harder level of the program says the word, then asks child to spell word without seeing it. Lists and reports can be printed. Minor technical problems.

Spellicopter

Spelling practice

◆◆◆◆◆◆ 66 FINAL RATING

◆◆◆◆◆ 59 User Friendliness

◆◆◆◆◆◆◆ 77 Educational Value

◆◆◆◆◆◆ 64 Instructional Design

Compton's New Media
1983
$39.95
Ages 6-10
Apple*, IBM, C64 ($29.95)
LA/5 SP/4

Child pilots helicopter (using joystick or arrow keys) over obstacles to pick up scattered letters of a spelling word. A sentence is given for a clue. Up to 400 words are available (40 lists of 10 words).

CL = Classification   **CP** = Creative projects   **LA** = Language   **NA** = Not applicable   **NB** = Number

Spelling and Reading Primer

Spelling and reading practice

◆◆◆◆◆ 51 FINAL RATING

◆◆◆◆ 46 User Friendliness

◆◆◆◆◆◆ 65 Educational Value

◆◆◆◆ 48 Instructional Design

Compton's New Media
1982
$39.95
Ages 4-8
Apple*, IBM, C64
LA/5

Two activities: Reading Primer—child uses spacebar to move cursor to match word with one of three line drawings. Spelling Primer—child sees drawing and must type in word. Twenty-two word-lists with 350 words ranging from "pin" to "circle." Keeps a running record for one child.

Spelling Bee, The

Spelling skills

◆◆◆ 32 FINAL RATING

◆◆◆ 34 User Friendliness

◆◆◆ 37 Educational Value

◆◆ 24 Instructional Design

Troll Associates
1985
$39.95
Ages 5-6
Apple
LA/5

Consists of a book, disk, and cassette tape. Three games: (1) Child sees three words, e.g., fan/me/mine, and selects one that is different; (2) child changes word to match picture; and (3) child matches picture to word. Reading required. Limited content. Cluttered graphics.

Stars & Planets

Counting, planets, prereading, creativity

◆◆◆◆◆◆ 62 FINAL RATING

◆◆◆◆◆◆ 68 User Friendliness

◆◆◆◆◆◆ 61 Educational Value

◆◆◆◆◆ 58 Instructional Design

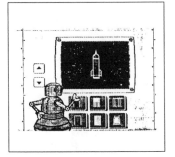

Advanced Ideas, Inc.
1989
$44.95
Ages 3-6
IIGS*, IBM (3.5" or 5.25")
NB/3 CL/2 SE/1 CP/4

Six activities about planets and stars. Child uses keyboard to (1) match planets, (2) put planets in order by orbit, (3) match constellation outline or word, (4) control a robot to match rockets, (5) gather and count moon rocks, or (6) match planets with their written names. Design limits child-control. Good sound, graphics. Does not use mouse.

| OT = Other topics | SE = Seriation | SP = Spatial relations | TI = Time | * = Version reviewed |

Stepping Stones Level I

Letters, numbers, and words

◆◆◆◆◆ 59 FINAL RATING

◆◆◆◆◆ 58 User Friendliness

◆◆◆◆◆◆◆ 84 Educational Value

◆◆◆◆ 47 Instructional Design

CompuTeach
1987
$39.95
Ages 2-4
Apple, IBM*, Mac
LA/4,5,6 NB/2,3,4

Three disks: Reading, Math, and Word Pieces. Five games that include pressing any letter to see a picture (e.g., a cat for C), counting, and typing simple words. Word Pieces is a clever game in which child sees incomplete word, e.g., _IG and tries any letter to make a word. Variety of content. Sold in combination with "Stepping Stones Level II" for $49.95.

Stepping Stones Level II

Vocabulary, counting, adding

◆◆◆◆◆ 58 FINAL RATING

◆◆◆◆◆◆ 60 User Friendliness

◆◆◆◆◆◆ 76 Educational Value

◆◆◆◆◆ 47 Instructional Design

CompuTeach
1987
$39.95
Ages 5-7
Apple*, IBM, Mac
LA/4,5,6 NB/3,4

Three activities on two disks. Language—Child uses spacebar to select pictures of elements of a sentence, which animates itself if correct. Reading—child matches pictures and words. Arithmetic—child counts up to 24 objects and enters answer. Menus require reading. Sold in combination with "Stepping Stones Level I" for $49.95.

Stickers

Creative activity

◆◆◆◆◆◆◆ 79 FINAL RATING

◆◆◆◆◆◆◆ 77 User Friendliness

◆◆◆◆◆◆◆ 74 Educational Value

◆◆◆◆◆◆◆ 81 Instructional Design

Queue, Inc.
1984
$34.95
Ages 4-12
Apple, IBM*
CP/1,4 SP/1,2,8

Using arrow keys or joystick, child moves geometric shapes on screen to either match existing patterns or create own. Easy-to-use picture menu requires no reading. Keyboard or joystick can be used.

Stickybear ABC

Letter recognition

◆◆◆◆◆ 59 FINAL RATING

◆◆◆◆◆◆◆ 76 User Friendliness

◆◆◆◆◆ 53 Educational Value

◆◆◆◆◆ 55 Instructional Design

Optimum Resource, Inc.
1982
$39.95
Ages 3-6
Apple*, Atari, C64
LA/4

Child presses any letter key to get one of two animated pictures related to letter. Easy-to-use program, but little challenge. Entertaining graphics. Talking version available for Apple IIGS (see "The New Talking Stickybear Alphabet").

Stickybear Math

Counting, addition, subtraction

◆◆◆◆◆◆◆◆ 81 FINAL RATING

◆◆◆◆◆◆◆ 70 User Friendliness

◆◆◆◆◆◆◆◆◆ 90 Educational Value

◆◆◆◆◆◆◆ 82 Instructional Design

Optimum Resource, Inc.
1984
$39.95
Ages 6-9
Apple*, IBM, C64
NB/3,4,7

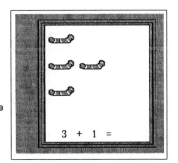

A 20-level math program that keeps names, levels, scores, and types of problems for up to 25 children. Automatically tracks and adjusts difficulty level. Content ranges from counting to three-place vertical-presentation subtraction with borrowing. Includes poster and stickers. Animated graphics illustrate problems.

Stickybear Numbers

Counting from 0 to 9

◆◆◆◆◆◆◆ 75 FINAL RATING

◆◆◆◆◆◆◆ 75 User Friendliness

◆◆◆◆◆◆◆ 79 Educational Value

◆◆◆◆◆◆◆ 71 Instructional Design

Optimum Resource, Inc.
1987
$39.95
Ages 3-6
Apple*, IBM, C64
NB/3,4,7,8

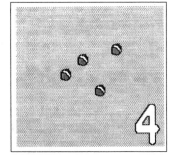

Child uses spacebar or number keys to see sets of colorful objects. Pressing the 4 key, for example, causes four bouncing balls to appear. Spacebar causes balls to disappear, one at a time. Each time a number key is pressed, a new set of objects (20 possible) appears. Entertaining graphics. Easy to use. Numbers are spoken if Echo speech synthesizer is used.

Stickybear Printer

"Printing fun for everyone"

◆◆◆◆ 43 FINAL RATING

◆◆◆◆ 40 User Friendliness

◆◆◆ 36 Educational Value

◆◆◆◆ 49 Instructional Design

Optimum Resource, Inc.
1985
$49.95
Ages 5-up
Apple
CP/4 OT/4

Allows creation of cards, stories, or posters. Multiple-menu design requires reading, limiting independent use by nonreaders. Can utilize Imagewriter II color printer. A second package, "Stickybear Printer Picture Library" ($39.95), contains two disks of additional graphics.

Stickybear Reading

Word and sentence fun

◆◆◆◆◆◆◆ 77 FINAL RATING

◆◆◆◆◆◆ 68 User Friendliness

◆◆◆◆◆◆◆◆ 89 Educational Value

◆◆◆◆◆◆◆ 78 Instructional Design

Optimum Resource, Inc.
1984
$39.95
Ages 5-8
Apple*, IBM, C64
LA/5,8,10

Three activities: Child can use joystick, arrow keys, or mouse to match words with pictures, complete a sentence, or build a sentence by selecting its parts. Graphics animate each sentence or word used. Includes 32-page book and poster.

Stickybear Shapes

Shape identification

◆◆◆◆◆◆◆ 70 FINAL RATING

◆◆◆◆◆ 56 User Friendliness

◆◆◆◆◆◆◆◆ 80 Educational Value

◆◆◆◆◆◆◆ 78 Instructional Design

Optimum Resource, Inc.
1983
$39.95
Ages 3-6
Apple*, Atari, C64, IBM
SP/8

The Stickybear series offers a book, a poster, and suggestions for extending concepts into noncomputer contexts. This program provides practice with five common shapes in three games: Pick It, Name It, and Find It. Paddles, arrow keys, or mouse can operate program. IBM version uses Covox Speech Adapter.

Stickybear Town Builder

Map skills

◆◆◆◆◆◆◆◆ 80 FINAL RATING

◆◆◆◆◆◆ 68 User Friendliness

◆◆◆◆◆◆◆◆◆ 97 Educational Value

◆◆◆◆◆◆◆ 80 Instructional Design

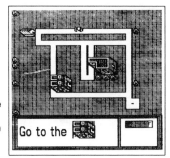

Go to the

Optimum Resource, Inc.
1984
$49.95
Ages 6-9
Apple*, C64
SP/3,4,6,7 TI/5,6 CL/2

Using joystick or arrow keys, child makes a town by placing 1 of 30 buildings on an empty map. The child can then drive car to find buildings in a matching game or to find hidden keys in the town. Towns can be saved. Joystick and color monitor recommended.

Stickybear Typing

Typing skills

◆◆◆◆ 42 FINAL RATING

◆◆◆◆ 49 User Friendliness

◆◆◆◆ 41 Educational Value

◆◆◆ 37 Instructional Design

Optimum Resource, Inc.
1985
$49.95
Ages 6-up
Apple*, IBM, C64
LA/4

Three activities give child practice with (1) finding letters with correct fingers, (2) building speed, and (3) typing stories. Includes 30 levels of difficulty, records scores, and gives WPM score. Slow key/screen response. Reading required.

Stone Soup

Creative writing

◆◆◆◆◆◆◆◆ 89 FINAL RATING

◆◆◆◆◆◆◆◆ 84 User Friendliness

◆◆◆◆◆◆◆◆◆ 92 Educational Value

◆◆◆◆◆◆◆◆◆ 93 Instructional Design

He roamed the countryside.
He slept with the rabbits.
He sang with the birds. But
there wasn't much food, and
the beggar was feeling hungry.

William K. Bradford Publishing
1989
$75.00
Ages 5-up
Apple*, IBM (3.5" or 5.25"),
  Mac LC
LA/3,8,9 NB/3 SP/1,2,4 CP/1,4

Contains three parts: Story Teller—presents clever version of the Stone Soup story. Story Maker—child uses mouse or keyboard to create and print, in color, versions of original stories. Activities—includes story-starters, a treasure-hunt, recipes, and a puppet kit. No sound. Excellent design puts the child in control of a wide range of content.

Storybook Weaver

Creating and illustrating stories

◆◆◆◆◆◆◆◆ 83 FINAL RATING

◆◆◆◆◆◆◆ 73 User Friendliness

◆◆◆◆◆◆◆◆◆ 91 Educational Value

◆◆◆◆◆◆◆◆ 86 Instructional Design

MECC
1990
$59.00
Ages 5-8
IIGS (note two 3 1/2 inch disk
　　drives required)
LA/3,8,9 CP/1,4 SP/7

Child uses mouse and keyboard to type stories and illustrates them by selecting various scenes and images. Resulting pictures can be printed or saved. Contains 12 background scenes, 6 fonts in two sizes, and over 300 realistic images that include people, animals, vehicles, and objects. Stories can be up to 50 pages.

Super GS Award Maker

Teacher's utility printing award certificates

Not rated

Orange Cherry Software
1990
$59.00
Ages na
IIGS
CP/4

Sixty-six ready-made award certificates listed under the following topics: language arts, science, social studies, physical education, math, achievement, sports, library, art, music and drama, holidays, and miscellaneous. Each award has a blank space for a name and a date. Awards can be printed in black and white or in color with an Imagewriter II printer.

SuperPrint !

Printing utility

◆◆◆◆◆◆ 62 FINAL RATING

◆◆◆◆ 42 User Friendliness

◆◆◆◆◆◆ 65 Educational Value

◆◆◆◆◆◆◆ 78 Instructional Design

Scholastic Software, Inc.
1987
$59.95
Ages 5-up
Apple*, IBM, Mac
CP/1,4

A program that prints signs, cards, banners, or posters that can be as large as 24 by 55 inches. All menus require reading. Four type styles and over 100 graphics. Prints in black and white or in color. Requires disk changing. See "Print Shop" for a better printing program.

CL = Classification　　　**CP** = Creative projects　　　**LA** = Language　　　**NA** = Not applicable　　　**NB** = Number

Surrounding Patterns

Visual imagery, symmetry

◆◆◆◆◆◆ 77 FINAL RATING

◆◆◆◆◆◆ 75 User Friendliness

◆◆◆◆◆◆◆◆ 98 Educational Value

◆◆◆◆◆◆ 65 Instructional Design

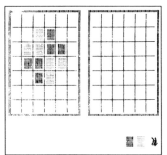

Strawberry Hill Software
1985
$19.00
Ages 3-10
Apple*, C64
SP/1,2,3,4,8,9 CP/1,4

Child sees a pattern of colored shapes and uses joystick or arrow keys to copy it. Seven levels are available, or child can make own designs, which can be saved. Program design is easy to use and encourages experimentation.

Talk About a Walk

Classifying household objects

◆◆◆◆◆ 56 FINAL RATING

◆◆◆◆◆ 59 User Friendliness

◆◆◆◆◆◆ 69 Educational Value

◆◆◆◆ 46 Instructional Design

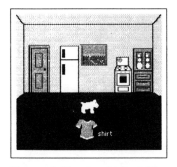

Queue, Inc.
1984
$39.95
Ages 4-6
Apple
LA/1,5 CL/2 SP/6

Two activities in which child sees 1 of 20 household items or words (spoon) and must place it in one of four rooms of a house. The second activity shows objects inside or outside a house. Child must press any key to indicate if the object is in the correct place.

Talking ABC's

Letter recognition

◆◆◆◆ 43 FINAL RATING

◆◆◆◆ 41 User Friendliness

◆◆◆◆◆ 50 Educational Value

◆◆◆◆ 40 Instructional Design

Orange-Cherry Software
1988
$59.00
Ages 3-7
IIGS (512K, 3.5")
LA/4 CL/2

Two disks—one for the letters A—M, the other for N—Z. Contains three activities: (1) Child presses any letter to hear letter name and see letter-related picture. (2) Child sees picture, hears letter, and must press a key. (3) Child sees on-screen keyboard, hears letter name, and must press that key. Limited content.

OT = Other topics　　**SE** = Seriation　　**SP** = Spatial relations　　**TI** = Time　　* = Version reviewed

Talking Alpha Chimp

Letter recognition, counting

◆◆◆◆◆◆◆ 84 FINAL RATING

◆◆◆◆◆◆◆ 85 User Friendliness

◆◆◆◆◆◆◆ 83 Educational Value

◆◆◆◆◆◆◆ 81 Instructional Design

Orange Cherry Software
1989
$59.00
Ages 3-7
IIGS*, IBM (3.5")
LA/4 NB/3 TI/6

Three activities on two disks. Alphabet Board—child clicks the mouse on a letter, sees a related picture, and gives the letter name. Number Tree—child clicks on a numeral, sees a corresponding sequence of events. Alphabet Story—child hears a letter named, presses its key, and sees and hears corresponding animation and sounds. Good graphics and sounds.

Talking Animals Activity Set

Matching six animals with their sounds, creating pictures

◆◆◆◆◆◆◆ 74 FINAL RATING

◆◆◆◆◆◆◆◆ 80 User Friendliness

◆◆◆◆◆◆ 67 Educational Value

◆◆◆◆◆◆◆ 71 Instructional Design

Orange Cherry Software
1989
$59.00
Ages 4-9
IIGS
CL/1 NB/3 CP/1

Four activities: Animal sounds—child clicks mouse on one of six animals to hear its sound. Animal rescue—a confusing game in which child "saves" animals by matching an animal with its sound. Animal Count—a limited activity in which child counts animals in a barnyard. Animal Builder—child combines animal parts and can color or print the result. Clear sounds and graphics. Some reading required.

Talking Classroom

A variety of school-related subjects

◆◆◆◆◆◆◆ 75 FINAL RATING

◆◆◆◆◆◆◆ 76 User Friendliness

◆◆◆◆◆◆ 65 Educational Value

◆◆◆◆◆◆◆◆ 80 Instructional Design

Orange Cherry Software
1990
$49.95
Ages 4-7
IIGS (1 MB), IBM (Covox)
LA/4 TI/9 SP/6 CP/1

Eight limited activities on two disks. Child uses mouse to click on a coin or dollar to see its equivalent in change; set the hands of a clock; press a letter key to hear the letter's name; match days of the week (spoken with written); watch an egg or cocoon hatch; click on a world map to learn about continents; color one of five line drawings; or print related worksheets. Some reading required. Uses clear speech and graphics. Requires disk swapping.

CL = Classification   **CP** = Creative projects   **LA** = Language   **NA** = Not applicable   **NB** = Number

Talking Clock

Clock-reading skills

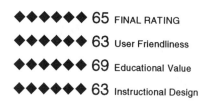

◆◆◆◆◆◆ 65 FINAL RATING

◆◆◆◆◆◆ 63 User Friendliness

◆◆◆◆◆◆ 69 Educational Value

◆◆◆◆◆◆ 63 Instructional Design

Orange Cherry Software
1988
$59.00
Ages 5-8
IIGS* (512K, 3.5"), IBM
TI/9

Child sets the hour, minute, and second hands on a clock by clicking mouse on one of two arrows. Uses pull-down menus to access options. Limited content. Reads time from clock and provides feedback statements in digitized speech. Reading required.

Talking Colors and Shapes

Basic colors and shapes

◆◆◆◆ 49 FINAL RATING

◆◆◆◆ 46 User Friendliness

◆◆◆◆◆◆ 64 Educational Value

◆◆◆◆ 44 Instructional Design

Orange Cherry Software
1989
$59.00
Ages 4-7
IIGS (3.5")
CL/2 SP/8

Two disks—one for colors and one for shapes. Each disk contains five activities that include selecting a shape or color and then hearing its name, matching colors or shapes ("find the square"), or filling in outlines of shapes with colors. Good speech and graphics. Poor range of content and design. Not recommended.

Talking Dinosaurs

Dinosaur names, counting

◆◆◆◆◆ 53 FINAL RATING

◆◆◆◆◆◆ 63 User Friendliness

◆◆◆◆◆ 59 Educational Value

◆◆◆◆ 43 Instructional Design

Orange Cherry Software
1989
$59.00
Ages 5-9
IIGS (3.5")
NB/3

Child clicks mouse on one of five dinosaurs to hear its name, finds the hidden dinosaurs in a picture, counts colored dinosaur bones and enters numeral (from 1 to 9), or fills in a dinosaur picture with one of four colors. Can also print four dinosaur outlines. The limited content and poor design diminish the value of the clear graphics and digitized speech.

Talking First Reader

Word sounds

◆◆◆◆◆ 63 FINAL RATING

◆◆◆◆◆◆ 63 User Friendliness

◆◆◆◆◆◆◆ 71 Educational Value

◆◆◆◆◆ 57 Instructional Design

Orange Cherry Software
1989
$59.00
Ages 5-8
IIGS (one 3.5" disk)
LA/5,8

Five activities in which child uses mouse to select one of three words (in lower-case) to match a picture, to select a word to end a sentence, or to move a bouncing ball along a sentence and thus hear each word. Each sentence is cleverly illustrated with good graphics. However, children lose interest quickly.

Talking First Words

Recognize and create words

◆◆◆◆◆◆ 62 FINAL RATING

◆◆◆◆◆◆ 61 User Friendliness

◆◆◆◆◆ 56 Educational Value

◆◆◆◆◆◆ 66 Instructional Design

Orange Cherry Software
1990
$49.95
Ages 4-7
IIGS
LA/4,5,6,8

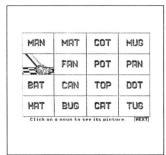

Five activities on two disks. (1) Child clicks on one of 18 action word cards to see a related animated sequence. (2) Child clicks on one of 32 noun word cards to hear word and see picture. (3) Child types missing letter after seeing a picture and listening to the word. (4) Child solves five simple word riddles. (5) Child clicks on a sentence-ending to match a picture. Excellent graphics and speech. Menu requires reading.

Talking First Writer

Experiment with words and sentences

◆◆◆◆◆◆◆ 74 FINAL RATING

◆◆◆◆◆◆ 61 User Friendliness

◆◆◆◆◆◆◆◆ 86 Educational Value

◆◆◆◆◆◆◆ 78 Instructional Design

Orange Cherry Software
1989
$59.00
Ages 6-9
IIGS (3.5")
LA/3,5,6,8,9,10

Three activities. In the first two, a child sees a picture and creates a three-word sentence (five-word, in level two) by selecting words with the mouse. The third activity (see picture) is the most fun, presenting 20 words a child can experiment with. Logical word combinations are illustrated and read in clear digitized speech. Limited content.

CL = Classification   **CP** = Creative projects   **LA** = Language   **NA** = Not applicable   **NB** = Number

Talking Money

Units of money

◆◆◆◆◆◆ 60 FINAL RATING

◆◆◆◆◆◆ 65 User Friendliness

◆◆◆◆◆◆◆ 72 Educational Value

◆◆◆◆◆ 50 Instructional Design

Orange Cherry Software
1989
$59.00
Ages 5-9
IIGS (3.5")
NB/3,7

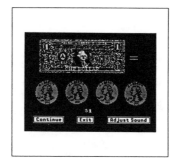

Five activities in which child uses the mouse to select a coin or bill, to hear its name, or to see its value (e.g., 1 dollar = 4 quarters). Child can match coins or bills with one of three amounts up to $10.00 or can select the correct amount of change for a purchase. Cumbersome design diminishes value of excellent graphics and clear digitized speech.

Talking Nouns I

Language development

◆◆◆◆◆◆◆◆ 80 FINAL RATING

◆◆◆◆◆◆◆◆◆ 95 User Friendliness

◆◆◆◆◆◆◆◆ 87 Educational Value

◆◆◆◆◆◆ 65 Instructional Design

Laureate Learning Systems
1987
$115.00
Ages 2.5-up
Apple (128K)
LA/5,8 CL/1,2

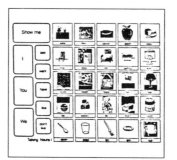

On an overlay for the TouchWindow (required), child presses a picture to hear its name said in a clear voice (Echo speech synthesizer required). Other words allow creation of simple sentences, e.g., "You see the bus." Fifty nouns available. Recommended for nonverbal children. Adult setup required.

Talking Nouns II

Language development

◆◆◆◆◆◆◆◆ 80 FINAL RATING

◆◆◆◆◆◆◆◆◆ 95 User Friendliness

◆◆◆◆◆◆◆◆ 87 Educational Value

◆◆◆◆◆◆ 65 Instructional Design

Laureate Learning Systems
1987
$115.00
Ages 2.5-up
Apple (128K)
LA/5,8 CL/1,2

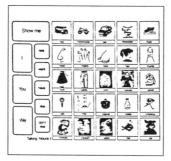

Same as "Talking Nouns I." Provides 50 additional nouns.

OT = Other topics   **SE** = Seriation   **SP** = Spatial relations   **TI** = Time   * = Version reviewed

Talking Numbers

Counting

◆◆◆◆ 41 FINAL RATING

◆◆◆◆ 46 User Friendliness

◆◆◆◆ 49 Educational Value

◆◆◆ 33 Instructional Design

Orange Cherry Software
1988
$59.00
Ages 5-7
IIGS (one 3.5" disk)
NB/4,8

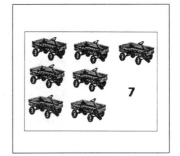

Four activities on one disk: (1) Child presses any number key to see and hear the number. (2) Child hears a number and must press its key. (3) Child hears and sees the computer count. (4) Child sees and hears number and must click mouse on the correct answer. Very limited content. Some reading required.

Talking Reading Railroad

Consonant and vowel sounds

◆◆◆◆ 54 FINAL RATING

◆◆◆◆◆ 63 User Friendliness

◆◆◆◆◆ 68 Educational Value

◆◆◆◆ 40 Instructional Design

Orange Cherry Software
1989
$59.00
Ages 5-9
IIGS (3.5")
LA/4,5,6,8

Two disks with four activities: (1) Child uses a mouse to match words with vowel sounds. (2) Child unscrambles a five-word sentence. (3) Child completes sentences by choosing one of three words. (4) Child hears the parts of a locomotive identified as mouse clicks on them. Limited content, same with each use. Requires "midstream" change of disk.

Talking School Bus

Directions, counting, animal sounds, and colors

◆◆◆◆◆◆◆ 77 FINAL RATING

◆◆◆◆◆◆◆ 82 User Friendliness

◆◆◆◆◆◆◆ 82 Educational Value

◆◆◆◆◆◆ 68 Instructional Design

Orange Cherry Software
1989
$59.00
Ages 5-8
IIGS*, IBM
SP/7 NB/3 CL/2

Consists of four simple activities on two disks. Bus Route—clicking mouse on directions moves a bus and picks up 4 children. At the Aquarium—a set of 1 to 10 fish are shown and counted by clicking on a number line. Farmer's Market—produce items are found and colored in. On the Farm—animals are matched with their sounds. Clear speech, sounds, and graphics. Limited content.

CL = Classification   **CP** = Creative projects   **LA** = Language   **NA** = Not applicable   **NB** = Number

Talking Speller

Spelling of 42 common words

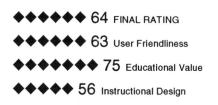

◆◆◆◆◆◆ 64 FINAL RATING

◆◆◆◆◆◆ 63 User Friendliness

◆◆◆◆◆◆◆ 75 Educational Value

◆◆◆◆◆ 56 Instructional Design

Orange Cherry Software
1989
$59.00
Ages 5-8
IIGS (3.5")
LA/6

Consists of six scenes based on travel, clothing, or the outdoors. In each, a child types a word, such as "train," to make a train appear in a scene. Letter hints are provided if needed. Also has a word-scramble activity where child sees a mixed-up word and uses the mouse to unscramble the letters. Combines great graphics and speech with poor design.

Talking Textwriter

Exploration of written language

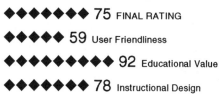

◆◆◆◆◆◆◆ 75 FINAL RATING

◆◆◆◆◆ 59 User Friendliness

◆◆◆◆◆◆◆◆◆ 92 Educational Value

◆◆◆◆◆◆◆ 78 Instructional Design

Scholastic Software, Inc.
1986
$187.45
Ages 3-9
Apple* (128K), IIGS, IBM
LA/3,4,5,6,7,9 CP/4 OT/4

A large-print word processor that says letters, words, or sentences as they are typed. Requires Echo speech synthesizer ($50 extra). Stories can be saved and printed. Requires adult setup. Comes on two disks. Apple IIGS and IBM versions do not require the Echo.

Talking Tiles

Letter and word sounds

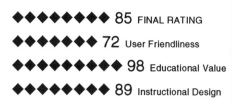

◆◆◆◆◆◆◆◆ 85 FINAL RATING

◆◆◆◆◆◆◆ 72 User Friendliness

◆◆◆◆◆◆◆◆◆ 98 Educational Value

◆◆◆◆◆◆◆◆ 89 Instructional Design

Bright Star Technology, Inc.
1988
$49.95
Ages 3-up
Mac (1 MB)
LA/3,4,5,6,7,8,9

Clicking the mouse on a letter produces an animated face that pronounces the letter. Letters can be "dragged" to the lower screen and combined with other letters to create any word, which is sounded out by the face. Children or adults can see, as well as hear, the phonics through the Mac's speech synthesizer.

| OT = Other topics | SE = Seriation | SP = Spatial relations | TI = Time | * = Version reviewed |

Talking TouchWindow

Creation of custom lessons

Not rated

Edmark Corporation
1989
$79.95
Ages na
Apple
OT/4

A utility program that allows a teacher to make multiple-choice-style lessons that make use of the TouchWindow and Echo speech synthesizer (requires both). Pictures can be created with graphics program such as "Color Me." A sample lesson could ask a child to "touch the red circle," for example. Up to 30 touch-active areas can be created per screen.

Talking Verbs

Language development

◆◆◆◆◆◆◆◆ 80 FINAL RATING

◆◆◆◆◆◆◆◆◆ 95 User Friendliness

◆◆◆◆◆◆◆◆ 87 Educational Value

◆◆◆◆◆◆ 65 Instructional Design

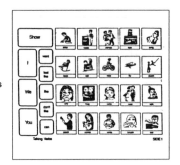

Laureate Learning Systems
1987
$115.00
Ages 2.5-up
Apple (128K)
LA/5,8 CL/1,2

On an overlay for the TouchWindow or Powerpad (required), child presses a verb picture (such as crying or talking). For picture pressed, word is said in a voice (Echo speech synthesizer required). Forty verbs and key-phrase words included. Adult setup required. Recommended for nonverbal children.

Ted Bear Games

Memory practice

◆◆◆◆◆◆◆◆ 83 FINAL RATING

◆◆◆◆◆◆◆◆ 82 User Friendliness

◆◆◆◆◆◆◆◆◆ 92 Educational Value

◆◆◆◆◆◆◆ 79 Instructional Design

Baudville
1985
$29.95
Ages 4-up
Apple*, C64, Atari, Mac
OT/1 CL/1,2

Contains three card games on one disk: Concentration, Old Maid, and Go Fish. Child uses mouse, joystick, arrow keys, or Koala Pad to move cards. Three difficulty levels offer a range in content. Well designed. Offers good level of child-control. Up to three players can play against the computer.

CL = Classification   **CP** = Creative projects   **LA** = Language   **NA** = Not applicable   **NB** = Number

Teddy and Iggy

Sequential memory practice

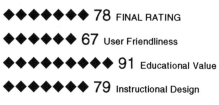

◆◆◆◆◆◆◆ 78 FINAL RATING

◆◆◆◆◆◆ 67 User Friendliness

◆◆◆◆◆◆◆◆◆ 91 Educational Value

◆◆◆◆◆◆◆ 79 Instructional Design

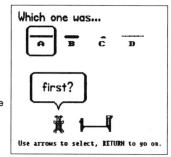

Sunburst Communications, Inc.
1987
$65.00
Ages 6-8
Apple*, C64
CL/1 OT/1

Three activities on one disk. Child must re-create order in which Teddy made his bed (recalling which color of sheet went on first), recall sequence in which several objects were flashed, or recall the order in which several boxes were opened. Uses keyboard, Muppet keyboard, or TouchWindow. Requires reading, color monitor.

Teddy Bear-rels of Fun

Creating pictures, graphics, and stories

◆◆◆◆◆ 56 FINAL RATING

◆◆◆ 37 User Friendliness

◆◆◆◆◆◆◆ 74 Educational Value

◆◆◆◆◆◆ 62 Instructional Design

DLM
1987
$39.95
Ages 5-up
Apple*, C64
CP/1,4 LA/3 SP/2

Child uses spacebar, RETURN, and arrow keys to create scenes with teddy bears. Includes over 200 pictures, backgrounds, and props that a child can arrange on the screen. Rather complex menus (a child must type CONTROL-C to go back) are better-suited to older children. Work can be saved or printed in color.

Teddy Bears Counting Fun

Counting skills

◆◆◆ 32 FINAL RATING

◆◆◆◆ 45 User Friendliness

◆◆◆ 30 Educational Value

◆◆ 27 Instructional Design

Micro-Learningware
1981
$30.00
Ages 3-6
Apple
NB/3

Presents nine scenes in which child counts bears (a random number from 1–9 appears), "reads" poem, and inputs number. Blocky graphics are hard to understand. Very limited content. Not recommended.

Teddy's Playground

Practice with color and shape attributes

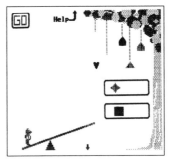

◆◆◆◆◆◆◆◆ 80 FINAL RATING

◆◆◆◆◆◆◆◆ 81 User Friendliness

◆◆◆◆◆◆◆◆ 88 Educational Value

◆◆◆◆◆◆◆ 75 Instructional Design

Sunburst Communications, Inc.
1985
$65.00
Ages 5-9
Apple
CL/2

Child uses joystick, mouse or arrow keys to move freely around three main areas of Teddy's playground to arrange pieces by shape, color, or shading. Includes supplementary materials. Similar in design to "Gertrude's Secrets." Color monitor required.

Telling Time

Clock practice

◆◆◆ 34 FINAL RATING

◆◆◆ 31 User Friendliness

◆◆◆ 31 Educational Value

◆◆◆ 37 Instructional Design

Orange Cherry Software
1984
$39.00
Ages 5-9
Apple*, C64, TRS 80, IBM,
    Atari, PET
TI/9

Provides practice with clock-reading skills. Multiple-choice questions are presented concerning the time shown on a rough clock. Child enters answer by typing letter. Reading required. A better clock-reading program is in "Learning About Numbers" by C&C Software.

This Land Is Your Land

Coloring pictures

◆◆◆◆◆◆◆◆ 80 FINAL RATING

◆◆◆◆◆◆◆◆ 79 User Friendliness

◆◆◆◆◆◆◆◆ 73 Educational Value

◆◆◆◆◆◆◆◆ 84 Instructional Design

Merit Software
1986
$14.95
Ages 3-up
Apple* (128K), IBM, C64
CP/1,4 SP/4

A coloring program with 30 blank scenes of the USA on one disk. Child moves cursor with mouse, joystick, or arrow keys to fill in sections of a picture with 1 of 16 available colors. Prints in color. Mouse and color monitor recommended. Very easy to use. Prints picture with calendar.

CL = Classification   **CP** = Creative projects   **LA** = Language   **NA** = Not applicable   **NB** = Number

Three Little Pigs, The

Creative writing

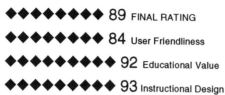

◆◆◆◆◆◆◆ 89 FINAL RATING

◆◆◆◆◆◆◆ 84 User Friendliness

◆◆◆◆◆◆◆◆ 92 Educational Value

◆◆◆◆◆◆◆◆ 93 Instructional Design

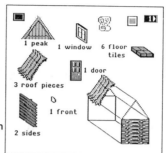

William K. Bradford Publishing
1989
$75.00
Ages 5-up
Apple*, Mac LC
LA/3,8,9 NB/3 SP/1,2,4,7 CP/1,4

Contains three parts: Story Teller—child reads through the story. Story Maker—child creates own story scenes, using animated objects or own text. Activities—contains story-starters, a tool hunt, a house-building activity, and a puppet kit. Mouse recommended. Good design, graphics. No sound. Can print in color with an Imagewriter II printer. Some reading required.

Tiger's Tales

Reading & vocabulary comprehension

◆◆◆◆◆◆◆ 80 FINAL RATING

◆◆◆◆◆◆ 66 User Friendliness

◆◆◆◆◆◆◆◆ 94 Educational Value

◆◆◆◆◆◆◆ 83 Instructional Design

Sunburst Communications, Inc.
1986
$65.00
Ages 5-7
Apple*, C64
LA/5,8

Five interactive stories in which child selects pictures related to the story. Includes a picture/word matching activity. Large, easy-to-read letters. Supplementary worksheets and activities are included. Can be used with Muppet Learning Keys. Reading required.

Time Master

Clock practice

◆◆ 25 FINAL RATING

◆◆ 28 User Friendliness

◆◆◆ 38 Educational Value

◆ 16 Instructional Design

Micro Power & Light Company
1980
$29.95
Ages 5-7
Apple
TI/9

Child must be able to read "set hand to half past seven" to use this program. Hands are moved with arrow keys. Choices are hours, half hours, quarter hours, minutes, or start and set the clock. Poor design. Not recommended.

Tink! Tonk!

Key location, alphabetical order

◆◆◆◆ 41 FINAL RATING

◆◆◆◆ 48 User Friendliness

◆◆◆◆◆ 54 Educational Value

◆◆ 28 Instructional Design

Mindscape, Inc.
1984
$24.00
Ages 4-8
Apple*, C64, IBM
LA/4 SP/4,7

Five games on one disk, designed to give practice with alphabet order (e.g., F,G,_,I) and key location. Games are played by using joystick or arrow keys to steer Tink's boat or helicopter to various islands. Most games are not at a preschool level. Color monitor recommended.

Tonk in the Land of Buddy-Bots

Problem solving

◆◆◆◆◆ 56 FINAL RATING

◆◆◆◆◆ 54 User Friendliness

◆◆◆◆◆◆ 66 Educational Value

◆◆◆◆ 49 Instructional Design

Mindscape, Inc.
1984
$29.95
Ages 4-8
Apple*, C64, IBM
SP/1,5,7 OT/1

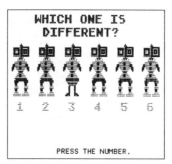

Child uses joystick or arrow keys to move "Tonk" through a 65-screen landscape filled with robot parts, sky holes, and enemy soldiers. Along the way, Tonk can stop to play one of six games on memory, matching, and spatial relations. Joystick use is optional.

Touch & Write

Printing practice

◆◆◆◆◆◆◆◆ 81 FINAL RATING

◆◆◆◆◆◆◆◆ 89 User Friendliness

◆◆◆◆◆◆◆◆ 87 Educational Value

◆◆◆◆◆◆◆ 72 Instructional Design

Sunburst Communications, Inc.
1986
$75.00
Ages 5-7
Apple
LA/4,5

Child touches screen (TouchWindow required) to make letters. Contains 4 stroke lessons and 19 letter lessons, based on the Palmer Manuscript style. Allows flexibility in design. Child can practice strokes, letters, or words. Work can be printed. D'Nealian version available.

CL = Classification   **CP** = Creative projects   **LA** = Language   **NA** = Not applicable   **NB** = Number

Touch and Match

Classification

◆◆◆◆◆ 65 FINAL RATING

◆◆◆◆◆ 62 User Friendliness

◆◆◆◆◆◆ 78 Educational Value

◆◆◆◆◆ 59 Instructional Design

Edmark Corporation
1986
$29.95
Ages 3-6
Apple
CL/2,4

Child needs only touch the screen (TouchWindow required) to identify identical, associated, or different pictures among four that are shown. Menu requires reading. Some setup required by adult. Clear but limited graphics. Easy for a child to use.

Touch and See

Memory skills

◆◆◆◆◆ 61 FINAL RATING

◆◆◆◆◆ 59 User Friendliness

◆◆◆◆◆◆◆ 80 Educational Value

◆◆◆◆ 49 Instructional Design

Edmark Corporation
1986
$39.95
Ages 4-7
Apple
OT/1 CL/2

A memory game in which children match 6 pairs of shapes, letters, pictures, or words hidden in 12 boxes. Timer shows time limit. Child touches screen to make matches. TouchWindow required. Written menus.

Toybox

Exploration of the computer

◆◆◆◆◆ 56 FINAL RATING

◆◆◆◆◆ 56 User Friendliness

◆◆◆◆◆◆ 72 Educational Value

◆◆◆◆◆ 64 Instructional Design

S.D.L.
1986
$10.00
Ages 1/2-up
C64*, Apple (128K), IBM
TI/1 CP/1,2,4

Each keystroke puts a different shape, color, or special effect on the screen in a random position. Effects accumulate on the screen, creating a composition that can be saved on the disk. Extremely easy to use.

OT = Other topics   **SE** = Seriation   **SP** = Spatial relations   **TI** = Time   * = Version reviewed

Treasure Mountain

Reading, thinking, math, and science skills

◆◆◆◆◆◆◆◆ 82 FINAL RATING

◆◆◆◆◆◆◆◆ 81 User Friendliness

◆◆◆◆◆◆◆◆ 84 Educational Value

◆◆◆◆◆◆◆◆ 80 Instructional Design

The Learning Company
1991
$37.99
Ages 5-9
IBM (CGA, VGA)
CL/1,2,3 LA/6,7,10 NB/7 SE/1
   OT/1

Child uses mouse or arrows to move through a maze of mountain paths. Along the way, hidden items can be discovered by following clues and carefully answering one of more than 350 multiple-choice word problems. Game and question difficulty increase as more treasures are discovered. Records can be saved, allowing many children to maintain ongoing games. Effectively combines good content with an engaging format.

Treehouse, The

Math skills, language, animals, music, and more

◆◆◆◆◆◆◆◆◆ 92 FINAL RATING

◆◆◆◆◆◆◆◆◆ 86 User Friendliness

◆◆◆◆◆◆◆◆◆ 98 Educational Value

◆◆◆◆◆◆◆◆◆ 92 Instructional Design

Broderbund Software
1991
$69.95
Ages 6-10
IBM* (VGA, hard disk, speech
   device), Apple, Mac
LA/8,9 TI/9 NB/1,3,5,7,8 CL/2
   CP/1-4 SP/6,7 SE/1

Child uses mouse (recommended), joystick, or arrows to explore a treehouse containing toys, animals, and six activities. Clicking on an object causes action or launches an activity. Primary activities cover sentence order, music creation and pitch, money and base ten, animal facts, and habitats. Includes 25 other entertaining objects to explore. Clear speech (separate device required) and graphics. Excellent design is rich in content and holds children's interest. Uses copy protection puzzle every fifth startup.

Vocabulary Skillbuilder Series

Vocabulary development

◆◆◆◆◆◆◆◆ 82 FINAL RATING

◆◆◆◆◆◆◆◆◆ 94 User Friendliness

◆◆◆◆◆◆◆ 71 Educational Value

◆◆◆◆◆◆◆ 76 Instructional Design

Edmark Corporation
1990
$179.95
Ages 3-6
Apple
LA/1

By touching screen (if used with TouchWindow) or selecting picture with arrow keys or single switch, child can hear name of a familiar object in a clear voice (Echo speech synthesizer required). The series contains 600 words on 8 disks, covering such common topics as body parts, animals, food, toys, people, and school. Content can be altered with the Edmark LessonMaker.

CL = Classification   **CP** = Creative projects   **LA** = Language   **NA** = Not applicable   **NB** = Number

Webster's Numbers

Basic math concepts

◆◆◆◆◆◆ 67 FINAL RATING

◆◆◆◆◆ 56 User Friendliness

◆◆◆◆◆◆◆ 86 Educational Value

◆◆◆◆◆◆ 65 Instructional Design

Compton's New Media
1983
$39.95
Ages 4-8
Apple*, C64
NB/3,4 SP/1,2,4

Four games: Ribbet—child moves through maze to catch numerals 1-9 in order. Balloon Race—child steers balloons to numerals to match a set. Shape Up—child moves shapes to match a model. Pushover—child unscrambles number blocks. Joystick or paddles required.

What Makes a Dinosaur Sore?

Language experience

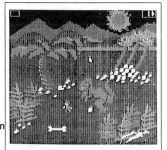

◆◆◆◆◆◆◆ 89 FINAL RATING

◆◆◆◆◆◆◆ 85 User Friendliness

◆◆◆◆◆◆◆◆ 94 Educational Value

◆◆◆◆◆◆◆◆ 91 Instructional Design

D. C. Heath & Company
1988
$75.00
Ages 5-10
Apple
LA/2,3,5,9 CP/4 SP/4,7

Children use mouse, Koala Pad, joystick, or arrow keys to select or move objects, backgrounds, words, or characters of a story. They can also add their own words. Resulting stories can be saved and printed in color. Includes four copies of the storybook. Good design. Fun to use. Part of the Explore-a-Story Series.

What's in a Frame?

Memory practice by context clues

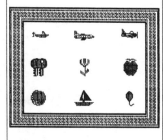

◆◆◆◆◆◆◆ 81 FINAL RATING

◆◆◆◆◆◆ 67 User Friendliness

◆◆◆◆◆◆◆◆ 91 Educational Value

◆◆◆◆◆◆◆ 88 Instructional Design

Sunburst Communications, Inc.
1987
$65.00
Ages 5-11
Apple
OT/1 CL/1,4

Two activities. Did You See This?—frame shows several objects for a timed period. Then one object at a time is shown, and child must decide if it was in the original frame. What's in a Frame?—from given objects, child marks ones that were in an original frame. Keeps records. TouchWindow optional.

OT = Other topics   SE = Seriation   SP = Spatial relations   TI = Time   * = Version reviewed

What's Next

Sequencing skills

◆◆◆◆◆◆◆ 74 FINAL RATING

◆◆◆◆◆◆ 69 User Friendliness

◆◆◆◆◆◆◆◆◆ 94 Educational Value

◆◆◆◆◆◆ 65 Instructional Design

Strawberry Hill Software
1985
$55.00
Ages 3-14
Apple*, C64
SE/1,2 CL/1,2 NB/1

Child sees a series of shapes or objects and must select which piece comes next in the series. There are eight levels of difficulty. Includes a "U-Design-It" feature that allows the design of custom patterns that can be saved. Offers a variety of sequences and objects.

Wheels on the Bus

Cause and effect

◆◆◆◆◆◆◆ 75 FINAL RATING

◆◆◆◆◆◆◆◆ 82 User Friendliness

◆◆◆◆◆◆ 68 Educational Value

◆◆◆◆◆◆◆ 74 Instructional Design

UCLA Intervention Program
1988
$35.00
Ages 3-6
Apple
TI/1,2

Child touches pictures on the PowerPad or TouchWindow that illustrate the song "Wheels on the Bus," hears verses of the song (Echo speech synthesizer required), and sees them animated on the screen. Easy to use. Designed for use in special education settings. UCLA sells 37 similar programs covering different themes.

Where Did My Toothbrush Go?

Language experience

◆◆◆◆◆◆◆◆ 89 FINAL RATING

◆◆◆◆◆◆◆◆ 85 User Friendliness

◆◆◆◆◆◆◆◆◆ 94 Educational Value

◆◆◆◆◆◆◆◆ 91 Instructional Design

D. C. Heath & Company
1988
$75.00
Ages 5-10
Apple
LA/2,3,5,9 CP/4 SP/4,7

Children use mouse, Koala Pad, joystick, or arrow keys to select or move objects, backgrounds, words, or characters of a story. Children can also add their own words. Resulting stories can be saved and printed in color. Includes four copies of the storybook. Good design. Fun to use.

CL = Classification   **CP** = Creative projects   **LA** = Language   **NA** = Not applicable   **NB** = Number

Where's My Checkered Ball?

Spatial relations

◆◆◆◆ 48 FINAL RATING

◆◆◆◆◆◆ 65 User Friendliness

◆◆◆◆ 41 Educational Value

◆◆◆ 35 Instructional Design

Intellimation
1990
$29.00
Ages 4-8
Mac
SP/4

An 11-page storybook designed for use by parent and child together. Pages are turned by clicking on page corner. On each page, the object is to find a hidden ball by clicking on items shown on the screen. A nice idea, but poorly implemented in this program. Some content too difficult or confusing for young children. Spanish or French versions available.

Which Number Is Missing?

Number order

◆◆◆◆◆ 59 FINAL RATING

◆◆◆◆◆◆ 61 User Friendliness

◆◆◆◆◆◆ 63 Educational Value

◆◆◆◆◆ 55 Instructional Design

MicroED, Inc.
1984
$7.99
Ages 5-6
Apple*, IBM, C64
NB/2

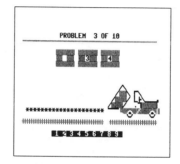

A simple program in which a child types a number to complete a random three-number sequence between 0 and 99. Correct answers cause a truck to drive across the screen. Keeps track of number of problems missed and the time spent on each problem. Limited content. Dry presentation. Menu requires reading.

Whole Neighborhood, The

A graphics program with text-writing feature

◆◆◆◆◆◆ 69 FINAL RATING

◆◆◆◆ 46 User Friendliness

◆◆◆◆◆◆◆◆ 83 Educational Value

◆◆◆◆◆◆◆ 81 Instructional Design

Queue, Inc.
1991
$49.95
Ages 6-13
Apple*, IBM
CP/4 LA/3,6,9 SP/2,5

Child selects from a variety of clip art (e.g., stores, workers, people, objects) to create town scenes that can be saved or printed in color. Words can be added and spoken on Echo synthesizer (optional). Our five-year-olds liked the graphics but needed help to use the program. Pages can be printed in seven sizes.

Winker's World of Numbers

Patterns in sequences of numbers

◆◆◆◆◆◆◆◆ 82 FINAL RATING

◆◆◆◆◆◆◆ 73 User Friendliness

◆◆◆◆◆◆◆◆◆ 92 Educational Value

◆◆◆◆◆◆◆◆ 82 Instructional Design

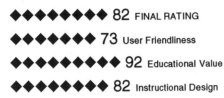

Wings for Learning
1989
$65.00
Ages 6-up
Apple
NB/3,8 OT/1

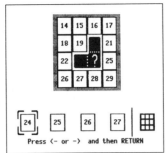

As Winker moves around a grid, numbers appear in the boxes of the grid, revealing parts of a number pattern. Child can stop Winker when ready to identify the pattern by guessing numbers in other boxes. Three difficulty levels offer a range of challenge. Picture menu is easy to use.

Winker's World of Patterns

Inferring and recognizing patterns

◆◆◆◆◆◆◆◆ 82 FINAL RATING

◆◆◆◆◆◆◆ 73 User Friendliness

◆◆◆◆◆◆◆◆◆ 92 Educational Value

◆◆◆◆◆◆◆◆ 82 Instructional Design

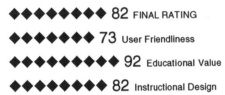

Wings for Learning
1989
$65.00
Ages 4-up
Apple
CL/2 SE/3 NB/4 LA/4 OT/1

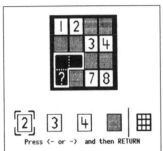

As Winker moves around a grid, colors, numbers, or letters appear in the boxes of a grid, revealing parts of a pattern. Child can stop Winker when ready to identify the pattern by guessing the colors, numbers, or letters in other boxes. Three difficulty levels. Picture menu is easy to use. Color monitor required.

Woolly Bounce

Force and motion

◆◆◆◆◆◆◆◆ 83 FINAL RATING

◆◆◆◆◆◆◆ 70 User Friendliness

◆◆◆◆◆◆◆◆◆ 92 Educational Value

◆◆◆◆◆◆◆◆ 87 Instructional Design

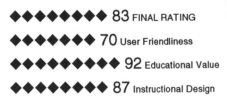

MECC
1991
$59.00
Ages 5-7
Apple
CL/1 TI/2,3 SE/1

A simple physics simulation involving influences on bouncing balls. The first activity allows free experimentation with variables of height, type of ball (e.g., bowling or tennis), and floor surface. In the second activity, a child must match a bounce by selecting the correct variables. Contains 15 kinds of balls and 2 types of surfaces. Graphs of information can be printed. Keeps records for each child.

CL = Classification   **CP** = Creative projects   **LA** = Language   **NA** = Not applicable   **NB** = Number

Word Factory

Word discrimination

◆◆ 22 FINAL RATING

◆◆ 25 User Friendliness

◆◆ 26 Educational Value

◆ 12 Instructional Design

Island Software
1983
$25.00
Ages 3-6
Apple
CL/2

Child uses < or > keys to discriminate between matching words. Leaves child with little control. Limited in content. Poor design. Not recommended.

Word Munchers

Vowel-sound discrimination

◆◆◆◆◆◆◆◆ 80 FINAL RATING

◆◆◆◆◆◆◆ 77 User Friendliness

◆◆◆◆◆◆◆◆◆ 92 Educational Value

◆◆◆◆◆◆◆ 73 Instructional Design

MECC
1985
$39.95
Ages 6-10
Apple*, IBM
LA/6,7

An enjoyable game in which child earns points by using arrow keys or joystick to move a creature around a grid of 30 word boxes in search of words containing a specific vowel sound (e.g., the vowel sound in "moon"). Game gets progressively harder. Teacher options allow control over which of 20 sounds are presented. A good way to practice with vowel sounds.

Word Processing for Kids

Word processing

◆◆◆◆◆◆◆ 78 FINAL RATING

◆◆◆◆◆◆◆ 70 User Friendliness

◆◆◆◆◆◆◆◆ 88 Educational Value

◆◆◆◆◆◆◆ 79 Instructional Design

Mobius Corporation
1984
See KidWare 2
Ages 3-5
IBM
LA/3

A simple 20- or 40-column word processor. A picture menu makes it easy for a child to create stories quickly. Text has a somewhat blocky appearance. Does not have speech capacity. Stories can be saved or printed. See "KidWare 2" for pricing information.

OT = Other topics   **SE** = Seriation   **SP** = Spatial relations   **TI** = Time   * = Version reviewed

Words

Letter disc., word experiences

◆◆◆◆◆◆ 61 FINAL RATING

◆◆◆◆ 49 User Friendliness

◆◆◆◆◆◆◆◆ 88 Educational Value

◆◆◆◆◆ 57 Instructional Design

Lawrence Hall of Science
1984
$34.95
Ages 4-6
Apple
LA/4,5,8

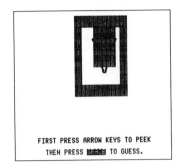

FIRST PRESS ARROW KEYS TO PEEK
THEN PRESS ▮▮▮▮ TO GUESS.

Presents three games, two on letter recognition and one on simple sentence structure. Kindergarten children were able to use the Funny Letters and Words activity. Activities effectively focus on the attributes of letters. Best for five-year-olds. Some reading used, e.g., "Press RETURN."

Words & Concepts

Vocabulary training

◆◆◆◆◆◆◆ 80 FINAL RATING

◆◆◆◆◆◆◆◆ 97 User Friendliness

◆◆◆◆◆◆◆ 86 Educational Value

◆◆◆◆◆◆ 69 Instructional Design

Laureate Learning Systems
1987
$200.00
Ages 3-adult
Apple
LA/5,8 CL/1,2,4

Find the table.

Shows three objects—using a TouchWindow, single switch, or number keys, a child responds to questions asked through an Echo speech synthesizer. Provides practice identifying, categorizing, associating, and discriminating 40 common nouns. Designed for children or adults who need training in vocabulary. Teacher setup allows much control over presentation. Keeps records.

Words & Concepts II

Vocabulary training

◆◆◆◆◆◆◆ 80 FINAL RATING

◆◆◆◆◆◆◆◆ 97 User Friendliness

◆◆◆◆◆◆◆ 86 Educational Value

◆◆◆◆◆◆ 69 Instructional Design

Laureate Learning Systems
1988
$200.00
Ages 3-adult
Apple
LA/5,8 CL/1,2,4

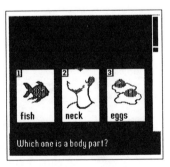

Which one is a body part?

Same as "Words & Concepts." Provides 40 additional nouns.

Words & Concepts III

Vocabulary training

◆◆◆◆◆◆◆◆ 80 FINAL RATING

◆◆◆◆◆◆◆◆ 97 User Friendliness

◆◆◆◆◆◆◆ 86 Educational Value

◆◆◆◆◆◆ 69 Instructional Design

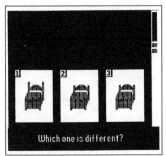

Which one is different?

Laureate Learning Systems
1988
$200.00
Ages 3-adult
Apple
LA/5,8 CL/1,2,4

Same as "Words & Concepts" and "Words & Concepts II."
Provides 40 additional nouns.

Working With Days and Months

Order of the days and months

◆◆◆◆◆◆ 63 FINAL RATING

◆◆◆◆◆◆ 63 User Friendliness

◆◆◆◆◆◆ 64 Educational Value

◆◆◆◆◆◆ 60 Instructional Design

S.R.A.
1985
$49.95
Ages 5-8
Apple
TI/9

Four activities on one disk. Child uses arrows and RETURN to
select a day or month and see an associated picture (e.g., a kite
for May), or to complete a short, three-day or three-month
sequence. Record-keeping system keeps track of progress.
Menu requires reading but is easy to use. Dry presentation.
Includes worksheets.

Working With Numbers

Counting and numerical order

◆◆◆◆◆◆ 63 FINAL RATING

◆◆◆◆◆◆ 63 User Friendliness

◆◆◆◆◆◆ 64 Educational Value

◆◆◆◆◆◆ 60 Instructional Design

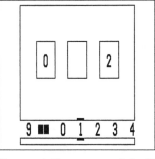

S.R.A.
1985
$49.95
Ages 5-8
Apple
NB/3,4

Four activities on one disk. Child uses arrows and RETURN to
select a number and see an associated set, or to complete a
short, three-number sequence. Some record keeping. Menu
requires reading but is easy to use. Includes worksheets. Dry
presentation.

Working With the Alphabet

Alphabetical order and letter recognition

◆◆◆◆◆◆ 63 FINAL RATING

◆◆◆◆◆◆ 63 User Friendliness

◆◆◆◆◆◆ 64 Educational Value

◆◆◆◆◆◆ 60 Instructional Design

S.R.A.
1985
$49.95
Ages 5-8
Apple
LA/4 CL/2

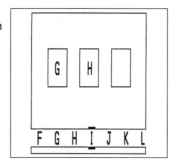

Four activities on one disk. Child uses arrows and RETURN to select a letter and see an associated picture (e.g., a ball for "b"), or to complete a short, three-letter alphabetical sequence. Can be set for upper/lower case. Some record keeping. Menu requires reading but is easy to use. Includes worksheets.

Working With Time

Matching clock faces

◆◆◆◆◆◆ 63 FINAL RATING

◆◆◆◆◆◆ 63 User Friendliness

◆◆◆◆◆◆ 64 Educational Value

◆◆◆◆◆◆ 60 Instructional Design

S.R.A.
1985
$49.95
Ages 5-8
Apple
TI/9

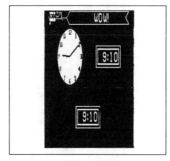

Three activities on one disk. Child uses arrows and RETURN to freely move the hands of a clock or to set hands to match the time shown on a digital or analog clock. Structured lessons have four steps: demonstration, practice, testing, and worksheets (included). Keeps record of progress. Menu requires reading. Dry presentation.

Write On: Primary Level

Writing

Not rated

Humanities Software
1988
$79.00 per disk
Ages 5-8
Apple*, IBM, Mac
LA/9 CP/4

Consists of 26 data disks compatible with any of 16 major word-processing programs (e.g., AppleWorks, Magic Slate, Microsoft Word). Disks consist of story starters, rhyming activities, cloze activities, poems, journal, forms, sentence starters, chants, couplets, and songs. Items typed by child can be saved or printed.

CL = Classification   **CP** = Creative projects   **LA** = Language   **NA** = Not applicable   **NB** = Number

Writing to Read 2.0

Reading skills

◆◆◆◆ 45 FINAL RATING

◆◆◆ 32 User Friendliness

◆◆◆◆◆◆◆ 74 Educational Value

◆◆◆◆ 41 Instructional Design

IBM Educational Systems
1982
$716.00
Ages 5-6
IBM
LA/4,5,6

A 14-disk computer-based curriculum designed to teach reading skills through writing, using phonetic spelling. Computers are only one component. Each disk covers three words. Child hears letter or word and must type. Speech synthesizer required. Available in Spanish. Ratings apply only to software.

Wunder Book

Matching, letter recognition, language practice

◆◆◆◆◆◆◆◆ 80 FINAL RATING

◆◆◆◆◆◆◆◆ 85 User Friendliness

◆◆◆◆◆◆◆◆ 88 Educational Value

◆◆◆◆◆◆◆ 71 Instructional Design

Software Excitement!
1991
Shareware
Ages 3-10
IBM (VGA)
CL/2,4 LA/4,5

Child uses mouse or keyboard to (1) select identical objects in a set of four, (2) select objects that are different, (3) type in the name of an object (e.g., "cat") with clues, and (4) type in the name of a pictured object without clues. The last two activities can be done in French, German, Spanish, or English for children/adults learning a language. Forty objects are available. Design promotes child-control.

Young Math

Addition & subtraction equations, patterns

◆◆◆◆◆◆◆ 75 FINAL RATING

◆◆◆◆◆◆ 68 User Friendliness

◆◆◆◆◆◆◆◆◆ 94 Educational Value

◆◆◆◆◆◆ 69 Instructional Design

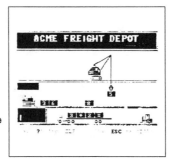

Stone & Associates
1986
$39.95
Ages 4-8
IBM*, Atari ST
NB/3,4,7,8 SE/2 SP/1

Four well-designed activities: Equations—child enters answer for equation to see answer animated. Construction—child sees equation and types answer to build a scene. Freight Depot—child uses arrow keys or joystick to load answers onto truck. Patterns—child selects next pattern element. Adult menu offers control over content.

OT = Other topics   **SE** = Seriation   **SP** = Spatial relations   **TI** = Time   * = Version reviewed

4

EVALUATION PROCESS

This chapter contains the Early Childhood Software
Evaluation Instrument that was developed to

1. Focus specifically on the early childhood category
   of software, covering issues important when working with three- to seven-year-old children

2. Generate numerical values in both specific and
   general categories to provide quick comparison of
   software packages

3. Record descriptive information about specific
   programs for purposes of recommendation,
   prescription, and documentation

Thirteen separate percentage scores ranging from 1 to
100 are generated by the Instrument and are defined in
Calculation of a Component Score, found in this chapter,
and Interpreting the Software Descriptions, found in
Chapter 2.

Terms used in the Instrument that may be unfamiliar to the
reader have been included in the Glossary (Appendix 6).

EARLY CHILDHOOD SOFTWARE EVALUATION INSTRUMENT

© 1985 High/Scope Educational Research Foundation

Title _____

Company _____

Author(s) _____

Address _____

_____

_____

Phone 1 (_____) _____/_____

Phone 2 (_____) _____/_____

Date _____

Age-range _____

Price _____

Notes:

SUMMARY OF RATINGS

Minimum User Competency _____ %

Menu Design _____ %

Technical Features _____ %

Content Presentation _____ %

Content Strength _____ %

Ease of Use _____ %

Feedback _____ %

Embedded Reinforcements _____ %

CMI Techniques _____ %

User Friendliness _____ %

Educational Value _____ %

Instructional Design _____ %

OVERALL RATING _____ %

Computer

_____ Apple II	_____ IBM PC	_____ C64	_____ Atari 400	_____ TRS 80
_____ Apple II +	_____ IBM PC jr	_____ C128	_____ Atari 800	_____ MacIntosh
_____ Apple IIe	_____ Acorn	_____ PET	_____ Atari ST	_____ Apple IIGS
_____ Apple IIc	_____ Adam	_____ Amiga	_____ Other	

Components

_____ 5¼" disk

_____ 3½" disk

_____ ROM cartridge

_____ Classroom applications

_____ User's guide

_____ Warranty (list terms)

Peripherals

Req.		Opt.
_____	Keyboard	_____
_____	Color monitor	_____
_____	Joystick(s)	_____
_____	Paddle(s)	_____
_____	Mouse	_____
_____	Muppet keyboard	_____
_____	Koala Pad	_____
_____	TouchWindow	_____
_____	Voice synthesis	_____
_____	Printer	_____
_____	Other (specify):	

Intentions

_____ Specified by developer

_____ Inferred by analyst

"This program is designed to provide experience with

_____ counting skills."

_____ letter recognition skills."

_____ matching or discrimination skills."

_____ computer skills."

_____ a medium for creative activity."

List the specific objectives of the program:

Mode of Interaction

_____ Drill and practice

_____ Tutorial

_____ Gaming

_____ Simulation

_____ Problem solving

_____ Open-ended/ divergent

Summary of Program: Provide a concise summary of the program's main points, content features, strengths, and weaknesses.

Classroom Observations

Conceptual Areas

Check the item(s) present in the program.

LANGUAGE (LA)

1 _____ Describing objects, events, and relations
2 _____ Describing feelings, one's own and others'
3 _____ Having one's own spoken language written and read aloud
4 _____ Recognizing letters
5 _____ Recognizing words — matching written words
6 _____ Matching sounds and symbols
7 _____ Matching rhyming words
8 _____ Using language to specify actions: sit, run fast, slow, into, toward, etc.
9 _____ Writing stories
10 _____ Following a simple (2- or 3-step) sequence of oral or written directions

NUMBER (NB)

1 _____ Comparing amounts: more, less, same
2 _____ Arranging two sets of symbols in one-to-one correspondence
3 _____ Counting objects; counting by 2s.
4 _____ Recognizing numerals
5 _____ Estimating the number of objects
6 _____ Measuring (length) using units
7 _____ Combining groups of objects; taking objects away
8 _____ Recognizing and naming the numerals 1, 2, 3, etc.

CLASSIFICATION (CL)

1 _____ Identifying attributes of things: color, shape, size, function
2 _____ Identifying how things are the same or different; sorting and matching
3 _____ Describing objects in different ways; sorting and re-sorting
4 _____ Identifying attributes an object does not possess; finding the object that does not belong to a set
5 _____ Holding more than one attribute in mind at a time
6 _____ Distinguishing between "all" and "some"

TIME (TI)

1 _____ Stopping and starting an action on signal
2 _____ Observing and describing changes
3 _____ Experiencing and describing different rates of speed
4 _____ Experiencing and describing time intervals — long, short, comparative terms
5 _____ Anticipating future events and making appropriate preparations
6 _____ Identifying the order of a sequence of events; reversing the order of events — before, after, at the same time
7 _____ Comparing the duration of events occurring at the same time — longer, shorter, etc.
8 _____ Using a timer to measure the duration of events
9 _____ Reading time from clocks and watches

SPATIAL RELATIONS (SP)

1 _____ Fitting things together and taking them apart
2 _____ Rearranging and reshaping objects
3 _____ Identifying things from different points of view
4 _____ Experiencing and describing the relative positions, directions, and distances of things — inside, outside, above, below, before, behind, on, under, toward, away
5 _____ Identifying and naming body parts: head, legs, arms, etc.
6 _____ Locating things in the classroom or school on simple maps
7 _____ Interpreting representations of spatial relations in drawings and pictures
8 _____ Distinguishing and describing shapes — circle, square, triangle, doughnut (open & closed shapes)
9 _____ Identifying and reversing spatial order
10 _____ Identifying shapes produced by cuts and folds

SERIATION (SE)

1 _____ Making comparisons — shape, shades of color, pitch, and/or speed
2 _____ Arranging several things in order and describing their relations by size, color, etc.
3 _____ Fitting one ordered set of objects to another through trial and error
4 _____ Inserting objects into an ordered sequence

CREATIVE PROJECTS (CP)

1 _____ Drawing pictures
2 _____ Creating sounds or music
3 _____ Programming
4 _____ Designing, changing, and printing a plan or product

OTHER TOPICS (OT)

1 _____ Practicing memory skills
2 _____ Recognizing and naming the parts of the computer
3 _____ Typing or practicing keyboard skills
4 _____ Making signs, word processing, or keeping records. (Of potential use to preschool and kindergarten teachers.)
5 _____ Nutrition, health, and safety

User Friendliness

Minimum User Competency

When considering the portions of the program designed or intended for the child's use, rate the method in which the child's answers are entered into the computer. (Numbers indicate the method's point-value.)

9 _____ Touch screen or use voice.
8 _____ Touch any key or one key.
7 _____ Move the cursor to a visual representation (icon) using a joystick, graphics tablet, light pen, or mouse.
6 _____ Use only 1-4 keys on the keyboard consistently, e.g, spacebar and RETURN.
5 _____ Move the cursor with the arrow keys.
4 _____ Find and press one of the number keys and/or RETURN.
3 _____ Find and press one of the letter keys and/or RETURN.
2 _____ Type in a word/RETURN.
1 _____ Press more than one key simultaneously, e.g., CONTROL-C.

Menu Design

6 _____ Picture or talking menu, touch screen to make the selection.
5 _____ Picture or talking menu, move cursor to selection with peripheral device, such as a joystick or a mouse.
4 _____ Picture or talking menu, move cursor to selection with arrow keys/RETURN to make the selection.
3 _____ Picture or talking menu, press specific key to make choice (e.g., a number key).
2 _____ Simple written menu, with less than six choices, using large letters.
1 _____ Written menu with more than six choices or small letters.

Technical Features

	always	some extent	never	N/A
• Program instructions can be reviewed on the screen	_____	_____	_____	_____
• When a child holds a key down, only one input is sent to the computer, except where intended, such as in a drawing program	_____	_____	_____	_____
• Getting to the part of the program to be used by the child requires only inserting a disk and starting the computer	_____	_____	_____	_____
• If there are data files. e.g., vocabulary words, that can be changed, doing so is easy	_____	_____	_____	_____
• Random generation is a part of the program's design	_____	_____	_____	_____
• Packaging of the program is well designed, providing storage capacity for the program materials	_____	_____	_____	_____
• Program package comes complete and ready-to-use	_____	_____	_____	_____
• Program design allows for quick loading time and minimal disk-reading time	_____	_____	_____	_____
• Program provides quick, obvious movement to and from the menu	_____	_____	_____	_____
• The title screen sequence is not long or can be bypassed	_____	_____	_____	_____
• Color is used	_____	_____	_____	_____
• Animated graphics are used	_____	_____	_____	_____
• Sound can be turned off or on from the program	_____	_____	_____	_____

total (13 possible)_____ _____ _____ _____

Educational Value

Content Presentation

	always	some extent	never	N/A
• The concept, rather than the game, is the central learning outcome	_____	_____	_____	_____
• The program is enjoyable to use	_____	_____	_____	_____
• Content is arranged in a challenging way	_____	_____	_____	_____
• Elements of the program are motivating to the child	_____	_____	_____	_____
• This program could be of interest to users other than the program's target audience, e.g., parents, older siblings, etc	_____	_____	_____	_____
• Content is applicable for early childhood age-range	_____	_____	_____	_____
• The child can control own sequence throughout the program	_____	_____	_____	_____
• Child can exit the activity at any point	_____	_____	_____	_____
• Language, text, or print is appropriate for the early childhood age-range	_____	_____	_____	_____
• The program includes data files (e.g., words, numbers) that can be changed	_____	_____	_____	_____
• The program provides demonstrations	_____	_____	_____	_____
• Practice is meaningful to the child (e.g., geographic location, home environment)	_____	_____	_____	_____
• The graphics — are not overly "cute"	_____	_____	_____	_____
— do not detract from the program's overall intentions	_____	_____	_____	_____
• Graphics do not promote unnecessary stimulation	_____	_____	_____	_____
• Music/sound does not promote unnecessary stimulation	_____	_____	_____	_____
• Content is free from racial bias	_____	_____	_____	_____
• Content is free from ethnic bias	_____	_____	_____	_____
• Content is free from sexual bias	_____	_____	_____	_____
total (19 possible)	_____	_____	_____	_____

Content Strength

	always	some extent	never	N/A
• This program provides a good presentation of one or more conceptual areas	_____	_____	_____	_____
• The program presents a clear focus on one or more conceptual areas	_____	_____	_____	_____
• The concept, rather than the game, is the central learning outcome	_____	_____	_____	_____
• The program provides practice with the concept in differing contexts	_____	_____	_____	_____
• Elements of the program match direct experiences	_____	_____	_____	_____
• The program is enjoyable to use	_____	_____	_____	_____
total (6 possible)	_____	_____	_____	_____

Instructional Design

Ease of Use

	always	some extent	never	N/A
• Can the child do the program the first time without help	____	____	____	____
• Can the child do the program after the first few times without help	____	____	____	____
• Does the child have control over:				
— time allowed for problems	____	____	____	____
— rate of display	____	____	____	____
— order of display	____	____	____	____
— exiting at any time	____	____	____	____
• The written instructions:				
— provide technical details for the program where needed	____	____	____	____
— provide stagies for extending the concepts into noncomputer contexts	____	____	____	____
— are well organized	____	____	____	____
total (9 possible)	____	____	____	____

Feedback

	always	some extent	never	N/A
• The child is aware of when he/she makes an incorrect response	____	____	____	____
• The child is aware of when he/she makes a correct response	____	____	____	____
• Feedback explains/shows why responses are not correct	____	____	____	____
• Feedback responses are varied	____	____	____	____
• Feedback is directly correlated to keystroke	____	____	____	____
• Feedback is appropriate because it				
— is nonthreatening	____	____	____	____
— reinforces content	____	____	____	____
— is understood by the child	____	____	____	____
• Feedback effectively makes use of sound and graphic capacities of the computer	____	____	____	____
• A record of the child's work				
— can be stored on disk	____	____	____	____
— can be printed	____	____	____	____
— is informative	____	____	____	____
total (12 possible)	____	____	____	____

Embedded Reinforcements

	always	some extent	never	N/A
• Graphic reinforcements are in support of, or reinforce, the content or concepts presented	____	____	____	____
• Sound reinforcements are in support of, or reinforce, the content or concepts presented	____	____	____	____
total (4 possible)	____	____	____	____

CMI Techniques

Techniques of Computer Managed Instruction
____ are not used in this convergent-style program (0 points)
____ are not appliable to this divergent-style program (NA)
____ are not applicable because the user or adult selects difficulty level (NA)
____ are used (check those that apply — 1 point each)
　　____ feedback is individualized to the child's response
　　____ program helps a child understand his or her progress, e.g., how many problems remaining
　　____ a record of the child's work is recorded
　　____ program is designed so that it can automatically adapt to an appropriate difficulty level

____ total (4 possible)

Comments of Reviewer to Software Producer

CALCULATION OF A COMPONENT SCORE

The following formula is used to compute the specific scores for each component of the program:

$$\frac{(X + Y/2)}{n - Z} \times 100 = S$$

Where
X = Total of checks in "always" column
Y = Total of checks in "some extent" column
Z = Total of checks in the "N/A" column
n = Number of items in a category (such as Feedback)
S = Score for a component of the program (as a percent)

For example:

Feedback

	always	some extent	never	N/A
The child is aware of when he/she makes an incorrect response	✓			
The child is aware of when he/she makes a correct response	✓			
Feedback explains/shows why responses are not correct			✓	
Feedback responses are varied	✓			
Feedback is directly correlated to keystroke	✓			
Feedback is appropriate because it	✓			
— is nonthreatening		✓		
— reinforces content		✓		
— is understood by the user				
Feedback effectively makes use of sound and graphic capacities of the computer	✓			
A record of the child's work			✓	
— can be stored on disk				✓
— can be printed				✓
— is informative				
Total (12 possible)	6	2	2	2

In this example

X = 6 (Total of checks under "always")
Y = 2 (Total of checks under "some extent")
Z = 2 (Total of checks under "N/A")
n = 12 (Number of items under the heading "Feedback")

So, when applying the formula above,

$$\frac{6 + 2/2}{12 - 2} \times 100 = 70$$

The component score (S) for Feedback is 70%.

APPENDIXES

APPENDIX 1
EARLY CHILDHOOD SOFTWARE PRODUCERS

Access Unlimited
3535 Briar Park
Suite 102
Houston TX 77042
713/461-0006
  Big and Small
  Fun With Colors
  Learning Directions
  Knowing Directions
  Learning Letters
  Learning Numbers
  Learning Shapes
  Learning Sight Words
  Learning the Alphabet
  Readiness Fun
  Same and Different
  Scanning Fun
  Silly Letters & Numbers
  Simple Addition
  Simple Cause and Effect
  Spell-A-Word

Advanced Ideas, Inc.
680 Hawthorne Drive
Tiburon, CA 94702
415/435-5086
Fax 415/435-2049
  Dinosaurs
  Stars & Planets

Agency Systems
7645 Production Drive
P.O. Box 37410
Cincinnati, OH 45237
513/761-5610
  Early-On

Alphaphonics
P.O. Box 2024
San Mateo, CA 94401
415/588-8082
  Alphaget
  Astro's ABCs

American Guidance Service
Publishers Building
Circle Pines, MN 55014
800/328-2560
  SocPix

Aquarius Instructional
P.O. Box 130
Indian Rocks Beach, FL 34635
800/338-2644
Fax 813/595-2685
In FL, 813/595-7890
  Jr. Typer

Artworx
1844 Penfield Road
Penfield, NY 14526
800/828-6573
  Hodge Podge
  Monkey Math

Barnum Software
2201 Broadway, Suite 201
Oakland, CA 94612
800/332-3638
415/268-0804
  Quarter Mile, The

Baudville
5380 52nd Street SE
Grand Rapids, MI 49508
616/698-0888
  Mad Match
  Ted Bear Games

BL Educational Software
2899 Agoura Rd. #529
Westlake Village, CA 91361
805/498-8121
  Caveman Clockwork

Bright Star Technology, Inc.
14450 NE 29th
Suite 220
Bellevue, WA 98007
206/885-5446
Fax 206/869-1582
  Alphabet Blocks
  Talking Tiles

Broderbund Software
500 Redwood Blvd.
P.O. Box 6121
Novato, CA 94948-6121
800/521-6263
415/382-4400
Fax 415/382-4671
  KidPix
  Playroom, The
  Print Shop, The
  Treehouse, The

C&C Software
5713 Kentford Circle
Wichita, KS 67220
316/683-6056
  Learning About Numbers
  Letters and First Words
  Magic Crayon

CBS Software
  Dr. Seuss Fix-Up the Mix-Up
    Puzzler
  *Note: In 1987, CBS Software
  was dissolved. See Hi Tech
  Expressions, Joyce Hakansson
  Associates, Inc., or Mindscape,
  for information on old CBS
  titles.*

Chariot Software Group
3659 India Street, Suite 100C
San Diego, CA 92103
800/242-7468
619/298-0202
Fax 619/491-0021
  Dot-to-Dot Construction Set
  Pattern Blocks 2.1

Compton's NewMedia
(Formerly Britannica Software)
345 Fourth Street
San Francisco, CA 94107
800/572-2272
In CA, 415/597-5555
  Berenstain Bears Fun With
    Colors, The
  Berenstain Bears Junior
    Jigsaw, The
  Berenstain Bears Learn About
    Counting, The
  Berenstain Bears Learn About
    Letters, The
  Creature Creator
  Designasaurus
  Introduction to Counting
  Math Maze
  Notable Phantom, The
  Spellicopter
  Spelling and Reading Primer
  Webster's Numbers

Compu-Tations
Suite A-150
5600 Maple
West Bloomfield, MI 48033
800/345-2964
  Early Elementary I
  Early Elementary II

Compu-Teach
78 Olive Street
New Haven, CT 06511
800/448-3224
In CT, 203/777-7738
  Once Upon a Time
  Stepping Stones Level I
  Stepping Stones Level II

Computer Curriculum Corp.
1287 Lawrence Station Road
Sunnyvale, CA 94089
800/227-8324
  CCC Instructional System

D.C. Heath & Company
125 Spring Street
Lexington, MA 02173
800/334-3284
  Bald-Headed Chicken, The
  Brand New View, A
  Great Leap, A
  Just Around the Block
  Not Too Messy, Not Too Neat
  Read, Write, & Publish 1
  Rosie the Counting Rabbit
  Sleepy Brown Cow, The
  What Makes a Dinosaur Sore?
  Where Did My Toothbrush Go?

Data Command
119 South Schuyler Avenue
P.O. Box 548
Kankakee, IL 60901-0548
800/528-7390
815/933-7735
  Alphabet Sounds
  One Banana More

Davidson and Associates, Inc.
P.O. Box 2961
Torrance, CA 90509
800/556-6141
In CA, 310/793-0601
  Eco-Saurus
  Kid Works
  Math and Me
  Math Blaster Plus
  Reading and Me

DIL International
2115, Boivin Street
Sainte-Foy, (Quebec) CANADA
G1V 1N6
800/463-5581
416/687-9786
Fax 418/527-0642
  Costume Ball, The
  Extrateletactograph, The
  Garden, The

DLM
One DLM Park
Allen, TX 75002
800/527-4747
In TX, 800/442-4711
  Alphabet Circus
  Animal Photo Fun
  Comparison Kitchen
  Curious George Goes
    Shopping
  Curious George in Outer Space
  Curious George Visits the
    Library
  Fish Scales
  Number Farm
  Shape & Color Rodeo
  Teddy Bear-rels of Fun

E.C.S.
Exceptional Children's
Software, Inc.
P.O. Box 487
Hays, KS 67601
913/625-9281
  Adventures of Jimmy Jumper,
    The
  Color Find
  Rabbit Scanner, The
  Run Rabbit Run
  Sight Word Spelling

Ebsco Curriculum Materials
P.O. Box 1943
Birmingham, AL 35201
800/633-8623
In AL, 205/991-1210
  IEP Generator 5.0

Edmark Corporation
6727 185th Ave N.E.
Redmond, WA 98052
800/426-0856
206/861-8200
Fax 206/746-3962
  Early Concepts Skillbuilder
    Series
  Edmark LessonMaker
  Edmark Reading Program
    Level 1
  Talking TouchWindow
  Touch and Match
  Touch and See
  Vocabulary Skillbuilder Series

Educational Activities, Inc.
P.O. Box 392
Freeport, NY 11520
800/645-3739
  ABC-123 Activities for Learning
  Adventures of Dobot, The
  Early Childhood Learning
    Program
  First Encounters
  It's No Game
  Spaceship Lost

First Byte, Inc.
Clauset Center
3100 South Harbor, Suite 150
Santa Ana, CA 92704
800/523-8070
In CA, 714/432-1740
  Dinosaur Discovery Kit, The
  Eco-Saurus
  First Letters and Words
  First Shapes
  KidTalk
  Puzzle Storybook, The
  Talking First Words

Fisher-Price
638 Grand Avenue
East Aurora, NY 14502
617/494-1200
See Queue, Inc., or
GameTek/IJE, Inc.

Gamco Industries, Inc.
P.O. Box 1911
Big Spring, TX 79721-1911
800/351-1404
Fax 915/267-7480
Alphabet Express
Clue in on Phonics
Number Sea Hunt
Shape Starship

Gametek/IJE, Inc.
Distributors for Fisher-Price
2999 NE 191 Street, Suite 800
North Miami Beach, FL 33180
305/935-3995
Chutes and Ladders
Firehouse Rescue
Fun Flyer
I Can Remember
Little People Bowling Alley
My Grand Piano
Perfect Fit
School Bus Driver

Great Wave Software
5353 Scotts Valley Drive
Scotts Valley, CA 95066
408/438-1990
KidsMath
KidsTime
NumberMaze
ReadingMaze

Hartley Courseware, Inc.
Box 419
Dimondale, MI 48821
800/247-1380
In MI, 517/646-6458
Alphabet Academy, The
Big Red Hat, The
Bird's Eye View
Colors and Shapes
Conservation and Counting
Consonant Capers
Dr. Peet's Talk/Writer
Early Skills
Fish Dish, The
Home Row
I Love You in the Sky, Butterfly
Jen the Hen
Letter Recognition
My Words
Observation and Classification
Ollie and Seymour

Parquetry and Pictures
Patterns and Sequences
Picture Parade
Pictures, Letters, and Sounds
Size and Logic

Hi Tech Expressions
584 Broadway, Suite 509
New York, NY 10012
800/447-6543
212/941-1224
Chip 'n Dale
Daffy Duck, P.I.
Electric Company: Bagasaurus
Electric Company: Picture
Place
Electric Company: Roll-A-Word
Looney Tunes Print Kit
Print Power
Sesame Street Astro-Grover
Sesame Street Big Bird's
Special Delivery
Sesame Street Ernie's Big
Splash
Sesame Street Ernie's Magic
Shapes
Sesame Street First Writer
Sesame Street Grover's Animal
Adventures
Sesame Street Learning
Library 1
Sesame Street Learning
Library 2
Sesame Street Letter-Go-
Round
Sesame Street Pals Around
Town
Sesame Street Print Kit

Houghton Mifflin Co.
Educational Software Division
1 Beacon Street, 30th floor
Boston, MA 02108
617/725-5000
FirstWriter
KinderMath II
Reading Comprehension:
Level 1
Reading Helpers
Reading Starters
Sound Ideas: Consonants
Sound Ideas: Vowels
Sound Ideas: Word Attack

Humanities Software
408 Columbia, Suite 209
P.O. Box 950
Hood River, OR 97031
800/245-6737
Write On: Primary Level

IBM Educational Systems
P.O. Box 2150
Atlanta, GA 30055
404/238-3245
Bouncy Bee Learns Letters 1.0
Bouncy Bee Learns Words 1.0
Exploring Measure, Time, &
Money
Juggle's Butterfly
Math Concepts Level P
Primary Editor Plus
Writing to Read 2.0

Intellimation
130 Cremona Drive
P.O. Box 1922
Santa Barbara, CA 93116-1922
800/346-8355
Alphabet for Everyone
Let's Go to Hannah's House
Where's My Checkered Ball?

IRI Group
200 East Wood, Suite 250
Palatine, IL 60067
800/922-4474
In IL, 312/991-6300
Perception, Inc.

Island Software
Box 300
Lake Grove, NY 11755
516/585-3755
Letter Games
Milk Bottles
Puss in Boot
Word Factory

Josten's Learning Corporation
6170 Cornerstone Court East
Suite 300
San Diego, CA 92121-3710
800/521-8538
619/587-0087
Dragon Tales
Emerging Literacy Program
Integrated Learning System

**Joyce Hakansson Associates,
Inc.**
2029 Durant
Berkeley, CA 94704
415/540-5963
Ducks Ahoy!
Great Gonzo in WordRider,
The
Kermit's Electronic Storymaker

Kidsview Software, Inc.
P.O. Box 98
Warner, NH 03278
603/927-4428
　　Kidsword
　　Mount Murdoch

KinderMagic Software
1680 Meadowglen Lane
Encinitas, CA 92024
619/632-6693
　　Mosaic Magic

Koala Technologies, Corp.
70 North Second Street
San Jose, CA 95113
408/287-6311
408/287-6278
　　Koala Pad Graphics Exhibitor
　　(Makers of the Koala Pad touch
　　tablet—$139.95)

Laureate Learning Systems
110 East Spring Street
Winooski, VT 05404
800/562-6801
　　Bozons' Quest
　　Concentrate!
　　Creature Chorus
　　First Verbs
　　Micro-LADS
　　My House: Language Activities
　　　of Daily Living
　　Sentence Master Level 1
　　Talking Nouns I
　　Talking Nouns II
　　Talking Verbs
　　Words & Concepts
　　Words & Concepts II
　　Words & Concepts III

Lawrence Hall of Science
University of California
Berkeley, CA 94720
415/642-3167
　　Estimation
　　Music
　　Numbers
　　Words

Lawrence Productions, Inc.
1800 South 35th Street
P.O. Box 458
Galesburg, MI 49053
800/421-4157
Fax 616/665-7060
In MI, 616/665-7075
　　Katie's Farm
　　McGee
　　McGee at the Fun Fair

Learning Box, The
4508 Valleycrest Drive
Arlington, TX 76013
800/743-9450
817/457-9459
　　Base Ten Blocks
　　Logic Blocks

Learning Company, The
6493 Kaiser Drive
Fremont, CA 94555
800/852-2255
415/792-2101
　　Bumble Games
　　Children's Writing and Publish-
　　　ing Center
　　Gertrude's Secrets
　　Math Rabbit
　　Moptown Parade
　　Reader Rabbit
　　Treasure Mountain, The

MECC
Minnesota Ed. Computing Corp.
6160 Summit Drive North
Minneapolis, MN 55430-4003
800/685-6322
612/569-1500
　　Arithmetic Critters
　　Counting Critters 1.0
　　Easy Color Paint 2.0
　　EZ Logo
　　First Letter Fun
　　Fun From A to Z
　　Measure Works
　　Money Works
　　Paint With Words
　　Path-Tactics
　　Patterns
　　Phonics Prime Time: Initial
　　　Consonants
　　Picture Chompers
　　Storybook Weaver
　　Woolly Bounce
　　Word Munchers

Merit Software
13635 Gamma Road
Dallas, TX 75244
800/238-4277
In TX, 214/385-2353
　　ABC's
　　Animal Hotel
　　Bike Hike
　　Dinosaurs Are Forever
　　Fun on the Farm
　　Holidays and Seasons
　　Lion's Workshop
　　Same or Different

Sesame Street Crayon: Letters
　for You
Sesame Street Crayon:
　Numbers Count
Sesame Street Crayon:
　Opposites Attract
Shutterbug's Patterns
Shutterbug's Pictures
This Land Is Your Land

Micro Power & Light Company
8814 Sanshire Avenue
Dallas, TX 75231
214/553-0105
　　Alphabet Recognition
　　Counting and Ordering
　　Country Combo
　　My Puzzles and Alphabet
　　Time Master

Micro-Learningware
Route 1, Box 162
Amboy, MN 56010
507/674-3705
　　Teddy Bears Counting Fun

MicroED, Inc.
P.O. Box 24750
Edina, MN 55424
612/929-2242
　　Begining Reading Skills
　　Early Math
　　Learning the Alphabet
　　Which Number Is Missing?

Micrograms, Inc.
1404 North Main Street
Rockford, IL 61103
800/338-4726
815/965-2464
　　Kinder Critters
　　Mathosaurus Level K
　　Professor Al's Sequencing Lab

Milliken Publishing Co.
P.O. Box 21579
1100 Research Boulevard
St. Louis, MO 63132-0579
800/325-4236
314/991-4220
　　Alphabetization & Letter
　　　Recognition
　　First "R": Kindergarten, The
　　Math Sequences
　　Milliken Storyteller, The

MindPlay
Methods & Solutions, Inc.
3130 North Dodge Boulevard
Tucson, AZ 85716
800/221-7911
Fax 602/322-0363
In AZ, 602/322-6163
    Bake & Taste
    Cat 'n Mouse
    Cotton Tales
    Cotton's First Files
    Easy Street
    Math Magic
    Picture Perfect
    Race the Clock

Mindscape Educational
Software
A Division of SVE
1345 West Diversey Parkway
Chicago, IL 60614
800/829-1900
312/525-1500
    Body Awareness
    Color Me
    Fun With Directions
    Knowing Numbers
    Letters and Words
    Shapes & Patterns
    Tink! Tonk!
    Tonk in the Land of Buddy-Bots

Mobius Corporation
405 North Henry Street
Alexandria, VA 22134
703/684-2911
    KidWare 2 Learning Center:
        Electronic Builder
        Electronic Easel
        Farm, The
        I Can Count the Petals of a
            Flower
        Mural Maker
        Music Maker
        Word Processing for Kids

Nordic Software, Inc.
3939 North 48th Street
Lincoln, NE 68504
800/228-0417
In NE, 402/466-6502
    Clock Works
    Coin Works
    Preschool Disk 1
    Preschool Disk 2
    Preschool Pack

Ohm Software Company
163 Richard Drive
Tiverton, RI 02878
401/253-9354
    Kieran

Optimum Resource, Inc.
Publishers of Weekly Reader
Software
10 Station Place
Norfolk, CT 06058
800/327-1473
In CT, 203/542-5553
    New Talking Stickybear
        Alphabet, The
    New Talking Stickybear
        Opposites, The
    New Talking Stickybear
        Shapes, The
    Stickybear ABC
    Stickybear Math
    Stickybear Numbers
    Stickybear Opposites
    Stickybear Printer
    Stickybear Reading
    Stickybear Shapes
    Stickybear Town Builder
    Stickybear Typing

Orange-Cherry Software
P.O. Box 390
Pound Ridge, NY 10576-0390
800/672-6002
    Jungle Safari
    Super GS Award Maker
    Talking ABC's
    Talking Alpha Chimp
    Talking Animals Activity Set
    Talking Classroom
    Talking Clock
    Talking Colors and Shapes
    Talking Dinosaurs
    Talking First Reader
    Talking First Writer
    Talking Money
    Talking Numbers
    Talking Reading Railroad
    Talking School Bus
    Talking Speller
    Telling Time

P.E.A.L. Software
P.O. Box 8188
Calabasas, CA 91372
818/883-7849
Action/Music
    Exploratory Play
    Keytalk
    Representational Play

Paperback Software
2830 Ninth Street
Berkeley, CA 94710
415/644-2116
    My ABC's

Power Industries LP
37 Walnut Street
Wellesley Hills, MA 02181
617/235-7733
800/395-5009
    Delta Drawing Today

Queue, Inc.
338 Commerce Drive
Fairfield, CT 06434
800/232-2224
203/335-0908
Fax 203/336-2481
    Alice in Wonderland
    Alphabet Arcade, The
    Alphabet Zoo
    Animal Alphabet and Other
        Things
    Big Book Maker
    Boars Tell Time, The
    Charlie Brown's 1-2-3's
    Charlie Brown's ABC's
    City Country Opposites
    Developing Language Skills
    Dinosaur Days Plus
    Diskovery Adding Machine
    Diskovery Take Away Zoo
    Early Games
    Easy as ABC
    Facemaker
    Facemaker Golden Edition
    Grandma's House
    Hey Diddle
    Inside Outside Opposites
    Inside Outside Shapes
    Jack and the Beanstalk
    Kids on Keys
    Kidwriter
    Kinder Koncepts MATH
    Kinder Koncepts Reading
    Kindercomp
    Kindercomp Golden Edition
    Learn the Alphabet
    Learn to Add
    Letters, Pictures & Words
    Mask Parade
    Monsters & Make-Believe
    Monsters & Make-Believe Plus
    Mr. and Mrs. Potato Head
    Peanuts Maze Marathon
    Peanuts Picture Puzzlers
    Preschool IQ Builder I
    Preschool IQ Builder II
    Puzzle Master
    Rainbow Painter
    Reading I
    Robot Writer Plus
    Stickers
    Talk About a Walk
    Whole Neighborhood, The

R.J. Cooper & Associates
Adaptive Technology Specialists
24843 Del Prado, Suite 283
Dana Point, CA 92629
714/240-1912
    Children's Switch Progressions
    Early & Advanced Switch
      Games
    Human Being Machine, The
    Joystick Trainer

Random House Software
See: McGraw-Hill Media

S.D.L.
285 32nd Avenue
San Fransisco, CA 94121
415/221-2479
    Toybox

S.R.A.
P.O. Box 5380
Chicago, IL 60680-5380
800/621-0476
312/984-7000
    Fact Track
    Mathematics Level A
    Ollie Begins It
    Ollie Compares It
    Ollie Finds It!
    Ollie Hears and Remembers
    Ollie Hears and Sequences
    Ollie Letters It
    Ollie Matches It
    Ollie Numbers It
    Ollie Remembers It
    Ollie Remembers Numbers!
    Ollie Sequences It!
    Spatial Concepts
    Working With Days and Months
    Working With Numbers
    Working With the Alphabet
    Working With Time

Scholastic Software, Inc.
P.O. Box 7502
2931 East McCarty Street
Jefferson City, Missouri 65102
800/541-5513
212/505-3000
    Bank Street Writer III, The
    Computergarten
    ESL Writer
    Kids at Work
    Microzine Jr. (Sept/Oct.'88)
    SuperPrint!
    Talking Textwriter

Sierra On-Line
Sierra On-Line Building
Coarsegold, CA 93614
209/683-6858
    Mixed-Up Mother Goose

Software Excitement!
P.O. Box 3072
6475 Crater Lake Highway
Central Point, OR 97502
800/444-5457
Fax 503/826-8090
    Amy's First Primer 2.2
    Animated Alphabet
    Animated Math
    Animated Memory
    Animated Shapes
    Brandon's Bigbox
    School Mom
    Wunder Book

SouthWest EdPsych Services
2001 West Silvergate
Chandler, AZ 85224
602/253-6528
    Reading Machine, The

Spinnaker Software Corp.
201 Broadway
Cambridge, MA 02139-1901
800/826-0706
    All Spinnaker educational
    titles are now available from
    Queue, Inc.

Springboard
See: Queue, Inc.

Stone & Associates
Suite 319
7910 Ivanhoe Avenue
La Jolla, CA 92037
800/733-1263
619/459-9173
    Kid's Stuff
    Memory Lane 2.0
    My Letters, Numbers, and
      Words
    Phonics Plus
    Young Math

Strawberry Hill Software
202-11961-88th Avenue
Delta, British Columbia
Canada V4C 3C9
604/594-5947
    Hobo's Luck
    Peter's Growing Patterns
    Surrounding Patterns
    What's Next

Sunburst Communications, Inc.
101 Castleton Street
Pleasantville, NY 10570-3498
800/628-8897
    1-2-3 Sequence Me
    Balancing Bear
    Getting Ready to Read and
      Add
    Hop To It!
    Magic Slate
    Memory Building Blocks
    Mickey's Magic Reader
    Muppet Slate
    Muppet Word Book
    Muppets On Stage
    Muppetville
    Now You See It, Now You
      Don't
    Odd One Out
    Playwrite
    Simon Says
    Space Waste Race
    Teddy and Iggy
    Teddy's Playground
    Tiger's Tales
    Touch & Write
    What's in a Frame?

**Teach Yourself By Computer
Software, Inc.**
3400 Monroe Avenue
Rochester, NY 14618
716/381-5450
    Match-On-A-Mac

Teacher Support Software
1035 N.W. 57th Street
Gainesville, FL 32605-4483
800/228-2871
Fax 904/332-6779
In FL, 904/332-6404
    Language Experience
      Recorder Plus
    Make-a-Book
    Read-a-Logo

Tom Snyder Productions, Inc.
90 Sherman Street
Cambridge, MA 02140
800/342-0236
Fax 617/876-0033
In MA, 617/876-4433
    Flodd, the Bad Guy
    Jack and the Beanstalk

Troll Associates
100 Corporate Drive
Mahwah, New Jersey 07430
800/526-5289
    Alphabet Fun: Big and Little
      Letters
    Alphabet Fun: Learning the
      Alphabet
    Bremen Town Musicians
    I Can Count
    Dino Speller
    Magic String, The
    Reading Fun: Beginning
      Consonants
    Reading Fun: Final Consonants
    Reading Fun: Vowel Sounds
    Rumpelstiltskin
    Spelling Bee, The

UCLA Intervention Program
for Handicapped Children
1000 Veteran Avenue, Rm. 23-10
Los Angeles, CA 90024
310/825-4821
    Wheels on the Bus

Walt Disney Computer Software
257 Park Avenue South
New York, NY 10010
212/475-8030
    Donald's Alphabet Chase
    Goofy's Railway Express
    Mickey & Minnie's Fun Time
      Print Kit
    Mickey's 123's

    Mickey's ABC's
    Mickey's Colors & Shapes
    Mickey's Crossword Puzzle
      Maker
    Mickey's Jigsaw Puzzles
    Mickey's Runaway Zoo: Fun
      With Numbers

Wescott Software
P.O. Box 7010
Evanston, IL 60204
800/669-9886
708/328-1367
    Fun With Drawing
    Fun With Letters and Words
    Fun With Memory
    Fun With Numbers
    Match Maker (Beginning)

Wes Horlacher's New Media
Values Center
P.O. Box 1462
Walnut, CA 91879
714/595-1355
    Magic Melody Box

William K. Bradford Publishing
Company, Inc.
310 School Street
Acton, MA 01720
800/421-2009
508/263-6996 Fax 508/263-9375
    Princess and the Pea, The
    Stone Soup
    Three Little Pigs, The

Wings for Learning
1600 Green Hills Road
P.O. Box 660002
Scotts Valley, CA 95067-0002
800/321-7511
408/438-5502
Fax 408/438-4214
    Color 'n' Canvas
    Counters
    Learn About: Animals
    Learn About: Plants
    Winker's World of Numbers
    Winker's World of Patterns

APPENDIX 2
OTHER USEFUL SOURCES OF INFORMATION

In the following list, you'll find names, addresses, and phone numbers of other software producers, sources of shareware, and suppliers of computer items relevant to early childhood software.

AC's Guide to the Amiga
PiM Publications
PO Box 869
Fall River, MA 02722
800/345-3360
508/678-4200
Produces an extensive listing of Commodore Amiga software titles ($9.95).

Ad Lib Inc.
220 Grand-Allee East, Suite 850
Quebec, QC, Canada
G1R 2J1
800/463-2686
Producers of the Ad Lib Card, a music synthesizer card for MS DOS computers ($75.00), that enhances the sound of some existing programs.

Apple Computer Company
20525 Mariani Avenue
Cupertino, CA 95014
408/973-3708
Makers of Apple computers.

Apple Support Center
5130 Plaza Boulevard Parkway
Charlotte, NC 28210
704/357-4500
Headquarters for Apple's special purchasing program for teachers.

Apple Support Center
5655 Meadowbrook Court
Rolling Meadows, IL 60008
312/806-3600

Apple Support Center
904 Caribbean Drive
Sunnyvale, CA 94089
408/734-9790

Chariot Software Group
3659 India Street, Suite 100C
San Diego, CA 92103
800/242-7468
619/298-0202
Fax 619/491-0021
A good source of freeware and shareware titles for the Mac. Each title costs $3.00.

Covox Inc.
675 Conger Street
Eugene, Oregon 97402
503/342-1271
Makers of sound enhancement hardware for IBM computers.

Developmental Equipment, Inc.
Building 115
1000 North Rand Road
Wauconda, IL 60084
312/526-2682
Makers of the Single Switch Software, The Adaptive Firmware Card (tm), and Keinx.

DIL International
2115, Boivin Street
Sainte-Foy, (Quebec) CANADA
G1V 1N6
800/463-5581
416/687-9786
Fax 418/527-0642
Makers of: The Extrateletactograph, The Mary Marvel and Willy Wiz at the Costume Ball, Mary Marvel and Willy Wiz in the Garden, The Wonderworker ($99.95).

Dunamis, Inc.
3620 Highway 317
Suwanee, GA 30174
404/932-0485
Producer of the PowerPad ($249.95). Also sells 10 special education programs for the PowerPad.

Edmark Corporation
6727 185th Ave N.E.
Redmond, WA 98052
800/426-0856
206/861-8200
Fax 206/746-3962
Producers of the Touch Window ($230.00) for the Apple or IBM.

Egghead Discount Software
22011 S.E. 51st Street
Issaquah, WA 98027
800-EGGHEAD
A good place to purchase software at discount prices.

Forty-Seventh Street Photo
36 East 19th Street
New York, NY 10003
800/221-7774
A discount mail order computer dealer. A good place to call to check hardware prices.

Hach Associates, Inc.
P.O. Box 10849
Winston-Salem, NC 27108
800/624-7968
Fax 919/759-9353
Producers of the Concept Keyboard ($495), a touch sensitive pad which attaches to Apple or IBM computers and allows more than one person to use a program. Useful for special education settings.

Koala Technologies, Corp.
70 North Second Street
San Jose, CA 95113
408/287-6311
408/287-6278
Makers of the Koala Pad touch tablet ($139.95) and Koala Pad Graphics Exhibitor.

Logitech
6505 Kaiser Drive
Fremont, CA
800/231-7717
Makers of the Kidz Mouse ($79.00), a mouse designed especially for children to use with IBM or compatible computers.

Only the Best
Software Guide
Education News Service
P.O. Box 1789
Carmichael, CA 95609
916/483-6159
A useful guide to highly rated software for K–12 ($27.95 per copy).

PC-SIG
1030-D East Duane Ave.
Sunnyvale, CA 94086
800/245-6717
A shareware vendor that distributes 2,700 titles for $3.99 per disk. Also publishes ShareWare Magazine.

Prodigy
445 Hamilton
White Plains, NY 10601
800/PRODIGY
An on-line service that includes some early childhood software (see Tom Snyder Productions). Service fee is $12.95 per month.

Public Brand Software
P.O. Box 51315
Indianapolis, IN 46251
800/426-3475
A ShareWare vendor that distributes 3,500 titles for $5.00 per disk.

Public (software) Library
P.O. Box 35705
Houston, TX 77235-5705
800/242-4775
A ShareWare vendor that distributes 5,000 programs for $5.00 per disk.

RC Systems, Inc.
121 West Winesap Road
Bothell, WA 98012
206/672-6909
Makers of the Slotbuster II ($149.95).

Reasonable Solutions
2101 West Main Street
Medford, Oregon 97501
800/876-3475
Fax 503/773-7803
A good source for ShareWare for MS-DOS computers.

ShareWare Magazine
1030 D East Duane Avenue
Sunnyvale, CA 94086
408/730-9291
Fax 408/730-2107
A bi-monthly magazine on ShareWare Software.

Software Excitement!
P.O. Box 3072
6475 Crater Lake Highway
Central Point, OR 97502
800/444-5457
Fax 503/826-8090
A ShareWare vendor that distributes titles for $3.00 each.

Street Electronics
6420 Via Real
Carpinteria, CA 93013
805/684-4593
Makers of speech synthesizers
For Apple
(Echo II $129.95 — IIGS, IIe)
(Echo LC $129.95 — for Mac LC, Apple IIc+, IIc)
For MS-DOS
(Echo PC II $99.95).

TSL
(The Software Labs)
3767 Overland Avenue, #112-115
Los Angeles, CA 90034
800/359-9998
A ShareWare vendor that distributes 1,000 titles at $3.69 each.

Unicorn Engineering, Inc.
5221 Central Ave., Suite 205
Richmond, CA 94804
800/899-6687
510/528-0670
Producers of the Unicorn Keyboard ($395), a touch-sensitive pad for Apple, Macintosh, or IBM computers.

APPENDIX 3
SOFTWARE LISTING BY TOPIC

The following lists classify software programs according to topic. A program is included under a topic if all or some of its content deals with that topic. The topics are as follows: classification, clocks, counting, creative projects, dinosaurs, drawing, keyboard skills, language, memory practice, ordering, plants and animals, spatial relations, special education, temporal relations, and word processing.

CLASSIFICATION
Title — Description **Final Rating**

Color Find — Matching colors	69 ◆◆◆◆◆◆
Colors and Shapes — Color ID, visual discrimination	76 ◆◆◆◆◆◆◆
Comparison Kitchen — Compare and categorize pictures	72 ◆◆◆◆◆◆◆
Costume Ball, The — Variety of basic skills	62 ◆◆◆◆◆◆
Cotton's First Files — Beginning database management	77 ◆◆◆◆◆◆◆
Country Combo — Creative experience	26 ◆◆
Curious George Goes Shopping — Classifying into categories	65 ◆◆◆◆◆◆
Dinosaur Discovery Kit, The — Matching, picture-word connections	65 ◆◆◆◆◆◆
Dinosaurs — Reading, math, and memory skills	65 ◆◆◆◆◆◆
Early & Advanced Switch Games — Cause/effect, matching, counting	75 ◆◆◆◆◆◆◆
Early Concepts Skillbuilder Series — Matching, prepositions	60 ◆◆◆◆◆◆
Early Elementary I — Counting and matching	27 ◆◆
Early Skills — Shape and word discrimination	61 ◆◆◆◆◆◆
Easy Street — Classification, matching, counting	84 ◆◆◆◆◆◆◆◆
First Shapes — Five basic shapes	75 ◆◆◆◆◆◆◆
Fun With Colors — Color recognition	66 ◆◆◆◆◆◆
Garden, The — Functional intelligence	62 ◆◆◆◆◆◆
Gertrude's Secrets — Classifying and seriating	84 ◆◆◆◆◆◆◆◆
Lion's Workshop — Visual discrimination	49 ◆◆◆◆
Mad Match — Matching, visual discrimination	81 ◆◆◆◆◆◆◆◆
Match Maker (Beginning) — Matching objects	77 ◆◆◆◆◆◆◆
Match-On-A-Mac — Matching letters, shapes, numbers	79 ◆◆◆◆◆◆◆
Mickey's Colors & Shapes — Colors and shapes	72 ◆◆◆◆◆◆◆

Moptown Parade — Classification and seriation   55 ◆◆◆◆◆

Muppetville — Classifying, memory skills   87 ◆◆◆◆◆◆◆◆

Observation and Classification — Classification skills   80 ◆◆◆◆◆◆◆◆

Odd One Out — Matching/discrimination   74 ◆◆◆◆◆◆◆

Ollie and Seymour — Pedestrian safety, readiness skills   77 ◆◆◆◆◆◆◆

Ollie Finds It! — Matching shapes, letters, and words   67 ◆◆◆◆◆◆

Ollie Hears and Remembers — Auditory memory skills   64 ◆◆◆◆◆◆

Ollie Hears and Sequences — Auditory memory skills   64 ◆◆◆◆◆◆

One Banana More — Reading readiness, counting   34 ◆◆◆

Patterns — Pattern recognition: shapes, sounds   79 ◆◆◆◆◆◆◆

Patterns and Sequences — Matching/discrimination   72 ◆◆◆◆◆◆◆

Perception, Inc. — Problem solving and thinking skills   71 ◆◆◆◆◆◆◆

Picture Chompers — Classification practice   79 ◆◆◆◆◆◆◆

Preschool Disk 2 — Matching, counting, adding, memory   75 ◆◆◆◆◆◆◆

Preschool IQ Builder I — Concepts of same and different   38 ◆◆◆

Preschool IQ Builder II — Matching, shapes, numbers, letters   43 ◆◆◆◆

Preschool Pack — Letters, numbers, and shapes   79 ◆◆◆◆◆◆◆

Reading and Me — Matching, classifying, recognizing   79 ◆◆◆◆◆◆◆

Same and Different — Matching   64 ◆◆◆◆◆◆

Same or Different — Visual discrimination, matching   55 ◆◆◆◆◆

Sesame Street Big Bird's Special Delivery — Object recognition   31 ◆◆◆

Sesame Street Ernie's Magic Shapes — Visual discrimination practice   45 ◆◆◆◆

Sesame Street Grover's Animal Adventures — Classifying animals   76 ◆◆◆◆◆◆◆

Sesame Street Learning Library 2 — Problem solving, classifying animals   NR

Shape & Color Rodeo — Recognizing shapes and colors   73 ◆◆◆◆◆◆◆

Shape Starship — Matching attributes   65 ◆◆◆◆◆◆

Shapes & Patterns — Visual discrimination, cognitive skills   66 ◆◆◆◆◆◆

Shutterbug's Patterns — Sequencing, pattern recognition   36 ◆◆◆

SocPix — Classification (class membership)   61 ◆◆◆◆◆◆

Talking Animals Activity Set — Matching animals with sounds   74 ◆◆◆◆◆◆◆

Talking Colors and Shapes — Basic colors and shapes   49 ◆◆◆◆

Teddy and Iggy — Sequential memory practice   78 ◆◆◆◆◆◆◆

Teddy's Playground — Practice with colors and shapes   80 ◆◆◆◆◆◆◆◆

Touch and Match — Classification   65 ◆◆◆◆◆◆

Treasure Mountain — Reading, thinking, math, and science   82 ◆◆◆◆◆◆◆

Winker's World of Patterns — Inferring and recognizing patterns   82 ◆◆◆◆◆◆◆◆

Woolly Bounce — Force and motion   83 ◆◆◆◆◆◆◆◆

Word Factory — Word discrimination   22 ◆◆

Wunder Book — Matching, letter recognition   80 ◆◆◆◆◆◆◆◆

CLOCKS

Title — Description **Final Rating**

Boars Tell Time, The — Clock skills   68 ◆◆◆◆◆◆

Caveman Clockwork — Time concepts   45 ◆◆◆◆
Clock Works — Clock-reading skills, units of time   72 ◆◆◆◆◆◆◆
Exploring Measure, Time, & Money — Units of time   86 ◆◆◆◆◆◆◆◆
Kieran — Letters, numbers, clocks   70 ◆◆◆◆◆◆◆
Learning About Numbers — Counting, clocks, basic math facts   78 ◆◆◆◆◆◆◆
Playroom, The — Letters, numbers, and time   91 ◆◆◆◆◆◆◆◆◆
School Mom — Basic skills practice, clocks   54 ◆◆◆◆◆
Talking Classroom — A variety of school-related subjects   75 ◆◆◆◆◆◆◆
Talking Clock — Clock reading skills   65 ◆◆◆◆◆◆
Telling Time — Clock practice   34 ◆◆◆
Time Master — Clock practice   25 ◆◆
Working With Time — Matching clock faces   63 ◆◆◆◆◆◆

COUNTING

Title — Description **Final Rating**

Amy's First Primer 2.2 — Letters, counting, shapes, etc.   71 ◆◆◆◆◆◆◆
Animated Math — Counting, math facts   71 ◆◆◆◆◆◆◆
Arithmetic Critters — Counting, addition, and subtraction   78 ◆◆◆◆◆◆◆
Balancing Bear — Comparing amounts, addition, etc.   77 ◆◆◆◆◆◆◆
Base Ten Blocks — Develop understanding of patterns   86 ◆◆◆◆◆◆◆◆
Berenstain Bears Learn About Counting, The — Counting up to 9   76 ◆◆◆◆◆◆◆
Bike Hike — Memory, recall of objects   41 ◆◆◆◆
Charlie Brown's 1-2-3's — Numeral recognition, counting   67 ◆◆◆◆◆◆
Chutes and Ladders — Counting   58 ◆◆◆◆◆
Clock Works — Clock-reading skills, units of time   72 ◆◆◆◆◆◆◆
Coin Works — Value of coins   71 ◆◆◆◆◆◆◆
Conservation and Counting — Counting skills   71 ◆◆◆◆◆◆◆
Counters — Counting experiences   69 ◆◆◆◆◆◆
Counting and Ordering — 1-9 counting, numeral recognition   56 ◆◆◆◆◆
Counting Critters 1.0 — Counting and early math concepts   81 ◆◆◆◆◆◆◆◆
Diskovery Adding Machine — Counting, addition skills   69 ◆◆◆◆◆◆
Diskovery Take Away Zoo — Counting, subtraction practice   68 ◆◆◆◆◆◆
Dot-to-Dot Construction Set — Counting, problem solving   72 ◆◆◆◆◆◆◆
Early Games — Counting, letters, and drawing   60 ◆◆◆◆◆◆
Early Math — Counting, numerical order   43 ◆◆◆◆
Easy Street — Classification, matching, counting   84 ◆◆◆◆◆◆◆◆
Estimation — Estimation of length, area, & time units   78 ◆◆◆◆◆◆◆
Fast Track — Addition, subtraction, multiplication, division   59 ◆◆◆◆◆
Fish Scales — Measurement   78 ◆◆◆◆◆◆◆
Fun With Numbers — Numeral recognition, adding, subtracting   59 ◆◆◆◆◆
Getting Ready to Read and Add — Numerals, U/L- case letters   63 ◆◆◆◆◆◆
Hobo's Luck — Counting and probability   54 ◆◆◆◆◆
Hop To It! — Number lines   80 ◆◆◆◆◆◆◆◆

I Can Count — Counting up to 10   40 ◆◆◆◆
I Can Count the Petals of a Flower — Counting   56 ◆◆◆◆◆
Introduction to Counting — Counting   66 ◆◆◆◆◆◆
KidsMath — Basic math skills   83 ◆◆◆◆◆◆◆◆
KidsTime — Letters, numbers, matching, etc.   82 ◆◆◆◆◆◆◆◆
Kieran — Letters, numbers, clocks, etc.   70 ◆◆◆◆◆◆◆
Kinder Koncepts MATH — Number and math skills   57 ◆◆◆◆◆
Kindercomp Golden Edition — Counting, letters, matching   70 ◆◆◆◆◆◆◆
Kindermath II — Math fundamentals   57 ◆◆◆◆◆
Knowing Numbers — Fundamental math skill practice   67 ◆◆◆◆◆◆
Learn to Add — Matching numbers, math facts   75 ◆◆◆◆◆◆◆
Learning Numbers — Counting from 1 to 5   63 ◆◆◆◆◆◆
Match-On-A-Mac — Matching letters, shapes, numbers   79 ◆◆◆◆◆◆◆
Math and Me — Shapes, patterns, numbers, addition   78 ◆◆◆◆◆◆◆
Math Blaster Plus — Basic math facts practice   85 ◆◆◆◆◆◆◆◆
Math Concepts Level P — Math concepts and symbols   73 ◆◆◆◆◆◆◆
Math Magic — Math facts (add, sub., mult., div.)   53 ◆◆◆◆◆
Math Maze — Basic math facts   52 ◆◆◆◆◆
Math Rabbit — Counting, matching sets, etc.   78 ◆◆◆◆◆◆◆
Math Sequences — Number readiness   69 ◆◆◆◆◆◆
Mathematics Level A — Whole numbers, addition, subtraction   69 ◆◆◆◆◆◆
Mathosaurus Level K — Beginning number concepts   72 ◆◆◆◆◆◆◆
Measure Works — Practice with measurements   80 ◆◆◆◆◆◆◆
Mickey's 123's — Counting from 1 to 9   74 ◆◆◆◆◆◆◆
Mickey's Runaway Zoo: Fun With Numbers — Counting 1 to 9   60 ◆◆◆◆◆◆
Money Works — Money skills   76 ◆◆◆◆◆◆◆
Monkey Math — Basic math facts, numerical order   49 ◆◆◆◆
Muppets on Stage — Counting skills, letter recognition   81 ◆◆◆◆◆◆◆◆
Muppetville — Classifying, memory skills   87 ◆◆◆◆◆◆◆◆
Number Farm — Counting skills   78 ◆◆◆◆◆◆◆
Number Sea Hunt — Counting, adding, number order, subtracting   66 ◆◆◆◆◆◆
NumberMaze — Practice with basic math facts   81 ◆◆◆◆◆◆◆◆
Numbers — Numeral discovery, counting   58 ◆◆◆◆◆
Ollie Numbers It — Numeral, set association   64 ◆◆◆◆◆◆
Path-Tactics — Counting, basic math facts   69 ◆◆◆◆◆◆
Peter's Growing Patterns — Pattern recognition   73 ◆◆◆◆◆◆◆
Playroom, The — Letters, numbers, and time   91 ◆◆◆◆◆◆◆◆◆
Preschool Disk 1 — Letters, counting, alphabet   62 ◆◆◆◆◆◆
Preschool Disk 2 — Matching, counting, adding, memory   75 ◆◆◆◆◆◆◆
Preschool Pack — Letters, numbers, and shapes   79 ◆◆◆◆◆◆◆
Rosie the Counting Rabbit — Language experience   89 ◆◆◆◆◆◆◆◆
School Bus Driver — Coordination, judgment, and recall   73 ◆◆◆◆◆◆◆
Sesame Street Astro-Grover — Counting, adding, and subtracting   41 ◆◆◆◆
Sesame Street Learning Library 1 — Matching, counting, adding, subtracting   NR
Silly Letters & Numbers — Letter and numeral recognition   70 ◆◆◆◆◆◆◆

Simple Addition — Addition with sums less than nine — 69 ◆◆◆◆◆◆

Stars & Planets — Counting, planets, etc. — 62 ◆◆◆◆◆◆

Stepping Stones Level I — Letters, numbers, and words — 59 ◆◆◆◆◆

Stepping Stones Level II — Vocabulary, counting, adding — 58 ◆◆◆◆◆

Stickybear Math — Counting, addition, subtraction — 81 ◆◆◆◆◆◆◆◆

Stickybear Numbers — Counting from 0 to 9 — 75 ◆◆◆◆◆◆◆

Talking Alpha Chimp — Letter recognition, counting — 84 ◆◆◆◆◆◆◆◆

Talking Animals Activity Set — Matching six animals with sounds — 74 ◆◆◆◆◆◆◆

Talking Dinosaurs — Dinosaur names, counting — 53 ◆◆◆◆◆

Talking Money — Units of money — 60 ◆◆◆◆◆◆

Talking Numbers — Counting — 41 ◆◆◆◆

Talking School Bus — Directions, counting, animal sounds — 77 ◆◆◆◆◆◆◆

Teddy Bears Counting Fun — Counting skills — 32 ◆◆◆

Treehouse, The — Math skills, base ten, carrying — 92 ◆◆◆◆◆◆◆◆◆

Webster's Numbers — Basic math concepts — 67 ◆◆◆◆◆◆

Winker's World of Numbers — Patterns in sequences of numbers — 82 ◆◆◆◆◆◆◆◆

Winker's World of Patterns — Inferring and recognizing patterns — 82 ◆◆◆◆◆◆◆◆

Working With Numbers — Counting and numerical order — 63 ◆◆◆◆◆◆

Young Math — Addition and subtraction equations — 75 ◆◆◆◆◆◆◆

CREATIVE PROJECTS

Title — Description **Final Rating**

ABC's — Coloring pictures — 80 ◆◆◆◆◆◆◆◆

Bake & Taste — Reading skills, following directions — 83 ◆◆◆◆◆◆◆◆

Bald-Headed Chicken, The — Language experience — 89 ◆◆◆◆◆◆◆◆

Berenstain Bears Fun With Colors, The — Coloring and creating with stickers — 86 ◆◆◆◆◆◆◆◆

Big Book Maker — Printing utility program — NR

Brand New View, A — Language experience — 89 ◆◆◆◆◆◆◆◆

Children's Writing & Publishing Center — Creative writing — 86 ◆◆◆◆◆◆◆◆

Color 'n' Canvas — Visual art, drawing, painting, etc. — 91 ◆◆◆◆◆◆◆◆◆

Color Me — Drawing, creating — 89 ◆◆◆◆◆◆◆◆

Cotton Tales — Word processing, language development — 78 ◆◆◆◆◆◆◆

Cotton's First Files — Beginning database management — 77 ◆◆◆◆◆◆◆

Country Combo — Creative experience — 26 ◆◆

Delta Drawing Today — Drawing, early programming concepts — 81 ◆◆◆◆◆◆◆◆

Dinosaur Days Plus — Creation of writing and graphics — 69 ◆◆◆◆◆◆

Dinosaur Discovery Kit, The — Matching, picture-word connections — 65 ◆◆◆◆◆◆

Dinosaurs Are Forever — Coloring pictures — 80 ◆◆◆◆◆◆◆◆

Dr. Peet's Talk/Writer — Language exploration and skills — 79 ◆◆◆◆◆◆◆

Early Childhood Learning Program — Conceptual skill development — 53 ◆◆◆◆◆

Early Games — Counting, letters, and drawing — 60 ◆◆◆◆◆◆

Easy Color Paint 2.0 — Drawing — 84 ◆◆◆◆◆◆◆◆

Electronic Builder — Shapes, spatial thinking — 82 ◆◆◆◆◆◆◆◆

Electronic Easel — Drawing pictures   73 ◆◆◆◆◆◆◆
ESL Writer — Word processing   79 ◆◆◆◆◆◆◆
Extrateletactograph, The — Drawing and writing stories   73 ◆◆◆◆◆◆◆
EZ Logo — Problem solving, directionality   74 ◆◆◆◆◆◆◆
Facemaker — Pattern matching, creative activity   54 ◆◆◆◆◆
Facemaker Golden Edition — Creativity, memory   75 ◆◆◆◆◆◆◆
Farm, The — Creation of a microworld   80 ◆◆◆◆◆◆◆◆
FirstWriter — Creative writing   76 ◆◆◆◆◆◆◆
Fun on the Farm — Coloring pictures   80 ◆◆◆◆◆◆◆◆
Fun With Colors — Color recognition   66 ◆◆◆◆◆◆
Fun With Drawing — Drawing pictures   71 ◆◆◆◆◆◆◆
Great Leap, A — Language experience   89 ◆◆◆◆◆◆◆◆
Holidays & Seasons — Coloring pictures   80 ◆◆◆◆◆◆◆◆
I Love You in the Sky, Butterfly — Language experience   89 ◆◆◆◆◆◆◆◆
Integrated Learning System — Math and reading, K-9   79 ◆◆◆◆◆◆◆
Just Around the Block — Language experience   89 ◆◆◆◆◆◆◆◆
Kermit's Electronic Storymaker — Words and their meaning   77 ◆◆◆◆◆◆◆
Keytalk — A beginning literacy activity   76 ◆◆◆◆◆◆◆
Kid Works — Creative writing, drawing, creating   90 ◆◆◆◆◆◆◆◆◆
KidPix — Creation of visual effects   93 ◆◆◆◆◆◆◆◆◆
Kids at Work — Creation of graphics   69 ◆◆◆◆◆◆
KidsTime — Letters, numbers, matching, writing   82 ◆◆◆◆◆◆◆◆
Kidsword — Large-type word processing   55 ◆◆◆◆◆
KidWare 2 Learning Center — Variety of skills and experiences   NR
Kidwriter — Creating computer storybooks   73 ◆◆◆◆◆◆◆
Kindercomp — Matching, drawing, etc.   68 ◆◆◆◆◆◆
Kindercomp Golden Edition — Counting, letters, drawing, etc.   70 ◆◆◆◆◆◆◆
Koala Pad Graphics Exhibitor — Drawing   76 ◆◆◆◆◆◆◆
Learn About: Animals — Animals, environments, etc.   80 ◆◆◆◆◆◆◆◆
Learn About: Plants — Plants, environments, etc.   80 ◆◆◆◆◆◆◆◆
Learning Shapes — Practice with four basic shapes   66 ◆◆◆◆◆◆
Let's Go To Hannah's House — Pre-literacy skills   48 ◆◆◆◆
Logic Blocks — Understanding of geometry, patterns   86 ◆◆◆◆◆◆◆◆
Looney Tunes Print Kit — Creating printed materials   46 ◆◆◆◆
Magic Crayon — Drawing with arrow keys   75 ◆◆◆◆◆◆◆
Magic Melody Box — Creating music   59 ◆◆◆◆◆
Magic Slate — Word processing   81 ◆◆◆◆◆◆◆◆
Make-A-Book — Creation of books   67 ◆◆◆◆◆◆
Mask Parade — Creative design   77 ◆◆◆◆◆◆◆
Measure Works — Practice with measurements   80 ◆◆◆◆◆◆◆◆
Mickey & Minnie's Fun Time Print Kit — Creating printed products   79 ◆◆◆◆◆◆◆
Microzine Jr. (Sept/Oct.'88) — Habitats, making masks, programming   81 ◆◆◆◆◆◆◆◆
Milliken Storyteller, The — Early reading skills   82 ◆◆◆◆◆◆◆◆
Monsters & Make-Believe — Creative writing, illustrations   71 ◆◆◆◆◆◆◆
Monsters & Make-Believe Plus — Creative writing, illustrations   69 ◆◆◆◆◆◆

Mr. and Mrs. Potato Head — Creative projects, imagination, etc.   71 ◆◆◆◆◆◆◆

Mural Maker — Creating print products   58 ◆◆◆◆◆

Music — Seriation of pitch   59 ◆◆◆◆◆

Music Maker — Creation of music   65 ◆◆◆◆◆◆

My Grand Piano — Learning notes, playing familiar songs   79 ◆◆◆◆◆◆◆

My Words — Language experience   78 ◆◆◆◆◆◆◆

Not Too Messy, Not Too Neat — Language experience   89 ◆◆◆◆◆◆◆◆

Notable Phantom, The — Musical notation, pitch recognition   66 ◆◆◆◆◆◆

Paint With Words — Word recognition   73 ◆◆◆◆◆◆◆

Pattern Blocks 2.1 — Visual imagery, symmetry   77 ◆◆◆◆◆◆◆

Patterns — Pattern recognition: shapes, sounds   79 ◆◆◆◆◆◆◆

Picture Perfect — Draw, color, and write   79 ◆◆◆◆◆◆◆

Playroom, The — Letters, numbers, and time   91 ◆◆◆◆◆◆◆◆◆

Primary Editor Plus — Word processing, drawing, making banners   74 ◆◆◆◆◆◆◆

Princess and the Pea, The — Creative writing   62 ◆◆◆◆◆◆

Print Power — Creating printed materials   46 ◆◆◆◆

Print Shop, The — Creation of printed materials   85 ◆◆◆◆◆◆◆◆

Puzzle Master — Problem solving (puzzles)   79 ◆◆◆◆◆◆◆

Puzzle Storybook, The — Writing, creating pictures   66 ◆◆◆◆◆◆

Rainbow Painter — Drawing   80 ◆◆◆◆◆◆◆◆

Read, Write, & Publish 1 — Word processing, illustrating   81 ◆◆◆◆◆◆◆◆

Robot Writer Plus — Creative writing   69 ◆◆◆◆◆◆

Rosie the Counting Rabbit — Language experience   89 ◆◆◆◆◆◆◆◆

School Mom — Basic skills practice   54 ◆◆◆◆◆

Sesame Street Crayon: Letters for You — Coloring pictures   80 ◆◆◆◆◆◆◆◆

Sesame Street Crayon: Numbers Count — Coloring pictures   80 ◆◆◆◆◆◆◆◆

Sesame Street Crayon: Opposites Attract — Coloring pictures   80 ◆◆◆◆◆◆◆◆

Sesame Street First Writer — Writing & printing   81 ◆◆◆◆◆◆◆◆

Sesame Street Print Kit — Creating printed materials   46 ◆◆◆◆

Sleepy Brown Cow, The — Language experience   89 ◆◆◆◆◆◆◆◆

Stickers — Creative activity   79 ◆◆◆◆◆◆◆

Stickybear Printer — "Printing fun for everyone"   43 ◆◆◆◆

Stone Soup — Creative writing   89 ◆◆◆◆◆◆◆◆

Storybook Weaver — Creating and illustrating stories   83 ◆◆◆◆◆◆◆◆

Super GS Award Maker — Teacher's utility: printing award certificates   NA

SuperPrint! — Printing utility   62 ◆◆◆◆◆◆

Surrounding Patterns — Visual imagery, symmetry   77 ◆◆◆◆◆◆◆

Talking Textwriter — Exploration of written language   75 ◆◆◆◆◆◆◆

Teddy Bear-rels of Fun — Creating pictures, graphics, and stories   56 ◆◆◆◆◆

This Land Is Your Land — Coloring pictures   80 ◆◆◆◆◆◆◆◆

Three Little Pigs, The — Creative writing   89 ◆◆◆◆◆◆◆◆

Toybox — Exploration of the computer   56 ◆◆◆◆◆

Treehouse, The — Math skills, language, animals, etc.   92 ◆◆◆◆◆◆◆◆◆

What Makes a Dinosaur Sore? — Language experience   89 ◆◆◆◆◆◆◆◆

Where Did My Toothbrush Go? — Language experience   89 ◆◆◆◆◆◆◆◆

Whole Neighborhood, The — Creation of text and graphics　　69 ◆◆◆◆◆◆

Write On: Primary Level — Writing　　NR

DINOSAURS
Title — Description **Final Rating**

Designasaurus — Learning about dinosaurs　　57 ◆◆◆◆◆

Dinosaur Days Plus — Writing and graphics　　69 ◆◆◆◆◆◆

Dinosaur Discovery Kit, The — Matching, picture-word connections　　65 ◆◆◆◆◆◆

Dinosaurs — Reading, math, and memory skills　　65 ◆◆◆◆◆◆

Dinosaurs Are Forever — Coloring pictures　　80 ◆◆◆◆◆◆◆◆

First Letters and Words — Letters & words, dinosaurs　　74 ◆◆◆◆◆◆◆

Once Upon a Time..., Volume I — Language experience, creation of stories　　59 ◆◆◆◆◆

Simple Addition — Addition with sums less than nine　　69 ◆◆◆◆◆◆

Talking Dinosaurs — Dinosaur names, counting　　53 ◆◆◆◆◆

What Makes a Dinosaur Sore? — Language experience　　89 ◆◆◆◆◆◆◆◆

DRAWING
Title — Description **Final Rating**

Color 'n' Canvas — Visual art, drawing, painting, symmetry　　91 ◆◆◆◆◆◆◆◆◆

Color Me — Drawing, creating　　89 ◆◆◆◆◆◆◆◆

Delta Drawing Today — Drawing, programming concepts　　81 ◆◆◆◆◆◆◆◆

Early Games — Counting, letters, and drawing　　60 ◆◆◆◆◆◆

Easy Color Paint 2.0 — Drawing, creation of visual product　　84 ◆◆◆◆◆◆◆◆

Electronic Easel — Drawing pictures　　73 ◆◆◆◆◆◆◆

Extrateletactograph, The — Drawing and writing stories　　73 ◆◆◆◆◆◆◆

EZ Logo — Problem solving, directionality　　74 ◆◆◆◆◆◆◆

Fun With Drawing — Drawing pictures　　71 ◆◆◆◆◆◆◆

Kid Works — Creative writing, drawing, creating　　90 ◆◆◆◆◆◆◆◆◆

KidPix — Creation of visual effects　　93 ◆◆◆◆◆◆◆◆◆

Kindercomp Golden Edition — Counting, letters, matching, and drawing　　70 ◆◆◆◆◆◆◆

Koala Pad Graphics Exhibitor — Drawing　　76 ◆◆◆◆◆◆◆

Magic Crayon — Drawing with arrow keys　　75 ◆◆◆◆◆◆◆

Picture Perfect — Draw, color, and write　　79 ◆◆◆◆◆◆◆

Treehouse, The — Math skills, language, animals, music, and more　　92 ◆◆◆◆◆◆◆◆◆

KEYBOARD SKILLS
Title — Description **Final Rating**

Computergarten — Keyboard skills, computer terms　　27 ◆◆

Home Row — Keyboarding skills (touch-typing)　　75 ◆◆◆◆◆◆◆

Jr. Typer — Touch typing 41 ♦♦♦♦
Kids on Keys — Letter recognition 62 ♦♦♦♦♦♦
Learning Letters — Matching letters 62 ♦♦♦♦♦♦

LANGUAGE

Title — Description **Final Rating**

ABC-123 Activities for Learning — Matching, alphabet order 48 ♦♦♦♦
Action/Music — Using the computer for speech 80 ♦♦♦♦♦♦♦♦
Adventures of Jimmy Jumper, The — Prepositional concepts 69 ♦♦♦♦♦♦
Alice in Wonderland — Remembering a sequence of events 69 ♦♦♦♦♦♦
Alphabet Academy, The — Alphabet sequencing, letters 78 ♦♦♦♦♦♦♦
Alphabet Arcade, The — Alphabetizing, dictionary skills 42 ♦♦♦♦
Alphabet Blocks — Letter names and sounds, alphabet 85 ♦♦♦♦♦♦♦♦
Alphabet Circus — Letter recognition, alphabet order 68 ♦♦♦♦♦♦
Alphabet Express — Alphabet skills 68 ♦♦♦♦♦♦
Alphabet for Everyone — Letter recognition, alphabet order 54 ♦♦♦♦♦
Alphabet Fun: Big and Little Letters — Upper-and lower-case letters 64 ♦♦♦♦♦♦
Alphabet Fun: Learning the Alphabet — Letter recognition, alphabet 78 ♦♦♦♦♦♦♦
Alphabet Recognition — Letter recognition 46 ♦♦♦♦
Alphabet Sounds — Letter sounds, initial consonants 29 ♦♦
Alphabet Zoo — Letter recognition 51 ♦♦♦♦♦
Alphabetization & Letter Recognition — Alphabetizing, letter discrimination 67 ♦♦♦♦♦♦
Alphaget — Letter recognition practice 51 ♦♦♦♦♦
Amy's First Primer 2.2 — Letters, counting, shapes, and space 71 ♦♦♦♦♦♦♦
Animal Alphabet and Other Things — Letter recognition, alphabet 81 ♦♦♦♦♦♦♦♦
Animated Alphabet — Letter recognition 65 ♦♦♦♦♦♦
Astro's ABCs — Letter recognition skills 62 ♦♦♦♦♦♦
Bald-Headed Chicken, The — Language experience 89 ♦♦♦♦♦♦♦♦
Bank Street Writer III, The — Word processing 71 ♦♦♦♦♦♦♦
Beginning Reading Skills — Beginning reading skills 57 ♦♦♦♦♦
Berenstain Bears Learn About Letters, The — Letter recognition, alphabet 73 ♦♦♦♦♦♦♦
Big Red Hat, The — Short "a" sound and reading comprehension 77 ♦♦♦♦♦♦♦
Bouncy Bee Learns Letters 1.0 — Letter recognition 72 ♦♦♦♦♦♦♦
Bouncy Bee Learns Words 1.0 — Word knowledge 62 ♦♦♦♦♦♦
Brand New View, A — Language experience 89 ♦♦♦♦♦♦♦♦
Brandon's Bigbox — Letter recognition 51 ♦♦♦♦♦
Bremen Town Musicians — Homonyms, context clues, comprehension 45 ♦♦♦♦
Cat 'n Mouse — Relational concepts 65 ♦♦♦♦♦♦
Charlie Brown's ABC's — Letter recognition & association 64 ♦♦♦♦♦♦
Children's Writing & Publishing Center — Creative writing, creating printed products 86 ♦♦♦♦♦♦♦♦
Clue in on Phonics — Practice with letter sounds 71 ♦♦♦♦♦♦♦
Consonant Capers — Letter recognition 64 ♦♦♦♦♦♦

Cotton Tales — Word processing   78 ◆◆◆◆◆◆◆

Daffy Duck, P.I. — Spelling practice   72 ◆◆◆◆◆◆◆

Developing Language Skills — Knowledge of words   45 ◆◆◆◆

Dino Speller — Alphabetization, letter recognition   63 ◆◆◆◆◆◆

Donald's Alphabet Chase — Letter recognition, alphabet   75 ◆◆◆◆◆◆◆

Dr. Peet's Talk/Writer — Language exploration and skills   79 ◆◆◆◆◆◆◆

Dragon Tales — Language development   NR

Early Elementary II — Letter recognition, counting   28 ◆◆

Easy as ABC — Letter recognition, alphabet   80 ◆◆◆◆◆◆◆◆

Edmark Reading Program Level 1 — Beginning reading skills   66 ◆◆◆◆◆◆

Electric Company: Bagasaurus — Vocabulary development   59 ◆◆◆◆◆

Electric Company: Picture Place — Vocabulary and word recognition   58 ◆◆◆◆◆

Electric Company: Roll-A-Word — Word recognition, vowel sounds   44 ◆◆◆◆

Emerging Literacy Program — Language skills   89 ◆◆◆◆◆◆◆◆

ESL Writer — Word processing   79 ◆◆◆◆◆◆◆

Exploratory Play — Early language acquisition   71 ◆◆◆◆◆◆◆

First "R": Kindergarten, The — Letter recognition   74 ◆◆◆◆◆◆◆

First Letter Fun — Letter recognition   82 ◆◆◆◆◆◆◆◆

First Verbs — Learning 40 common verbs   73 ◆◆◆◆◆◆◆

FirstWriter — Creative writing   76 ◆◆◆◆◆◆◆

Fish Dish, The — Short "i" sound and comprehension   77 ◆◆◆◆◆◆◆

Flodd, the Bad Guy — Letter and word recognition   70 ◆◆◆◆◆◆◆

Fun From A to Z — Alphabet skills practice   81 ◆◆◆◆◆◆◆◆

Fun With Letters and Words — Letter recognition   76 ◆◆◆◆◆◆◆

Getting Ready to Read and Add — Numerals, upper/lower-case letters   63 ◆◆◆◆◆◆

Great Gonzo in Word Rider, The — Fun with words, timing, strategy   73 ◆◆◆◆◆◆◆

Great Leap, A — Language experience   89 ◆◆◆◆◆◆◆◆

Hey Diddle — Rhyming words and phrases   47 ◆◆◆◆

Hodge Podge — Letter recognition   51 ◆◆◆◆◆

I Love You in the Sky, Butterfly — Language experience, themes   89 ◆◆◆◆◆◆◆◆

Integrated Learning System — Math and reading, K-9   79 ◆◆◆◆◆◆◆

It's No Game — Personal safety skills   62 ◆◆◆◆◆◆

Jack and the Beanstalk — Word recognition, event sequence   69 ◆◆◆◆◆◆

Jack and the Beanstalk — Letter and word recognition, reading   70 ◆◆◆◆◆◆◆

Jen the Hen — Short "e" sound and reading comprehension   77 ◆◆◆◆◆◆◆

Just Around the Block — Language experience   89 ◆◆◆◆◆◆◆◆

Katie's Farm — Exploring, talking about actions   83 ◆◆◆◆◆◆◆◆

Kermit's Electronic Storymaker — Words and their meaning   77 ◆◆◆◆◆◆◆

Keytalk — A beginning literacy activity   76 ◆◆◆◆◆◆◆

Kid's Stuff — Counting skills, letter recognition   76 ◆◆◆◆◆◆◆

KidsTime — Letters, numbers, matching, writing   82 ◆◆◆◆◆◆◆◆

Kidsword — Large-type word processing   55 ◆◆◆◆◆

KidTalk — Language experience   86 ◆◆◆◆◆◆◆◆

KidWare 2 Learning Center — Variety of skills and experiences   NR

Kidwriter — Creating computer storybooks   73 ◆◆◆◆◆◆◆

Kieran — Letters, numbers, clocks, upper/lower-case letters 70 ◆◆◆◆◆◆◆

Kinder Critters — Addresses, phone numbers 70 ◆◆◆◆◆◆◆

Kinder Koncepts Reading — Reading readiness 44 ◆◆◆◆

Language Experience Recorder Plus — Word processing 55 ◆◆◆◆◆

Learn the Alphabet — Upper/lower-case letters, alphabet 56 ◆◆◆◆◆

Learning the Alphabet — Alphabet skills 66 ◆◆◆◆◆◆

Learning the Alphabet — Matching letters, alphabet 50 ◆◆◆◆◆

Learning Sight Words — Matching and typing sight words 56 ◆◆◆◆◆

Let's Go To Hannah's House — Pre-literacy skills 48 ◆◆◆◆

Letter Games — Letter recognition 34 ◆◆◆

Letter Recognition — Location of letters on keyboard 48 ◆◆◆◆

Letters and First Words — Letters, initial consonants 68 ◆◆◆◆◆◆

Letters and Words — Letter recognition, alphabet order 68 ◆◆◆◆◆◆

Letters, Pictures & Words — Letter recognition 67 ◆◆◆◆◆◆

Magic Slate — Word processing 81 ◆◆◆◆◆◆◆◆

Magic String, The — Reading skills 46 ◆◆◆◆

Make-A-Book — Creation of books 67 ◆◆◆◆◆◆

McGee at the Fun Fair — Exploring, talking about actions 83 ◆◆◆◆◆◆◆◆

Memory Lane 2.0 — Matching, sequencing, memory skills 68 ◆◆◆◆◆◆

Mickey's ABC's — Recognizing upper or upper/lower-case letters 78 ◆◆◆◆◆◆◆

Mickey's Crossword Puzzle Maker — Reading, problem solving 76 ◆◆◆◆◆◆◆

Mickey's Magic Reader — Reading for enjoyment 75 ◆◆◆◆◆◆◆

Micro-LADS — Covers 46 fundamental syntax rules 75 ◆◆◆◆◆◆◆

Milliken Storyteller, The — Early reading skills 82 ◆◆◆◆◆◆◆◆

Mount Murdoch — Adventure game and word processor 45 ◆◆◆◆

Muppet Slate — Language experiences 88 ◆◆◆◆◆◆◆◆

Muppet Word Book — Letters and words 82 ◆◆◆◆◆◆◆◆

Muppets On Stage — Counting skills, letter recognition 81 ◆◆◆◆◆◆◆◆

My ABC's — Letter and numeral recognition 63 ◆◆◆◆◆◆

My House: Language Activities of Daily Living — Practice with names of common things 77 ◆◆◆◆◆◆◆

My Letters, Numbers, and Words — Letter recognition 46 ◆◆◆◆

My Puzzles and Alphabet — Letter recognition 49 ◆◆◆◆

My Words — Language experience 78 ◆◆◆◆◆◆◆

New Talking Stickybear Alphabet, The — Letter recognition 64 ◆◆◆◆◆◆

Not Too Messy, Not Too Neat — Language experience 89 ◆◆◆◆◆◆◆◆

Ollie Begins It — Matching beginning sounds, letters 64 ◆◆◆◆◆◆

Ollie Compares It — Avoiding common letter reversals 64 ◆◆◆◆◆◆

Ollie Letters It — Matching upper/lower-case letters 64 ◆◆◆◆◆◆

Ollie Matches It — Matching letters 64 ◆◆◆◆◆◆

Paint With Words — Word recognition 73 ◆◆◆◆◆◆◆

Phonics Plus — Letter/word relationships 78 ◆◆◆◆◆◆◆

Phonics Prime Time: Initial Consonant — Initial consonant phonics skills 83 ◆◆◆◆◆◆◆◆

Pictures, Letters, and Sounds — Letter recognition 78 ◆◆◆◆◆◆◆

Playroom, The — Letters, numbers, and time 91 ◆◆◆◆◆◆◆◆◆

Playwrite — Writing scripts　　82 ◆◆◆◆◆◆◆◆

Preschool Disk 1 — Letters, counting, alphabet　　62 ◆◆◆◆◆◆

Primary Editor Plus — Word processing, drawing　　74 ◆◆◆◆◆◆◆

Princess and the Pea, The — Creative writing　　62 ◆◆◆◆◆◆

Puzzle Storybook, The — Writing, creating pictures　　66 ◆◆◆◆◆◆

Race the Clock — Memory　　69 ◆◆◆◆◆◆

Read, Write, & Publish 1 — Word processing　　81 ◆◆◆◆◆◆◆◆

Read-a-Logo — Use of commercial logos　　70 ◆◆◆◆◆◆◆

Reader Rabbit — Basic reading skills/comprehension　　71 ◆◆◆◆◆◆◆

Reading Comprehension: Level 1 — Reading comprehension skills　　82 ◆◆◆◆◆◆◆◆

Reading Fun: Beginning Consonants — Beginning consonants　　56 ◆◆◆◆◆

Reading Fun: Final Consonants — Final consonants　　56 ◆◆◆◆◆

Reading Fun: Vowel Sounds — Long and short vowel sounds　　46 ◆◆◆◆

Reading Helpers — Reading skills　　69 ◆◆◆◆◆◆

Reading I — Letters, letter sounds, and words　　79 ◆◆◆◆◆◆◆

Reading Machine, The — Various language skills　　65 ◆◆◆◆◆◆

Reading Starters — Reading skills　　63 ◆◆◆◆◆◆

ReadingMaze — Basic language skills　　74 ◆◆◆◆◆◆◆

Representational Play — Early language acquisition　　71 ◆◆◆◆◆◆◆

Rosie the Counting Rabbit — Language experience　　89 ◆◆◆◆◆◆◆◆

Rumpelstiltskin — Reading comprehension　　43 ◆◆◆◆

School Mom — Basic skills practice　　54 ◆◆◆◆◆

Sentence Master Level 1 — Reading skills, vocabulary development　　75 ◆◆◆◆◆◆◆

Sesame Street First Writer — Writing and printing words, sentences　　81 ◆◆◆◆◆◆◆◆

Sesame Street Letter-Go-Round — Letter matching　　56 ◆◆◆◆◆

Sight Word Spelling — Letter, word, and numeral recognition　　39 ◆◆◆

Silly Letters & Numbers — Letter and numeral recognition　　70 ◆◆◆◆◆◆◆

Sleepy Brown Cow, The — Language experience　　89 ◆◆◆◆◆◆◆◆

Sound Ideas: Consonants — Consonant sounds　　80 ◆◆◆◆◆◆◆◆

Sound Ideas: Vowels — Five vowel sounds (long, short)　　80 ◆◆◆◆◆◆◆◆

Sound Ideas: Word Attack — Consonant blends, clusters, etc.　　72 ◆◆◆◆◆◆◆

Space Waste Race — Letter/numeral recognition　　49 ◆◆◆◆

Spell-A-Word — Spelling　　53 ◆◆◆◆◆

Spellicopter — Spelling practice　　66 ◆◆◆◆◆◆

Spelling and Reading Primer — Spelling and reading practice　　51 ◆◆◆◆◆

Spelling Bee, The — Spelling skills　　32 ◆◆◆

Stepping Stones Level I — Letters, numbers, and words　　59 ◆◆◆◆◆

Stepping Stones Level II — Vocabulary, counting, adding　　58 ◆◆◆◆◆

Stickybear ABC — Letter recognition　　59 ◆◆◆◆◆

Stickybear Reading — Word and sentence fun　　77 ◆◆◆◆◆◆◆

Stickybear Typing — Typing skills　　42 ◆◆◆◆

Stone Soup — Creative writing　　89 ◆◆◆◆◆◆◆◆

Storybook Weaver — Creating and illustrating stories　　83 ◆◆◆◆◆◆◆◆

Talk About a Walk — Classifying household objects　　56 ◆◆◆◆◆

Talking ABC's — Letter recognition　　43 ◆◆◆◆

Talking Alpha Chimp — Letter recognition, counting   84 ◆◆◆◆◆◆◆◆

Talking Classroom — A variety of school subjects   75 ◆◆◆◆◆◆◆

Talking First Reader — Word sounds   63 ◆◆◆◆◆◆

Talking First Words — Recognize and create words   62 ◆◆◆◆◆◆

Talking First Writer — Experiment with words and sentences   74 ◆◆◆◆◆◆◆

Talking Nouns I — Language development   80 ◆◆◆◆◆◆◆◆

Talking Nouns II — Language development   80 ◆◆◆◆◆◆◆◆

Talking Reading Railroad — Consonant and vowel sounds   54 ◆◆◆◆◆

Talking Speller — Spelling of 42 common words   64 ◆◆◆◆◆◆

Talking Textwriter — Exploration of written language   75 ◆◆◆◆◆◆◆

Talking Tiles — Letter and word sounds   85 ◆◆◆◆◆◆◆◆

Talking Verbs — Language development   80 ◆◆◆◆◆◆◆◆

Three Little Pigs, The — Creative writing   89 ◆◆◆◆◆◆◆◆

Tiger's Tales — Reading vocabulary and comprehension   80 ◆◆◆◆◆◆◆◆

Tink! Tonk! — Key location, alphabetical order   41 ◆◆◆◆

Touch & Write — Printing practice   81 ◆◆◆◆◆◆◆◆

Treehouse, The — Parts of sentences   93 ◆◆◆◆◆◆◆◆◆

Vocabulary Skillbuilder Series — Vocabulary development   82 ◆◆◆◆◆◆◆◆

Where Did My Toothbrush Go? — Language experience   89 ◆◆◆◆◆◆◆◆

Word Munchers — Vowel-sound discrimination   80 ◆◆◆◆◆◆◆◆

Word Processing for Kids — Word processing   78 ◆◆◆◆◆◆◆

Words — Letter discrimination, word experiences   61 ◆◆◆◆◆◆

Words & Concepts — Vocabulary training   80 ◆◆◆◆◆◆◆◆

Words & Concepts II — Vocabulary training   80 ◆◆◆◆◆◆◆◆

Words & Concepts III — Vocabulary training   80 ◆◆◆◆◆◆◆◆

Working With the Alphabet — Alphabetical order and letter recognition   63 ◆◆◆◆◆◆

Write On: Primary Level — Writing   NR

Writing To Read 2.0 — Reading skills   45 ◆◆◆◆

MEMORY PRACTICE

Title — Description **Final Rating**

Animal Hotel — Memory skills   45 ◆◆◆◆

Animated Memory — Matching, memory practice   70 ◆◆◆◆◆◆◆

Bike Hike — Memory, recall of objects   41 ◆◆◆◆

Concentrate! — Short-term memory skills   60 ◆◆◆◆◆◆

Facemaker Golden Edition — Creativity, memory practice   75 ◆◆◆◆◆◆◆

Fun With Memory — Memory   77 ◆◆◆◆◆◆◆

I Can Remember — Memory skills   64 ◆◆◆◆◆◆

Match Maker (Beginning) — Matching objects   77 ◆◆◆◆◆◆◆

Math Rabbit — Counting, matching sets, addition   78 ◆◆◆◆◆◆◆

Memory Building Blocks — Visual and auditory memory skills   83 ◆◆◆◆◆◆◆◆

Memory Lane 2.0 — Matching, sequencing, memory skills   68 ◆◆◆◆◆◆

Mixed-Up Mother Goose — Nursery rhymes, using maps, memory   80 ◆◆◆◆◆◆◆◆

Muppetville — Classifying, memory skills   87 ◆◆◆◆◆◆◆◆

Now You See It, Now You Don't — Memory skills   79 ◆◆◆◆◆◆◆

Ollie and Seymour — Pedestrian safety, memory   77 ◆◆◆◆◆◆◆

Ollie Hears and Remembers — Auditory memory skills   64 ◆◆◆◆◆◆

Ollie Hears and Sequences — Auditory memory skills   64 ◆◆◆◆◆◆

Ollie Remembers It — Visual memory   66 ◆◆◆◆◆◆

Ollie Remembers Numbers! — Visual memory   66 ◆◆◆◆◆◆

Ollie Sequences It! — Visual memory   66 ◆◆◆◆◆◆

Preschool Disk 2 — Matching, counting, adding, memory   75 ◆◆◆◆◆◆◆

Race the Clock — Memory   69 ◆◆◆◆◆◆

Reader Rabbit — Basic reading skills   71 ◆◆◆◆◆◆◆

Shutterbug's Pictures — Memory skills, reading readiness   61 ◆◆◆◆◆◆

Sight Word Spelling — Letter, word, and numeral recognition   39 ◆◆◆

Simon Says — Chaining memory exercise   80 ◆◆◆◆◆◆◆◆

Ted Bear Games — Memory practice   83 ◆◆◆◆◆◆◆◆

Teddy and Iggy — Sequential memory practice   78 ◆◆◆◆◆◆◆

Touch and See — Memory skills   61 ◆◆◆◆◆◆

Treasure Mountain — Reading, thinking, math, and science   82 ◆◆◆◆◆◆◆◆

What's in a Frame? — Memory practice by context clues   81 ◆◆◆◆◆◆◆◆

Winker's World of Numbers — Patterns in sequences of numbers   82 ◆◆◆◆◆◆◆◆

Winker's World of Patterns — Inferring and recognizing patterns   82 ◆◆◆◆◆◆◆◆

ORDERING

Title — Description **Final Rating**

1-2-3 Sequence Me — Sequencing skills   75 ◆◆◆◆◆◆◆

Big and Small — Concepts of big and small   66 ◆◆◆◆◆◆

City Country Opposites — Word meanings through context   78 ◆◆◆◆◆◆◆

Colors and Shapes — Color ID, visual discrimination   76 ◆◆◆◆◆◆◆

Curious George in Outer Space — Size comparisons   62 ◆◆◆◆◆◆

Inside Outside Opposites — Opposites   72 ◆◆◆◆◆◆◆

Logic Blocks — Understanding of geometry, patterns   86 ◆◆◆◆◆◆◆◆

Magic Melody Box — Creating music   59 ◆◆◆◆◆

Math and Me — Shapes, patterns, numbers   78 ◆◆◆◆◆◆◆

Moptown Parade — Classification and seriation   55 ◆◆◆◆◆

Music — Seriation of pitch   59 ◆◆◆◆◆

Music Maker — Creation of music   65 ◆◆◆◆◆◆

My Grand Piano — Learning notes and playing familiar songs   79 ◆◆◆◆◆◆◆

New Talking Stickybear Opposites, The — Opposites, e.g., "near/far"   73 ◆◆◆◆◆◆◆

Notable Phantom, The — Musical notation, pitch recognition   66 ◆◆◆◆◆◆

Patterns — Pattern recognition: shapes, sounds   79 ◆◆◆◆◆◆◆

Patterns and Sequences — Matching/discrimination   72 ◆◆◆◆◆◆◆

Perception, Inc. — Problem solving and thinking skills   71 ◆◆◆◆◆◆◆

Peter's Growing Patterns — Pattern recognition   73 ◆◆◆◆◆◆◆

Shape Starship — Matching shape and size attributes 65 ◆◆◆◆◆◆

Shapes & Patterns — Visual discrimination, cognitive skills 66 ◆◆◆◆◆◆

Simon Says — Chaining memory exercise 80 ◆◆◆◆◆◆◆◆

Size and Logic — Size discrimination, patterns 77 ◆◆◆◆◆◆◆

Stickybear Opposites — Opposites, e.g., "near/far" 73 ◆◆◆◆◆◆◆

Treasure Mountain — Reading, thinking, math, and science 82 ◆◆◆◆◆◆◆◆

Treehouse, The — Comparing pitches of tones 92 ◆◆◆◆◆◆◆◆◆

What's Next — Sequencing skills 74 ◆◆◆◆◆◆◆

Winker's World of Patterns — Inferring and recognizing patterns 82 ◆◆◆◆◆◆◆◆

Woolly Bounce — Force and motion 83 ◆◆◆◆◆◆◆◆

PLANTS AND ANIMALS
Title — Description **Final Rating**

Animal Alphabet and Other Things — Letter recognition, alphabet 81 ◆◆◆◆◆◆◆◆

Animal Photo Fun — Animals and their habitats 70 ◆◆◆◆◆◆◆

Eco-saurus — Ecology facts 59 ◆◆◆◆◆

Farm, The — Creation of a microworld 80 ◆◆◆◆◆◆◆◆

Jungle Safari — African plants and animals 82 ◆◆◆◆◆◆◆◆

Learn About: Animals — Animals, environments, and creative writing 80 ◆◆◆◆◆◆◆◆

Learn About: Plants — Plants, environments, and creative writing 80 ◆◆◆◆◆◆◆◆

Sesame Street Grover's Animal Adventure — Classifying animals 76 ◆◆◆◆◆◆◆

Talking Animals Activity Set — Matching six animals with sounds 74 ◆◆◆◆◆◆◆

Treehouse, The — Animal facts, habitats, and classes 92 ◆◆◆◆◆◆◆◆◆

SPATIAL RELATIONS
Title — Description **Final Rating**

Adventures of Dobot, The — Problem solving, critical thinking 70 ◆◆◆◆◆◆◆

Adventures of Jimmy Jumper, The — Prepositional concepts 69 ◆◆◆◆◆◆

Amy's First Primer 2.2 — Letters, counting, shapes 71 ◆◆◆◆◆◆◆

Animated Shapes — Shapes and colors 71 ◆◆◆◆◆◆◆

Berenstain Bears Junior Jigsaw, The — Spatial problem solving 71 ◆◆◆◆◆◆◆

Bird's Eye View — Perspective and positions 73 ◆◆◆◆◆◆◆

Body Awareness — Location of body parts 64 ◆◆◆◆◆◆

Bozons' Quest — Cognitive strategies, left/right 78 ◆◆◆◆◆◆◆

Color 'n' Canvas — Symmetry, drawing, painting 91 ◆◆◆◆◆◆◆◆◆

Comparison Kitchen — Compare and categorize pictures 72 ◆◆◆◆◆◆◆

Curious George Visits the Library — Position words such as "up," "down" 59 ◆◆◆◆◆

Delta Drawing Today — Drawing, programming concepts 81 ◆◆◆◆◆◆◆◆

Dot-to-Dot Construction Set — Counting, problem solving 72 ◆◆◆◆◆◆◆

Dr. Seuss Fix-Up the Mix-Up Puzzler — Problem solving 70 ◆◆◆◆◆◆◆

Easy Color Paint 2.0 — Drawing, symmetry 84 ◆◆◆◆◆◆◆◆

Easy Street — Classification, matching	84	◆◆◆◆◆◆◆◆
Electronic Builder — Shapes, spatial thinking	82	◆◆◆◆◆◆◆◆
EZ Logo — Problem solving, directionality	74	◆◆◆◆◆◆◆
Firehouse Rescue — Maze navigation	72	◆◆◆◆◆◆◆
First Shapes — Five basic shapes	75	◆◆◆◆◆◆◆
Fun Flyer — Eye-hand coordination, directions	64	◆◆◆◆◆◆
Fun With Directions — Perceptual and cognitive skills	62	◆◆◆◆◆◆
Fun With Drawing — Drawing pictures	71	◆◆◆◆◆◆◆
Gertrude's Secrets — Classifying and seriating	84	◆◆◆◆◆◆◆◆
Goofy's Railway Express — Noticing common shapes	62	◆◆◆◆◆◆
Grandma's House — Exploring and arranging	68	◆◆◆◆◆◆
Inside Outside Shapes — Six shapes and corresponding words	76	◆◆◆◆◆◆◆
Joystick Trainer — Joystick skill practice for children in powered wheelchairs	78	◆◆◆◆◆◆◆
Juggle's Butterfly — Spatial relationships	62	◆◆◆◆◆◆
KidPix — Creation of visual effects	93	◆◆◆◆◆◆◆◆◆
Knowing Directions — Directions of up, down, left, right	66	◆◆◆◆◆◆
Learning Directions — Directions of up, down, left, right	62	◆◆◆◆◆◆
Learning Shapes — Practice with four basic shapes	66	◆◆◆◆◆◆
Little People Bowling Alley — Spatial relationships, addition	70	◆◆◆◆◆◆◆
Logic Blocks — Understanding of geometry, patterns	86	◆◆◆◆◆◆◆◆
McGee — Independent exploration	78	◆◆◆◆◆◆◆
Mickey's Colors & Shapes — Colors and shapes	72	◆◆◆◆◆◆◆
Mickey's Jigsaw Puzzles — Spatial problem solving	85	◆◆◆◆◆◆◆◆
Mixed-Up Mother Goose — Nursery rhymes, using maps, memory	80	◆◆◆◆◆◆◆◆
Mosaic Magic — Spatial problem solving	79	◆◆◆◆◆◆◆
My Puzzles and Alphabet — Spatial problem solving	49	◆◆◆◆
New Talking Stickybear Shapes, The — Identification of five common shapes	75	◆◆◆◆◆◆◆
Parquetry and Pictures — Visual perception, parts and wholes	76	◆◆◆◆◆◆◆
Pattern Blocks 2.1 — Visual imagery, symmetry	77	◆◆◆◆◆◆◆
Peanuts Maze Marathon — Problem solving (mazes)	46	◆◆◆◆
Peanuts Picture Puzzlers — Problem solving (puzzles)	59	◆◆◆◆◆
Perfect Fit — Spatial relationships	70	◆◆◆◆◆◆◆
Peter's Growing Patterns — Pattern recognition	73	◆◆◆◆◆◆◆
Playroom, The — Letters, numbers, and time	91	◆◆◆◆◆◆◆◆◆
Puss in Boot — Spatial concepts	34	◆◆◆
Puzzle Master — Problem solving (puzzles)	79	◆◆◆◆◆◆◆
Puzzle Storybook, The — Writing, creating pictures	66	◆◆◆◆◆◆
Rainbow Painter — Drawing	80	◆◆◆◆◆◆◆◆
School Bus Driver — Coordination, judgment, and recall of details	73	◆◆◆◆◆◆◆
Sesame Street Pals Around Town — Problem solving, classifying animals	NR	
Spaceship Lost — Spatial relationships	45	◆◆◆◆
Spatial Concepts — 24 spatial concepts	61	◆◆◆◆◆◆
Stickers — Creative activity	79	◆◆◆◆◆◆◆
Stickybear Opposites — Opposites, e.g., "near/far"	73	◆◆◆◆◆◆◆
Stickybear Shapes — Shape identification	70	◆◆◆◆◆◆◆

Stickybear Town Builder — Map skills   80 ◆◆◆◆◆◆◆◆
Stone Soup — Creative writing   89 ◆◆◆◆◆◆◆◆
Storybook Weaver — Creating and illustrating stories   83 ◆◆◆◆◆◆◆◆
Surrounding Patterns — Visual imagery, symmetry   77 ◆◆◆◆◆◆◆
Talking Colors and Shapes — Basic colors and shapes   49 ◆◆◆◆
Talking School Bus — Directions, counting, animal sounds 77 ◆◆◆◆◆◆◆
Treehouse, The — Math skills, language, animals   92 ◆◆◆◆◆◆◆◆◆
Where's My Checkered Ball? — Spatial relations   48 ◆◆◆◆

SPECIAL EDUCATION
Title — Description **Final Rating**

Action/Music — Using the computer for speech   80 ◆◆◆◆◆◆◆◆
Adventures of Jimmy Jumper, The — Prepositional concepts   69 ◆◆◆◆◆◆
Big and Small — Concepts of big and small   66 ◆◆◆◆◆◆
Bozons' Quest — Cognitive strategies, left/right   78 ◆◆◆◆◆◆◆
Children's Switch Progressions — Cause and effect, progressions   65 ◆◆◆◆◆◆
Color Find — Matching colors   69 ◆◆◆◆◆◆
Concentrate! — Short-term memory skills   60 ◆◆◆◆◆◆
Creature Chorus — Cause and effect, switch use   78 ◆◆◆◆◆◆◆
Early & Advanced Switch Games — Cause/effect, matching, counting   75 ◆◆◆◆◆◆◆
Early Concepts Skillbuilder Series — Matching, prepositions   60 ◆◆◆◆◆◆
Early-On — Individual case management   NR
Edmark LessonMaker — A utility program   NR
Edmark Reading Program Level 1 — Beginning reading and language   66 ◆◆◆◆◆◆
Exploratory Play — Early language acquisition   71 ◆◆◆◆◆◆◆
First Verbs — Learning 40 common verbs   73 ◆◆◆◆◆◆◆
Fun With Colors — Color recognition   66 ◆◆◆◆◆◆
Human Being Machine, The — Recreation, body parts, sequencing   78 ◆◆◆◆◆◆◆
Joystick Trainer — Joystick skill practice for children in powered wheelchairs 78 ◆◆◆◆◆◆◆
Keytalk — A beginning literacy activity   76 ◆◆◆◆◆◆◆
Knowing Directions — Directions of up, down, left, right   66 ◆◆◆◆◆◆
Learning Directions — Directions of up, down, left, right   62 ◆◆◆◆◆◆
Learning Letters — Matching letters   62 ◆◆◆◆◆◆
Learning Numbers — Counting from 1 to 5   63 ◆◆◆◆◆◆
Learning Shapes — Practice with four basic shapes   66 ◆◆◆◆◆◆
Learning Sight Words — Matching and typing sight words   56 ◆◆◆◆◆
Learning the Alphabet — Alphabet skills   66 ◆◆◆◆◆◆
Micro-LADS — Covers 46 syntax rules   75 ◆◆◆◆◆◆◆
My House: Language Activities of Daily Living — Practice with names of
     common things   77 ◆◆◆◆◆◆◆
Playroom, The — Letters, numbers, and time   91 ◆◆◆◆◆◆◆◆◆
Rabbit Scanner, The — Eye tracking, matching   67 ◆◆◆◆◆◆
Readiness Fun — Cause and effect, scanning   70 ◆◆◆◆◆◆◆
Representational Play — Early language acquisition   71 ◆◆◆◆◆◆◆

Run Rabbit Run — Scanning, directionality, attention   70 ◆◆◆◆◆◆◆

Same and Different — Matching   64 ◆◆◆◆◆◆

Scanning Fun — Visual scanning   72 ◆◆◆◆◆◆◆

Sentence Master Level 1 — Reading skills, vocabulary   75 ◆◆◆◆◆◆◆

Sight Word Spelling — Letter, words, and numerals   39 ◆◆◆

Silly Letters & Numbers — Letter and numeral recognition   70 ◆◆◆◆◆◆◆

Simple Addition — Addition with sums less than nine   69 ◆◆◆◆◆◆

Simple Cause and Effect — Cause and effect   73 ◆◆◆◆◆◆◆

Spell-A-Word — Spelling   53 ◆◆◆◆◆

Talking Nouns I — Language development   80 ◆◆◆◆◆◆◆◆

Talking Nouns II — Language development   80 ◆◆◆◆◆◆◆◆

Talking TouchWindow — Creation of custom lessons   NR

Talking Verbs — Language development   80 ◆◆◆◆◆◆◆◆

Touch and Match — Classification   65 ◆◆◆◆◆◆

Touch and See — Memory skills   61 ◆◆◆◆◆◆

Vocabulary Skillbuilder Series — Vocabulary development   82 ◆◆◆◆◆◆◆◆

Wheels on the Bus — Cause and effect   75 ◆◆◆◆◆◆◆

Words & Concepts — Vocabulary training   80 ◆◆◆◆◆◆◆◆

Words & Concepts II — Vocabulary training   80 ◆◆◆◆◆◆◆◆

Words & Concepts III — Vocabulary training   80 ◆◆◆◆◆◆◆◆

TEMPORAL RELATIONS

Title — Description **Final Rating**

1-2-3 Sequence Me — Sequencing skills   75 ◆◆◆◆◆◆◆

Alice in Wonderland — Remembering a sequence of events   69 ◆◆◆◆◆◆

Animated Memory — Animation concepts   70 ◆◆◆◆◆◆◆

Bake & Taste — Using timers, sequencing   83 ◆◆◆◆◆◆◆◆

Boars Tell Time, The — Clock skills   68 ◆◆◆◆◆◆

Bozons' Quest — Using timing strategies   78 ◆◆◆◆◆◆◆

Caveman Clockwork — Clock drill and practice   45 ◆◆◆◆

Children's Switch Progressions — Cause and effect, progressions   65 ◆◆◆◆◆◆

Chip 'n Dale — Entertainment   53 ◆◆◆◆◆

City Country Opposites — Word meanings through context   78 ◆◆◆◆◆◆◆

Clock Works — Clock-reading skills, units of time   72 ◆◆◆◆◆◆◆

Creature Creator — Pattern matching, programming   62 ◆◆◆◆◆◆

Ducks Ahoy! — Logical reasoning skills   78 ◆◆◆◆◆◆◆

Early & Advanced Switch Games — Cause/effect   75 ◆◆◆◆◆◆◆

Estimation — Estimation of length, area, and time units   78 ◆◆◆◆◆◆◆

Exploring Measure, Time, & Money — Practice with units of time   86 ◆◆◆◆◆◆◆◆

Facemaker — Pattern matching, creative activity   54 ◆◆◆◆◆

Jack and the Beanstalk — Word recognition, event sequence   69 ◆◆◆◆◆◆

Learning About Numbers — Counting, clocks, basic math facts   78 ◆◆◆◆◆◆◆

Picture Parade — Ordering of events   63 ◆◆◆◆◆◆

Playroom, The — Clock practice and exploration   91 ◆◆◆◆◆◆◆◆◆
Professor Al's Sequencing Lab — Sequencing pictures and sentences   64 ◆◆◆◆◆◆
Rabbit Scanner, The — Eye tracking, matching   67 ◆◆◆◆◆◆
Readiness Fun — Cause and effect, scanning   70 ◆◆◆◆◆◆◆
Simple Cause and Effect — Cause and effect   73 ◆◆◆◆◆◆◆
Talking Clock — Clock reading skills   65 ◆◆◆◆◆◆
Telling Time — Clock practice   34 ◆◆◆
Time Master — Clock practice   25 ◆◆
Treehouse, The — Sequencing, clocks, and calendars   92 ◆◆◆◆◆◆◆◆◆
Wheels on the Bus — Cause and effect   75 ◆◆◆◆◆◆◆
Woolly Bounce — Force and motion   83 ◆◆◆◆◆◆◆◆
Working With Days and Months — Order of the days and months   63 ◆◆◆◆◆◆
Working With Time — Matching clock faces   63 ◆◆◆◆◆◆

WORD PROCESSING

Title — Description **Final Rating**

Bank Street Writer III, The — Word processing   71 ◆◆◆◆◆◆◆
Cotton Tales — Word processing   78 ◆◆◆◆◆◆◆
Dr. Peet's Talk/Writer — Language exploration and skills   79 ◆◆◆◆◆◆◆
ESL Writer — Word processing   79 ◆◆◆◆◆◆◆
FirstWriter — Creative writing   76 ◆◆◆◆◆◆◆
Jr. Typer — Touch typing   41 ◆◆◆◆
Keytalk — A beginning literacy activity   76 ◆◆◆◆◆◆◆
Kid Works — Creative writing, drawing, creating   90 ◆◆◆◆◆◆◆◆◆
Kid's Stuff — Counting skills, letter recognition   76 ◆◆◆◆◆◆◆
Kidsword — Large-type word processing   55 ◆◆◆◆◆
KidTalk — Language experience   86 ◆◆◆◆◆◆◆◆
Kidwriter — Creating computer storybooks   73 ◆◆◆◆◆◆◆
Language Experience Recorder Plus — Word processing   55 ◆◆◆◆◆
Magic Slate — Word processing   81 ◆◆◆◆◆◆◆◆
Make-A-Book — Creation of books   67 ◆◆◆◆◆◆
Mount Murdoch — Adventure game and word processor   45 ◆◆◆◆
Muppet Slate — Language experiences   88 ◆◆◆◆◆◆◆◆
Muppet Word Book — Letters and words   82 ◆◆◆◆◆◆◆◆
My Words — Language experience   78 ◆◆◆◆◆◆◆
Playwrite — Writing scripts   82 ◆◆◆◆◆◆◆◆
Primary Editor Plus — Word processing, drawing   74 ◆◆◆◆◆◆◆
Puzzle Storybook, The — Writing, creating pictures   66 ◆◆◆◆◆◆
Read, Write, & Publish 1 — Word processing and story illustrating   81 ◆◆◆◆◆◆◆◆
Rosie the Counting Rabbit — Language experience   89 ◆◆◆◆◆◆◆◆
Sesame Street Print Kit — Creating printed materials   46 ◆◆◆◆
SuperPrint! — Printing utility   62 ◆◆◆◆◆◆
Talking Textwriter — Exploration of written language   75 ◆◆◆◆◆◆◆
Word Processing for Kids — Word processing   78 ◆◆◆◆◆◆◆

APPENDIX 4
SOFTWARE LISTING BY COMPUTER BRAND

APPLE (376 titles)

Title — Computer (* = version reviewed)

1-2-3 Sequence Me — Apple
ABC's — Apple* (128K), IBM, C64
ABC-123 Activities for Learning — Apple*, C64
Action/Music — Apple
Adventures of Dobot, The — Apple*, IBM, C64
Adventures of Jimmy Jumper, The — Apple
Alice in Wonderland — Apple
Alphabet Academy, The — Apple
Alphabet Arcade, The — Apple
Alphabet Circus — Apple*, IBM, C64
Alphabet Express — Apple*, C64, TRS 80
Alphabet Fun: Big and Little Letters — Apple
Alphabet Fun: Learning the Alphabet — Apple
Alphabet Recognition — Apple
Alphabet Sounds — Apple
Alphabet Zoo — Apple*, IBM
Alphabetization & Letter Recognition — Apple
Alphaget — Apple
Animal Alphabet and Other Things — Apple
Animal Hotel — Apple*, IBM, C64
Animal Photo Fun — Apple
Arithmetic Critters — Apple (64K)
Astro's ABCs — Apple
Bake & Taste — Apple, IBM (VGA)
Balancing Bear — Apple
Bald-Headed Chicken, The — Apple (128K)
Bank Street Writer III, The — Apple*, IBM
Big and Small — Apple
Big Book Maker — Apple
Big Red Hat, The — Apple
Bike Hike — Apple*, IBM, C64
Bird's Eye View — Apple*, IBM

Boars Tell Time, The — Apple
Body Awareness — Apple
Bozons' Quest — Apple
Brand New View, A — Apple (128K)
Bremen Town Musicians — Apple
Bumble Games — Apple
Cat 'n Mouse — Apple*, IBM
Charlie Brown's 1-2-3's — Apple
Charlie Brown's ABC's — Apple*, IIGS, IBM
Children's Switch Progressions — Apple
Children's Writing & Publishing Center — Apple*, IBM
City Country Opposites — Apple*
Clue in on Phonics — Apple*, C64, TRS
Color Find — Apple
Color Me — Apple*, IBM, C64
Colors and Shapes — Apple
Comparison Kitchen — Apple*, IBM
Computergarten — Apple*, C64
Concentrate! — Apple
Conservation and Counting — Apple
Consonant Capers — Apple (Echo or Ufonic synthesizer)
Costume Ball, The — Apple*, IBM
Cotton Tales — Apple*, IBM, Mac
Cotton's First Files — Apple
Counters — Apple
Counting and Ordering — Apple
Counting Critters 1.0 — Apple (64K)
Country Combo — Apple
Creature Chorus — Apple
Creature Creator — Apple*, IBM
Curious George Goes Shopping — Apple (2-sided disk)

Curious George in Outer Space — Apple
Curious George Visits the Library — Apple*, IBM
Designasaurus — Apple*, Amiga, IBM, C64
Developing Language Skills — Apple
Dino Speller — Apple
Dinosaur Days Plus — Apple (128K)
Dinosaurs — Apple*, IBM, C64
Dinosaurs Are Forever — Apple* (128K), IBM, C64
Diskovery Adding Machine — Apple
Diskovery Take Away Zoo — Apple
Donald's Alphabet Chase — Apple*, IBM, C64
Dr. Peet's Talk/Writer — Apple
Dr. Seuss Fix-Up the Mix-Up Puzzler — Apple, C64*
Early & Advanced Switch Games — Apple
Early Childhood Learning Program — Apple*, C64
Early Concepts Skillbuilder Series — Apple
Early Elementary I — Apple*, Atari, IBM
Early Elementary II — Apple
Early Games — Apple*, IBM, Mac
Early Skills — Apple
Easy as ABC — Apple*, Mac, IBM
Easy Street — Apple*, IBM, Mac, IIGS
Edmark LessonMaker — Apple
Edmark Reading Program Level 1 — Apple
Electric Company: Bagasaurus — Apple (128K)*, IBM, C64
Electric Company: Picture Place — Apple* (128K), IBM, C64
Electric Company: Roll-A-Word — Apple (128K)*, IBM, C64
Emerging Literacy Program — Apple*, IBM, Mac LC
ESL Writer — Apple
Estimation — Apple
Exploratory Play — Apple (64K)
Extrateletactograph, The — IBM, Apple II+ or IIe* (not IIc)
EZ Logo — Apple (64K)
Facemaker — Apple, IBM*, C64, Atari
Facemaker Golden Edition — Apple*, IBM
Fact Track — Apple*, Atari, IBM, TRS 80
Firehouse Rescue — Apple, IBM*, C64
First "R": Kindergarten, The — Apple
First Encounters — Apple
First Letter Fun — Apple (64K)
FirstWriter — Apple
Fish Dish, The — Apple
Fish Scales — Apple
Flodd, the Bad Guy — Apple*, IBM, Mac
Fun From A to Z — Apple (64K)
Fun on the Farm — Apple* (128K), IBM, C64
Fun With Colors — Apple
Fun With Directions — Apple

Garden, The — IBM, Apple*
Gertrude's Secrets — Apple*, IBM*, C64
Getting Ready to Read and Add — Apple, IBM*, Atari, C64*
Grandma's House — Apple*, C64, Atari
Great Gonzo in WordRider, The — Apple
Great Leap, A — Apple (128K)
Hey Diddle — Apple*, IBM
Hobo's Luck — Apple*, C64
Hodge Podge — Apple*, C64, IBM, Atari
Holidays & Seasons — Apple* (128K), IBM, C64
Home Row — Apple
Hop To It! — Apple
Human Being Machine, The — Apple
I Can Count — Apple
I Can Remember — Apple, IBM*, C64
I Love You in the Sky, Butterfly — Apple*, IBM (3.5" or 5.25")
IEP Generator Version 5.0 — Apple*, IBM
Inside Outside Opposites — Apple
Inside Outside Shapes — Apple
Introduction to Counting — Apple*, IBM, Atari
It's No Game — Apple
Jack and the Beanstalk — Apple
Jack and the Beanstalk — Apple*, IBM, Mac
Jen the Hen — Apple
Joystick Trainer — Apple
Jr. Typer — Apple*, TRS 80
Juggle's Butterfly — Apple*, IBM
Just Around the Block — Apple (128K)
Keytalk — Apple* (64K), IBM
Kid's Stuff — IBM*, Apple, Atari ST
Kids at Work — Apple
Kids on Keys — Apple*, IBM
Kidsword — Apple*, C64
Kidwriter — Apple*, IBM (3.5")
Kinder Critters — Apple
Kinder Koncepts MATH — Apple
Kinder Koncepts Reading — Apple
Kindercomp — Apple, IBM*
Kindercomp Golden Edition — Apple*, IBM (3.5")
Kindermath II — Apple (64K)
Knowing Directions — Apple
Knowing Numbers — Apple
Koala Pad Graphics Exhibitor — Apple IIe*, IBM
Language Experience Recorder Plus — Apple
Learn About: Animals — Apple (128K, 3.5" or 5.25")
Learn About: Plants — Apple (128K, 3.5" or 5.25")
Learn the Alphabet — Apple*, IBM, C64 (cartridge)
Learn to Add — Apple*, IBM
Learning About Numbers — Apple
Learning Directions — Apple

Learning Letters — Apple
Learning Numbers — Apple
Learning Shapes — Apple
Learning Sight Words — Apple
Learning the Alphabet — Apple
Letter Games — Apple
Letter Recognition — Apple
Letters and First Words — Apple
Letters and Words — Apple*, IBM
Letters, Pictures & Words — Apple
Lion's Workshop — Apple*, C64
Little People Bowling Alley — Apple, IBM*, C64
Looney Tunes Print Kit — Apple*, IBM, C64, Atari
Magic Crayon — Apple
Magic Slate — Apple
Magic String, The — Apple
Mask Parade — Apple*, IBM
Math and Me — Apple* (128K), IBM, IIGS
Math Magic — Apple*, IBM
Math Maze — Apple*, IBM, Atari, C64
Math Rabbit — Apple*, IBM
Math Sequences — Apple
Mathematics Level A — Apple* (128K), IBM
Mathosaurus Level K — Apple
Measure Works — Apple (128K, 3.5" or 5.25")
Memory Building Blocks — Apple
Mickey's Crossword Puzzle Maker — IBM, Apple*
Mickey's Magic Reader — Apple
Micro-LADS — Apple
Microzine Jr. (Sept/Oct.'88) — Apple
Milk Bottles — Apple
Mixed-Up Mother Goose — Apple*, IBM*, Mac, IIGS, Atari ST
Money Works — Apple (128K)
Monkey Math — Apple*, C64, Atari
Monsters & Make-Believe — Apple*, Mac, IBM
Monsters & Make-Believe Plus — Apple (128K)
Moptown Parade — Apple*, IBM*, C64
Mount Murdoch — Apple*, IBM, C64
Mr. and Mrs. Potato Head — Apple
Muppet Slate — Apple
Muppet Word Book — Apple
Muppets On Stage — Apple*, IBM, C64
Muppetville — Apple
Music — Apple
My Grand Piano — Apple, IBM, C64*
My House: Language Activities of Daily Living — Apple* (Echo)
My Letters, Numbers, and Words — Apple, IBM*, Atari ST
My Words — Apple (64K)
Not Too Messy, Not Too Neat — Apple

Notable Phantom, The — Apple*, IBM, C64
Now You See It, Now You Don't — Apple
Number Farm — Apple*, C64, IBM
Number Sea Hunt — Apple*, TRS 80, C64
Numbers — Apple
Observation and Classification — Apple
Odd One Out — Apple*, C64
Ollie and Seymour — Apple
Ollie Begins It — Apple
Ollie Compares It — Apple
Ollie Finds It! — Apple
Ollie Hears and Remembers — Apple
Ollie Hears and Sequences — Apple
Ollie Letters It — Apple
Ollie Matches It — Apple
Ollie Numbers It — Apple
Ollie Remembers It — Apple
Ollie Remembers Numbers! — Apple
Ollie Sequences It! — Apple
Once Upon a Time... — Apple (128K), IBM* (256K), Mac
One Banana More — Apple
Paint With Words — Apple (64K)
Parquetry and Pictures — Apple
Path-Tactics — Apple*, IBM, C64
Patterns — Apple
Patterns and Sequences — Apple
Peanuts Maze Marathon — Apple*, IBM
Peanuts Picture Puzzlers — Apple*, IBM
Perception, Inc. — Apple
Perfect Fit — Apple, IBM*, C64
Peter's Growing Patterns — Apple
Phonics Prime Time: Initial Consonants — Apple
Picture Chompers — Apple
Picture Parade — Apple
Picture Perfect — Apple*, IBM
Pictures, Letters, and Sounds — Apple
Playroom, The — IBM, Mac* (color version available), Apple
Preschool IQ Builder I — Apple*
Preschool IQ Builder II — Apple*
Princess and the Pea, The — Apple* (3.5" or 5.25"), Mac LC
Print Power — Apple (128K)
Print Shop, The — Apple*, Mac, IBM, C64, Atari, IIGS*
Professor Al's Sequencing Lab — Apple
Puss in Boot — Apple
Puzzle Master — Apple*
Quarter Mile, The — Apple
Rabbit Scanner, The — Apple
Race the Clock — Apple*, IBM
Rainbow Painter — Apple*
Read, Write, & Publish 1 — Apple* (128K), IBM

Read-a-Logo — Apple (network version available)
Reader Rabbit — Apple*, IBM, C64, Mac, IIGS
Readiness Fun — Apple
Reading and Me — Apple* (128K), IBM, IIGS
Reading Comprehension: Level 1 — Apple (64K)
Reading Fun: Beginning Consonants — Apple
Reading Fun: Final Consonants — Apple
Reading Fun: Vowel Sounds — Apple
Reading Helpers — Apple (64K)
Reading I — Apple*, C64
Reading Machine, The — Apple
Reading Starters — Apple (64K)
Representational Play — Apple (64K)
Robot Writer Plus — Apple*, IBM
Rosie the Counting Rabbit — Apple (128K), Mac LC
Rumpelstiltskin — Apple
Run Rabbit Run — Apple
Same and Different — Apple
Same or Different — Apple*, C64
Scanning Fun — Apple
School Bus Driver — IBM*, Apple, C64
Sentence Master Level 1 — Apple (Echo synthesizer required)
Sesame Street Astro-Grover — Apple, IBM, C64*
Sesame Street Big Bird's Special Delivery — C64*, IBM, Apple
Sesame Street Crayon: Letters for You — Apple* (128K), IBM, C64, Amiga
Sesame Street Crayon: Numbers Count — Apple* (128K), IBM, C64, Amiga
Sesame Street Crayon: Opposites Attract — Apple* (128K), IBM, C64, Amiga
Sesame Street Ernie's Magic Shapes — C64*, Atari, IBM, Apple
Sesame Street First Writer — Apple* (128K), IBM
Sesame Street Learning Library 1 — Apple, IBM, Nintendo
Sesame Street Letter-Go-Round — Apple, C64*, IBM, Atari
Sesame Street Print Kit — Apple*, IBM, C64, Atari
Shape & Color Rodeo — Apple*, IBM, C64
Shape Starship — Apple*, C64, TRS 80
Shapes & Patterns — Apple
Shutterbug's Patterns — Apple*, C64
Shutterbug's Pictures — Apple*, C64
Sight Word Spelling — Apple
Silly Letters & Numbers — Apple
Simon Says — Apple*, C64
Simple Addition — Apple
Simple Cause and Effect — Apple
Size and Logic — Apple
Sleepy Brown Cow, The — Apple (128K)
SocPix — Apple

Sound Ideas: Consonants — Apple (64K)
Sound Ideas: Vowels — Apple (64K)
Sound Ideas: Word Attack — Apple (64K)
Space Waste Race — Apple*, Atari, TRS 80
Spaceship Lost — Apple
Spatial Concepts — Apple
Spell-A-Word — Apple
Spellicopter — Apple*, IBM, C64
Spelling and Reading Primer — Apple*, IBM, C64
Spelling Bee, The — Apple
Stepping Stones Level I — Apple, IBM*, Mac
Stepping Stones Level II — Apple*, IBM, Mac
Stickers — Apple, IBM*
Stickybear ABC — Apple*, Atari, C64
Stickybear Math — Apple*, IBM, C64
Stickybear Numbers — Apple*, IBM, C64
Stickybear Opposites — Apple*, Atari, C64
Stickybear Printer — Apple
Stickybear Reading — Apple*, IBM, C64
Stickybear Shapes — Apple*, Atari, C64, IBM
Stickybear Town Builder — Apple*, C64
Stickybear Typing — Apple*, IBM, C64
Stone Soup — Apple*, IBM (3.5" or 5.25"), Mac LC
SuperPrint! — Apple*, Mac, IBM
Surrounding Patterns — Apple*, C64
Talk About a Walk — Apple
Talking Nouns I — Apple (128K)
Talking Nouns II — Apple (128K)
Talking Textwriter — Apple* (128K), IIGS, IBM
Talking TouchWindow — Apple
Talking Verbs — Apple (128K)
Ted Bear Games — Apple*, C64, Atari, Mac
Teddy and Iggy — Apple*, C64
Teddy Bear-rels of Fun — Apple*, C64
Teddy Bears Counting Fun — Apple
Teddy's Playground — Apple
Telling Time — Apple*, C64, TRS 80, IBM, Atari, PET
This Land Is Your Land — Apple* (128K), IBM, C64
Three Little Pigs, The — Apple*, Mac LC
Tiger's Tales — Apple*, C64
Time Master — Apple
Tink! Tonk! — Apple*, C64, IBM
Tonk in the Land of Buddy-Bots — Apple*, C64, IBM
Touch & Write — Apple
Touch and Match — Apple
Touch and See — Apple
Toybox — Apple (128K), IBM, C64*
Treehouse, The — IBM*, Apple
Vocabulary Skillbuilder Series — Apple
Webster's Numbers — Apple*, C64
What Makes a Dinosaur Sore? — Apple

What's in a Frame? — Apple
What's Next — Apple*, C64
Wheels on the Bus — Apple
Where Did My Toothbrush Go? — Apple
Which Number Is Missing? — Apple*, IBM, C64
Whole Neighborhood, The — Apple*, IBM
Winker's World of Numbers — Apple
Winker's World of Patterns — Apple
Woolly Bounce — Apple
Word Factory — Apple

Word Munchers — Apple*, IBM
Words — Apple
Words & Concepts — Apple
Words & Concepts II — Apple
Words & Concepts III — Apple
Working With Days and Months — Apple
Working With Numbers — Apple
Working With the Alphabet — Apple
Working With Time — Apple
Write On: Primary Level — Apple*, IBM, Mac

IBM (202 titles)

Title — Computer (* = version reviewed)

ABC's — Apple* (128K), IBM, C64
Adventures of Dobot, The — Apple*, IBM, C64
Alphabet Circus — Apple*, IBM, C64
Alphabet Zoo — Apple*, IBM, C64
Amy's First Primer 2.2 — IBM
Animal Hotel — Apple*, IBM, C64
Animated Alphabet — IBM (VGA)
Animated Math — IBM (hard disk and EGA)
Animated Memory — IBM (VGA and hard drive)
Animated Shapes — IBM (VGA and hard drive)
Bake & Taste — Apple, IBM (VGA)
Bank Street Writer III, The — Apple*, IBM
Berenstain Bears Fun With Colors, The — IBM (VGA, hard disk)
Berenstain Bears Junior Jigsaw, The — IBM
Berenstain Bears Learn About Counting, The — IBM (VGA, CGA)
Berenstain Bears Learn About Letters, The — IBM* (CGA, VGA, 2.6MB of hard disk required)
Bike Hike — Apple*, IBM, C64
Bird's Eye View — Apple*, IBM
Bouncy Bee Learns Letters 1.0 — IBM
Bouncy Bee Learns Words 1.0 — IBM
Brandon's Bigbox — IBM (CGA)
Cat 'n Mouse — Apple*, IBM
Caveman Clockwork — IBM (VGA)
Charlie Brown's ABC's — Apple*, IIGS, IBM
Children's Writing & Publishing Center — Apple*, IBM
Chip 'n Dale — IBM (CGA or EGA)
Chutes and Ladders — IBM
Color Me — Apple*, IBM, C64
Comparison Kitchen — Apple*, IBM
Costume Ball, The — Apple*, IBM
Cotton Tales — Apple*, IBM, Mac
Creature Creator — Apple*, IBM

Curious George Visits the Library — Apple*, IBM
Daffy Duck, P.I. — IBM (CGA or VGA)
Delta Drawing Today — IBM
Designasaurus — Apple*, Amiga, IBM, C64
Dinosaur Discovery Kit, The — IBM*, IIGS, Mac, Amiga
Dinosaurs — Apple*, IBM, C64
Dinosaurs Are Forever — Apple* (128K), IBM, C64
Donald's Alphabet Chase — Apple*, IBM, C64
Early Elementary I — Apple*, Atari, IBM
Early Games — Apple*, IBM, Mac
Early-On — IBM
Easy as ABC — Apple*, Mac, IBM
Easy Street — Apple*, IBM, Mac, IIGS
Eco-Saurus — Mac, IBM* (VGA, hard disk, speech device)
Electric Company: Bagasaurus — Apple (128K)*, IBM, C64
Electric Company: Picture Place — Apple* (128K), IBM, C64
Electric Company: Roll-A-Word — Apple (128K)*, IBM, C64
Electronic Builder — IBM
Electronic Easel — IBM
Emerging Literacy Program — Apple*, IBM, Mac LC
Exploring Measure, Time, & Money — IBM (3.5")
Extrateletactograph, The — IBM, Apple II+ or IIe* (not IIc)
Facemaker — Apple, IBM*, C64, Atari
Facemaker Golden Edition — Apple*, IBM (3.5" disk)
Fact Track — Apple*, Atari, IBM, TRS 80
Farm, The — IBM
Firehouse Rescue — Apple, IBM*, C64
Flodd, the Bad Guy — Apple*, IBM, Mac
Fun Flyer — IBM, 5 1/4 inch disk, CGA, 256K
Fun on the Farm — Apple* (128K), IBM, C64

Fun With Drawing — IBM
Fun With Letters and Words — IBM
Fun With Memory — IBM
Fun With Numbers — IBM
Garden, The — Apple*, IBM
Gertrude's Secrets — Apple*, IBM*, C64
Getting Ready to Read and Add — Apple, IBM*, Atari, C64*
Goofy's Railway Express — IBM, C64
Hey Diddle — Apple*, IBM
Hodge Podge — Apple*, C64, IBM, Atari
Holidays & Seasons — Apple* (128K), IBM, C64
I Can Count the Petals of a Flower — IBM
I Can Remember — Apple, IBM*, C64
I Love You in the Sky, Butterfly — Apple*, IBM
IEP Generator Version 5.0 — Apple*, IBM
Integrated Learning System — IIGS, IBM*, Mac
Introduction to Counting — Apple*, IBM, Atari
Jack and the Beanstalk — Apple*, IBM, Mac
Juggle's Butterfly — IBM, Apple*
Jungle Safari — IIGS* (1 MB), IBM (with Covox)
Katie's Farm — IIGS*, Mac, IBM (VGA or CGA), Mac II, Amiga
Keytalk — Apple* (64K), IBM
Kid Works — IBM (640K, VGA, printer, mouse, hard disk)
Kid's Stuff — IBM*, Apple, Atari ST
KidPix — Mac* (color or B&W), IBM (VGA and hard disk)
Kids on Keys — Apple*, IBM
KidsTime — Mac*, IIGS, IBM
KidWare 2 Learning Center — IBM
Kidwriter — Apple*, IBM (3.5")
Kindercomp — Apple, IBM*
Kindercomp Golden Edition — Apple*, IBM (3.5")
Koala Pad Graphics Exhibitor — Apple IIe*, IBM
Learn the Alphabet — Apple*, IBM, C64 (cartridge)
Learn to Add — Apple*, IBM
Letters and Words — Apple*, IBM
Little People Bowling Alley — Apple, IBM*, C64
Looney Tunes Print Kit — Apple*, IBM, C64, Atari
Make-A-Book — IBM
Mask Parade — Apple*, IBM
Match Maker (Beginning) — IBM
Math and Me — Apple* (128K), IBM, IIGS
Math Blaster Plus — Mac* 1 MB (2MB for color), IBM (CGA and VGA)
Math Concepts Level P — IBM
Math Magic — Apple*, IBM
Math Maze — Apple*, IBM, Atari, C64
Math Rabbit — Apple*, IBM
Mathematics Level A — Apple* (128K), IBM

McGee — IIGS (3.5"), IBM (VGA or CGA), Mac, Amiga
McGee at the Fun Fair — IIGS*, Mac, IBM (VGA or CGA)
Memory Lane 2.0 — IBM* (VGA or CGA), Atari ST
Mickey & Minnie's Fun Time Print Kit — IBM (CGA, VGA)
Mickey's 123's — IBM
Mickey's ABC's — IBM
Mickey's Colors & Shapes — IBM (VGA, Sound Source recommended)
Mickey's Crossword Puzzle Maker — IBM, Apple*
Mickey's Jigsaw Puzzles — IBM (VGA)
Mickey's Runaway Zoo: Fun With Numbers — IBM*, C64
Milliken Storyteller, The — IIGS*, Mac, IBM (requires Covox for speech)
Mixed-Up Mother Goose — Apple*, IBM*, Mac, IIGS, Atari ST
Monsters & Make-Believe — Apple*, Mac, IBM
Moptown Parade — Apple*, IBM*, C64
Mosaic Magic — IBM (CGA, VGA)
Mount Murdoch — Apple*, IBM, C64
Muppets On Stage — Apple*, IBM, C64
Mural Maker — IBM
Music Maker — IBM
My ABC's — IBM
My Grand Piano — C64*, Apple, IBM
My Letters, Numbers, and Words — IBM*, Apple, Atari ST
My Puzzles and Alphabet — IBM
New Talking Stickybear Alphabet, The — IIGS (512K, 3.5"), IBM with Echo or Covox
New Talking Stickybear Shapes, The — IIGS (3.5"), IBM with Covox or Echo)
Notable Phantom, The — Apple*, IBM, C64
Number Farm — Apple*, C64, IBM
Once Upon a Time... — IBM* (256K), Apple (128K), Mac
Path-Tactics — Apple*, IBM, C64
Peanuts Maze Marathon — Apple*, IBM
Peanuts Picture Puzzlers — Apple*, IBM
Perfect Fit — Apple, IBM*, C64
Phonics Plus — IBM
Picture Perfect — Apple*, IBM
Playroom, The — Apple, IBM, Mac* (color version available)
Primary Editor Plus — IBM PS/2
Print Shop, The — Apple*, Mac, IBM, C64, Atari, IIGS*
Puzzle Storybook, The — IBM*, IIGS, Mac, Amiga
Race the Clock — Apple*, IBM
Read, Write, & Publish 1 — Apple* (128K), IBM
Reader Rabbit — Apple*, IBM, C64, Mac, IIGS
Reading and Me — Apple* (128K), IBM, IIGS
Robot Writer Plus — Apple*, IBM

School Bus Driver — IBM*, Apple, C64

School Mom — IBM (CGA)

Sesame Street Astro-Grover — Apple, IBM, C64*

Sesame Street Big Bird's Special Delivery — C64*, IBM, Apple

Sesame Street Crayon: Letters for You — Apple* (128K), IBM, C64, Amiga

Sesame Street Crayon: Numbers Count — Apple* (128K), IBM, C64, Amiga

Sesame Street Crayon: Opposites Attract — Apple* (128K), IBM, C64, Amiga

Sesame Street Ernie's Big Splash — C64*, IBM

Sesame Street Ernie's Magic Shapes — C64*, Atari, IBM, Apple

Sesame Street First Writer — Apple* (128K), IBM

Sesame Street Grover's Animal Adventures — C64*, IBM

Sesame Street Learning Library 1 — Apple, IBM, Nintendo

Sesame Street Learning Library 2 — IBM, Nintendo

Sesame Street Letter-Go-Round — C64*, IBM, Atari, Apple

Sesame Street Pals Around Town — C64*, IBM

Sesame Street Print Kit — Apple*, IBM, C64, Atari

Shape & Color Rodeo — Apple*, IBM, C64

Spellicopter — Apple*, IBM, C64

Spelling and Reading Primer — Apple*, IBM, C64

Stars & Planets — IIGS*, IBM (3.5" or 5.25")

Stepping Stones Level I — Apple, IBM*, Mac

Stepping Stones Level II — Apple*, IBM, Mac

Stickers — Apple, IBM*

Stickybear Math — Apple*, IBM, C64

Stickybear Numbers — Apple*, IBM, C64

Stickybear Reading — Apple*, IBM, C64

Stickybear Shapes — Apple*, Atari, C64, IBM

Stickybear Typing — Apple*, IBM, C64

Stone Soup — Apple*, IBM (3.5" or 5.25"), Mac LC

SuperPrint! — Apple*, Mac, IBM

Talking Alpha Chimp — IIGS*, IBM (3.5")

Talking Classroom — IIGS (1 MB), IBM (Covox)

Talking Clock — IIGS* (512K, 3.5"), IBM

Talking School Bus — IIGS*, IBM

Talking Textwriter — Apple* (128K), IIGS, IBM

Telling Time — Apple*, C64, TRS 80, IBM, Atari, PET

This Land Is Your Land — Apple* (128K), IBM, C64

Tink! Tonk! — Apple*, C64, IBM

Tonk in the Land of Buddy-Bots — Apple*, C64, IBM

Toybox — C64*, Apple (128K), IBM

Treasure Mountain — IBM (CGA, VGA)

Treehouse, The — IBM* (VGA, hard disk, speech device)

Which Number Is Missing? — Apple*, IBM, C64

Whole Neighborhood, The — Apple*, IBM

Word Munchers — Apple*, IBM

Word Processing for Kids — IBM

Write On: Primary Level — Apple*, IBM, Mac

Writing To Read 2.0 — IBM

Wunder Book — IBM (VGA)

Young Math — IBM*, Atari ST

C64 (97 titles)

Title — Computer (* = version reviewed)

ABC's — Apple* (128K), IBM, C64

ABC-123 Activities for Learning — Apple*, C64

Adventures of Dobot, The — Apple*, IBM, C64

Alphabet Circus — Apple*, IBM, C64

Alphabet Express — Apple*, C64, TRS 80

Alphabet Zoo — Apple*, IBM, C64

Animal Hotel — Apple*, IBM, C64

Bike Hike — Apple*, IBM, C64

Clue in on Phonics — Apple*, C64, TRS

Color Me — Apple*, IBM, C64

Computergarten — Apple*, C64

Designasaurus — Apple*, IBM, C64

Dinosaurs — Apple*, IBM, C64

Dinosaurs Are Forever — Apple* (128K), IBM, C64

Donald's Alphabet Chase — Apple*, IBM, C64

Dr. Seuss Fix-Up the Mix-Up Puzzler — Apple, C64*

Ducks Ahoy! — C64 (cartridge)

Early Childhood Learning Program — Apple*, C64

Electric Company: Bagasaurus — Apple (128K)*, IBM, C64

Electric Company: Picture Place — Apple* (128K), IBM, C64

Electric Company: Roll-A-Word — Apple (128K)*, IBM, C64

Facemaker — Apple, IBM*, C64, Atari

Firehouse Rescue — Apple, IBM*, C64

Fun on the Farm — Apple* (128K), IBM, C64

Gertrude's Secrets — Apple*, IBM*, C64

Getting Ready to Read and Add — Apple, IBM*, Atari, C64*

Goofy's Railway Express — IBM, C64

Grandma's House — Apple*, C64, Atari

Hobo's Luck — Apple*, C64

Hodge Podge — Apple*, C64, IBM, Atari

Holidays & Seasons — Apple* (128K), IBM, C64

I Can Remember — Apple, IBM*, C64

Kermit's Electronic Storymaker — C64

Kidsword — Apple*, C64

Kindercomp — Apple, IBM*

Learn the Alphabet — Apple*, IBM, C64 (cartridge)

Lion's Workshop — Apple*, C64

Little People Bowling Alley — Apple, IBM*, C64

Looney Tunes Print Kit — Apple*, IBM, C64, Atari

Math Maze — Apple*, IBM, Atari, C64

Mickey's Runaway Zoo: Fun With Numbers — IBM*, C64

Monkey Math — Apple*, C64, Atari

Moptown Parade — Apple*, IBM*, C64

Mount Murdoch — Apple*, IBM, C64

Muppets On Stage — Apple*, IBM, C64

My Grand Piano — C64*, Apple, IBM

Notable Phantom, The — Apple*, IBM, C64

Number Farm — Apple*, C64, IBM

Number Sea Hunt — Apple*, TRS 80, C64

Odd One Out — Apple*, C64

Path-Tactics — Apple*, IBM, C64

Perfect Fit — Apple, IBM*, C64

Print Shop, The — Apple*, Mac, IBM, C64, Atari, IIGS*

Reader Rabbit — Apple*, IBM, C64, Mac, IIGS

Reading I — Apple*, C64

Same or Different — Apple*, C64

School Bus Driver — IBM*, Apple, C64

Sesame Street Astro-Grover — Apple, IBM, C64*

Sesame Street Big Bird's Special Delivery — C64*, IBM, Apple

Sesame Street Crayon: Letters for You — Apple* (128K), IBM, C64, Amiga

Sesame Street Crayon: Numbers Count — Apple* (128K), IBM, C64, Amiga

Sesame Street Crayon: Opposites Attract — Apple* (128K), IBM, C64, Amiga

Sesame Street Ernie's Big Splash — C64*, IBM

Sesame Street Ernie's Magic Shapes — C64*, Atari, IBM, Apple

Sesame Street Grover's Animal Adventures — C64*, IBM

Sesame Street Letter-Go-Round — C64*, IBM, Atari, Apple

Sesame Street Pals Around Town — C64*, IBM

Sesame Street Print Kit — Apple*, IBM, C64, Atari

Shape & Color Rodeo — Apple*, IBM, C64

Shape Starship — Apple*, C64, TRS 80

Shutterbug's Patterns — Apple*, C64

Shutterbug's Pictures — Apple*, C64

Simon Says — Apple*, C64

Spellicopter — Apple*, IBM, C64

Spelling and Reading Primer — Apple*, IBM, C64

Stickybear ABC — Apple*, Atari, C64

Stickybear Math — Apple*, IBM, C64

Stickybear Numbers — Apple*, IBM, C64

Stickybear Opposites — Apple*, Atari, C64

Stickybear Reading — Apple*, IBM, C64

Stickybear Shapes — Apple*, Atari, C64, IBM

Stickybear Town Builder — Apple*, C64

Stickybear Typing — Apple*, IBM, C64

Surrounding Patterns — Apple*, C64

Ted Bear Games — Apple*, C64, Atari, Mac

Teddy and Iggy — Apple*, C64

Teddy Bear-rels of Fun — Apple*, C64

Telling Time — Apple*, C64, TRS 80, IBM, Atari, PET

This Land Is Your Land — Apple* (128K), IBM, C64

Tiger's Tales — Apple*, C64

Tink! Tonk! — Apple*, C64, IBM

Tonk in the Land of Buddy-Bots — Apple*, C64, IBM

Toybox — Apple (128K), IBM, C64*

Webster's Numbers — Apple*, C64

What's Next — Apple*, C64

Which Number Is Missing? — Apple*, IBM, C64

Whole Neighborhood, The — Apple*, IBM

MACINTOSH (56 titles)

Title — Computer (* = version reviewed)

Alphabet Blocks — Mac (1 MB)

Alphabet for Everyone — Mac (Hypercard 1.2.2)

Clock Works — Mac

Coin Works — Mac

Cotton Tales — Apple*, IBM, Mac

Dinosaur Discovery Kit, The — IBM*, IIGS, Mac, Amiga

Dot-to-Dot Construction Set — Mac

Dragon Tales — Mac LC (CD ROM fileserver required)

Early Games — Apple*, IBM, Mac

Easy as ABC — Apple*, Mac, IBM

Easy Color Paint 2.0 — Mac
Easy Street — Apple*, IBM, Mac, IIGS
Eco-Saurus — Mac, IBM* (VGA, hard disk, speech device)
Emerging Literacy Program — Apple*, IBM, Mac LC
First Letters and Words — IIGS*, Mac, Amiga, Atari ST
First Shapes — IIGS*, Mac, Amiga, Atari ST
Flodd, the Bad Guy — Apple*, IBM, Mac
Integrated Learning System — IIGS, IBM*, Mac
Jack and the Beanstalk — Apple*, IBM, Mac
Katie's Farm — IIGS*, Mac, IBM (VGA or CGA), Mac II, Amiga
KidPix — Mac* (color or B&W), IBM (VGA and hard drive)
KidsMath — Mac (512K)
KidsTime — Mac*, IIGS, IBM
KidTalk — Mac*, IIGS*, Atari ST, Amiga
Kieran — Mac
Let's Go To Hannah's House — Mac (hard disk, Hypercard)
Match-On-A-Mac — Mac
Math Blaster Plus — Mac* 1 MB (2MB for color), IBM (CGA and VGA)
McGee — IIGS (3.5"), IBM (VGA or CGA), Mac, Amiga
McGee at the Fun Fair — IIGS*, Mac, IBM (VGA or CGA), Mac II
Milliken Storyteller, The — IIGS*, Mac, IBM
Mixed-Up Mother Goose — Apple*, IBM*, Mac, IIGS, Atari ST

Monsters & Make-Believe — Apple*, Mac, IBM
NumberMaze — Mac (512K)
Once Upon a Time... — IBM* (256K), — Apple (128K), Mac
Pattern Blocks 2.1 — Mac
Playroom, The — IBM, Mac* (color version available), Apple
Preschool Disk 1 — Mac (512K)
Preschool Disk 2 — Mac (512K)
Preschool Pack — Mac (1 MB, hard disk recommended)
Princess and the Pea, The — Apple* (3.5" or 5.25"), Mac LC
Print Shop, The — Apple*, Mac, IBM, C64, Atari, IIGS*
Puzzle Storybook, The — IBM*, IIGS, Mac, Amiga
Reader Rabbit — Apple*, IBM, C64, Mac, IIGS
ReadingMaze — Mac
Rosie the Counting Rabbit — Apple (128K), Mac LC
Stepping Stones Level I — Apple, IBM*, Mac
Stepping Stones Level II — Apple*, IBM, Mac
Stone Soup — Apple*, IBM (3.5" or 5.25"), Mac LC
SuperPrint! — Apple*, Mac, IBM
Talking Tiles — Mac (1 MB)
Ted Bear Games — Apple*, C64, Atari, Mac
Three Little Pigs, The — Apple*, Mac LC
Treehouse, The — IBM* (VGA, hard disk, speech device), Mac
Where's My Checkered Ball? — Mac
Write On: Primary Level — Apple*, IBM, Mac

APPLE IIGS (48 titles)

Title — Computer (* = version reviewed)
Note: These titles are specially designed for the Apple IIGS. They will not run on Apple IIe or IIc computers. Software listed in this Appendix for the Apple IIe or IIc computers will generally run on Apple IIGS computers.

Base Ten Blocks — IIGS
Charlie Brown's ABC's — Apple*, IIGS, IBM
Color 'n' Canvas — IIGS (1 mb)
Dinosaur Discovery Kit, The — IBM*, IIGS, Mac, Amiga
Easy Street — Apple*, IBM, Mac, IIGS
First Letters and Words — IIGS*, Mac, Amiga, Atari ST
First Shapes — IIGS*, Mac, Amiga, Atari ST
First Verbs — IIGS
Integrated Learning System — IIGS, IBM*, Mac
Jungle Safari — IIGS* (1 MB), IBM (with Covox)
Katie's Farm — IIGS*, Mac, IBM (VGA or CGA), Mac II, Amiga
KidsTime — Mac*, IIGS, IBM
KidTalk — Mac*, IIGS*, Atari ST, Amiga
Logic Blocks — IIGS

Mad Match — IIGS
Math and Me — Apple* (128K), IBM, IIGS
McGee — IIGS (3.5"), IBM (VGA or CGA), Mac, Amiga
McGee at the Fun Fair — IIGS*, Mac, IBM (VGA or CGA), Mac II
Milliken Storyteller, The — IIGS*, Mac, IBM (requires Covox for speech)
Mixed-Up Mother Goose — Apple*, IBM*, Mac, IIGS, Atari ST
My House: Language Activities of Daily Living — Apple* (Echo synthesizer required), IIGS
New Talking Stickybear Alphabet, The — IIGS (512K, 3.5"), IBM (with Echo or Covox)
New Talking Stickybear Opposites, The — IIGS
New Talking Stickybear Shapes, The — IIGS (3.5"), IBM (with Covox or Echo)

Playwrite — IIGS (1 MB)
Print Shop, The — Apple*, Mac, IBM, C64, Atari, IIGS*
Puzzle Storybook, The — IBM*, IIGS, Mac, Amiga
Reader Rabbit — Apple*, IBM, C64, Mac, IIGS
Reading and Me — Apple* (128K), IBM, IIGS
Stars & Planets — IIGS*, IBM (3.5" or 5.25")
Storybook Weaver — IIGS (note: two 3 1/2 inch disk drives required)
Super GS Award Maker — IIGS
Talking ABC's — IIGS (512K, 3.5")
Talking Alpha Chimp — IIGS*, IBM (3.5")
Talking Animals Activity Set — IIGS
Talking Classroom — IIGS (1 MB), IBM (Covox)

Talking Clock — IIGS* (512K, 3.5"), IBM
Talking Colors and Shapes — IIGS (3.5")
Talking Dinosaurs — IIGS (3.5")
Talking First Reader — IIGS (one 3.5" disk)
Talking First Words — IIGS
Talking First Writer — IIGS (3.5")
Talking Money — IIGS (3.5")
Talking Numbers — IIGS (one 3.5" disk)
Talking Reading Railroad — IIGS (3.5")
Talking School Bus — IIGS*, IBM
Talking Speller — IIGS (3.5")
Talking Textwriter — Apple* (128K), IIGS, IBM

ATARI (28 titles)

Title — Computer (* = version reviewed)

Early Elementary — Apple*, Atari, IBM
Facemaker — Apple, IBM*, C64, Atari
Fact Track — Apple*, Atari, IBM, TRS 80
First Letters and Words — IIGS*, Mac, Amiga, Atari ST
First Shapes — IIGS*, Mac, Amiga, Atari ST
Getting Ready to Read and Add — Apple, IBM*, Atari, C64*
Grandma's House — Apple*, C64, Atari
Hodge Podge — Apple*, C64, IBM, Atari
Introduction to Counting — Apple*, IBM, Atari
Kid's Stuff — IBM*, Apple, Atari ST
KidTalk — Mac*, IIGS*, Atari ST, Amiga
Looney Tunes Print Kit — Apple*, IBM, C64, Atari
Math Maze — Apple*, IBM, Atari, C64
Memory Lane 2.0 — IBM* (VGA or CGA), Atari ST
Mixed-Up Mother Goose — Apple*, IBM*, Mac, IIGS, Atari ST

Monkey Math — Apple*, C64, Atari
My Letters, Numbers, and Words — Apple, IBM*, Atari ST
Print Shop, The — Apple*, Mac, IBM, C64, Atari, IIGS*
Sesame Street Ernie's Magic Shapes — C64*, Atari, IBM, Apple
Sesame Street Letter-Go-Round — Apple, C64*, IBM, Atari
Sesame Street Print Kit — Apple*, IBM, C64, Atari
Space Waste Race — Apple*, Atari, TRS 80
Stickybear ABC — Apple*, Atari, C64
Stickybear Opposites — Apple*, Atari, C64
Stickybear Shapes — Apple*, Atari, C64, IBM
Ted Bear Games — Apple*, C64, Atari, Mac
Telling Time — Apple*, C64, TRS 80, IBM, Atari, PET
Young Math — IBM*, Atari ST

AMIGA (14 titles)

Title — Computer (* = version reviewed)

Beginning Reading Skills — Amiga (512K)
Dinosaur Discovery Kit, The — IBM*, IIGS, Mac, Amiga
Early Math — Amiga (512K)
First Letters and Words — IIGS*, Mac, Amiga, Atari ST
First Shapes — IIGS*, Mac, Amiga, Atari ST
Katie's Farm — IIGS*, Mac, IBM (VGA or CGA), Mac II, Amiga
KidTalk — Mac*, IIGS*, Atari ST, Amiga
Learning the Alphabet — Amiga (512K)

McGee — IIGS (3.5"), IBM (VGA or CGA), Mac, Amiga
McGee at the Fun Fair — IIGS*, Mac, IBM (VGA or CGA), Mac II
Puzzle Storybook, The — IBM*, IIGS, Mac, Amiga
Sesame Street Crayon: Letters for You — Apple* (128K), IBM, C64, Amiga
Sesame Street Crayon: Numbers Count — Apple* (128K), IBM, C64, Amiga
Sesame Street Crayon: Opposites Attract — Apple* (128K), IBM, C64, Amiga

APPENDIX 5
SOFTWARE NO LONGER AVAILABLE

Following are titles reviewed in previous editions that have been taken off the market or that we have been unable to locate. Each listing contains the title, the producer, and the *Buyer's Guide* edition in which it was reviewed.

Adventures in Space — Scandura Training Systems — *1989*

Alpha Teach — Aquarius People Materials — *1989*

Alphabet Song and Count — Edusoft — *1989*

Alphabots — D.C. Heath & Company — *1990*

Beginner Reader — Scandura Training Systems — *1989*

Beginning Counting — MicroEd, Inc. — *1989*

Best Electronic Word Book Ever! — Mindscape — *1991*

Build a Book About You — Mindscape, Inc. — *1990*

Castle Clobber — Mindscape, Inc. — *1989*

Come Play With Pockets — World Book, Inc. — *1991*

Counting — MECC — *1989*

Counting Critters — Mindscape, Inc. — *1990*

Counting Skills — Aquarius Instructional — *1991*

Critter Count — Aquarius People Materials — *1990*

Delta Drawing — Spinnaker — *1990*

Early Learning Friends — Spinnaker — *1990*

Exploring Your World: The Weather — Grolier Electronic Publishing — *1991*

Fantastic Animals — Firebird Licensees, Inc. — *1989*

First Numbers: First Words — Educational Activities — *1990*

First Steps to Reading — Grolier Electronic Publishing — *1991*

Flying Carpet, The — Merit Software — *1989*

Fruit Tree/Gumball — BeCi Software — *1989*

Grabbit Factory — D.C. Heath & Company — *1990*

Grownup and Small — Mindscape, Inc. — *1990*

Happy Birthday Pockets — World Book, Inc. — *1991*

Hey Diddle Diddle — Spinnaker — *1990*

How to Weigh an Elephant — Merit Software — *1989*

I Love My Alphabet — First Star Software — *1990*

Juggle's Rainbow — The Learning Company — *1989*

Language Arts — Aquarius Instructional — *1991*

Learning Line, The — D.C. Heath & Company — *1990*

Learning With Fuzzywomp — Sierra On-Line — *1989*

Learning With Leeper — Sierra On-Line — *1991*

Let's Go Fishing — Merit Software — *1989*

LOGO Power — Mindscape, Inc. — *1990*

Make a Match — Springboard — *1990*

Many Ways to Say I Love You — Mindscape, Inc. — *1990*

Math Facts Level 1 — THESIS — *1989*

Maze-o — D.C. Heath & Company — *1990*

Memory Master — Stone & Associates — *1991*

Music Maestro — Springboard — *1990*

My Book — BeCi Software — *1989*

Number BeCi — BeCi Software — *1989*

Number Master — The Home School — *1991*

Ordering Sequencing — Aquarius Instructional — *1991*

Peter and the Wolf Music — Spinnaker — *1990*

Picture Dictionary — D.C. Heath & Company — *1989*

Play Together Learn Together — Grolier Electronic Publishing — *1991*

Pockets and Her New Sneakers — World Book, Inc. — *1991*

Pockets Goes on a Picnic — World Book, Inc. — *1991*

Pockets Goes on Vacation — World Book, Inc. — *1991*

Pockets Goes to the Carnival — World Book, Inc. — *1991*

Pockets Leads the Parade — World Book, Inc. — *1991*

Preschool Fun — THESIS — *1989*

Rhyming to Read — Grolier Electronic Publishing — *1991*

Sesame Street: Big Bird's Funhouse — Hi Tech Expressions — *1990*

Shape Games — BeCi Software — *1989*

Sound Tracks — MECC — *1989*

Spatial Relationships — Aquarius People Materials — *1990*

Story Machine — Spinnaker Software Corp. — *1989*

Sweet Shop — D.C. Heath & Company — *1990*

Talking Teacher — Firebird Licensees, Inc. — *1989*

Video Smarts — Connor Toy Corp. — *1991*

Which Number is Missing? — MicroEd — *1991*

APPENDIX 6
GLOSSARY

Definitions are given here for *Survey* terms or computer terms that may be unfamiliar to the reader.

Apple IIe Card—A circuit board containing the components of an Apple IIe computer. Makes the Macintosh LC computer compatible with older versions of Apple II software. Costs $139.95.

BASIC—Acronym for Beginners All-purpose Symbolic Instruction Code. A language often used with microcomputers, using word-like commands rather than numerical codes. A relatively easy language to learn.

branching—The capacity of a program to adjust its level of challenge to match the child's performance, an important component of computer-managed instruction (CMI). For example, if the child performs a task poorly, the program automatically presents a simpler task.

button—A clearly distinguished spot on the screen that a user may click on with a mouse to activate a command. No typing is necessary.

CD-ROM (compact disk-read only memory)—A device that stores a vast amount of information (such as an encyclopedia series) on a compact disk. The user may scan the disk for pertinent information.

chip—A tiny silicon surface containing a computer circuit.

clicking—Pressing and releasing the mouse button.

computer literacy—Familiarity with the parts of a microcomputer and some measure of programming skill.

computer-managed instruction (CMI)—A capacity of a computer program that allows a teacher to set up individualized activities. This often includes the ability to sort, print, and automatically update performance records of children who use the program. See *branching*.

Concept Keyboard—A vinyl-covered keypad that can be customized for different types of computer applications. Two Concept Keyboards can be plugged into the same computer, enabling two children to work together on the same program. Useful for special education settings. Produced by Hach Associates, it costs $495.

Contact Keyboard—An adaptive keyboard device for the Apple IIGS computer. Offers ten large keys and snaps into place over the Apple IIGS keyboard. Designed for use in special education settings.

copy protection puzzle—A method used by some software producers to prevent illegal copying of their programs. Consists of a simple puzzle (e.g., "Find the third word on page 6 of the user's manual"), the answer to which is found in the original program documentation. May complicate programs operated by children.

Covox Speech Adapter—A computer attachment that permits computer output to be spoken. Plugs inside the computer. For use in special education settings.

Cricket speech synthesizer—An attachment for the Apple IIc computer. Plugs into the modem port of the computer. Equivalent to the Echo IIb speech synthesizer. Made by Street Electronics Corporation. Costs about $100. See *Echo speech synthesizer.*

cursor—A symbol, such as a dash or box, that marks on the screen where the next keystroke will occur.

disk—See *floppy disk.*

disk drive—The mechanism into which the disk or diskette is inserted. Makes the disk rotate as on a record player.

divergent—See *open-ended.*

DOS—An acronym for disk operating sytem, a program that controls a computer's basic functions, such as reading disks or creating files.

dragging—Placing the cursor on an on-screen object, clicking the mouse button, and moving the mouse. As you move the mouse, the object on the screen also moves.

drill and practice—A program design that provides repeated practice with specific skills or concepts. Frequently involves answer checking, performance feedback, or chances to review missed problems.

Echo speech synthesizer—A computer attachment that permits computer output to be spoken. Plugs inside the computer. Requires special software that takes advantage of speech capability. Costs about $140. Made by Street Electronics Corporation. See *Cricket speech synthesizer.*

embedded reinforcements—A program's pictures or sounds that relate to and work with the content, rather than being merely entertaining or attention-getting.

file server—The computer that contains all the programs used by computers in a *network*.

floppy disk—A vinyl disk, coated with magnetic material, on which computer programs can be recorded for storage. Also called *diskette*.

freeware—See *shareware*.

graphics—The pictorial part of a program presented on the screen. Often animated and in color.

hard disk—In a computer, a nonremovable device on which information (files) can be stored. Also called a fixed disk. Hard (or fixed) disk storage is similar to floppy disk storage but provides much greater storage capacity.

hardware—The physical equipment that makes up a computer system, such as the monitor, computer, keyboard, printer.

Hypercard—A software application for the Macintosh computer that allows user with a minimal knowledge of computer programming to create custom programs.

icon—A picture or symbol that stands for a word. Often used in menus to make a program usable by nonreaders.

Imagewriter—A printer designed for Apple computers. The Imagewriter II can print in color if it has a special ribbon.

joystick—A computer attachment. Moving the joystick handle up, down, left, or right makes an object or cursor move in corresponding directions on the screen. A button on the joystick may also be used to stop or start action or pick up an object.

K—An abbreviation for Kilo, or thousand, usually referring to a computer's memory size in bytes. A 64K computer, for example, has 64 thousand bytes of memory. A byte can be roughly translated as one alphabet character.

key experiences—The learning objectives of the High/Scope Curriculum. Approximately 50 guideposts for planning classroom activities and evaluating learning progress.

Kidz Mouse—A computer mouse designed for children's use. Shaped like a mouse (a real mouse, not the computer device), it can be programmed for right- or left-handed children. For IBM or compatibles, it costs $79.

Koala Pad—A book-sized, touch-sensitive pad that allows information to be entered into the computer by drawing with a stylus or finger on the pad. Mostly used for drawing.

light pen—A pen-shaped attachment sensitive to the light of the computer's TV display. Can be used to "draw" on the screen or to point to and select objects or areas on the screen.

load—To copy a program's instructions from a disk or tape into the computer's memory.

LOGO—A computer language that uses a combination of simple instructions and graphics. Commonly used to introduce programming procedures to children.

memory—An ability of a computer system to store information for later retrieval.

menu—A list of a computer program's choices displayed on the screen.

microcomputer—A desktop-sized computer with many of the capabilities of larger computers.

monitor—The video display device attached to most microcomputers. Like a television screen without a channel tuner.

mouse—A handheld computer attachment whose movement (left, right, up, or down) on a desk moves objects or a cursor in corresponding directions on the screen. A button on the mouse may also be used to stop or start an action or pick up an object.

Muppet Learning Keys—A separate keyboard that plugs into a joystick port. Contains numbers 0-9 in left-to-right order and letters in alphabetical order, plus eight color keys. It requires specially designed software. Produced by Sunburst Communications, it costs about $100.

network—A system that links computers together. Networked computers can share printers or other equipment.

open-ended—The quality of computer programs, such as word processing, programming, and drawing programs, that allows many different results to be produced.

paddles—A computer attachment with dials that can be turned to move an object or cursor on the screen. Similar in operation to knobs of an Etch-a-Sketch game.

password—A word or code that allows a child to use parts of a computer program or gives access to his or her stored files.

peripheral—An attachment to the computer, such as a keyboard, monitor, printer, mouse, or voice synthesizer.

PowerPad—A large (12" by 12") touch-sensitive graphics tablet that plugs into the Apple II, IIe, or IIGS computer (not the IIc). Often used with picture templates that can be laid over its surface, allowing children to press pictures to enter answers into the computer. Also called *WonderWorker*. Produced by Dunamis, Inc., it costs about $200.

program—An organized set of instructions, written in a computer language, that makes the computer perform a specified task. Programs are referred to as "software."

programming—The process of giving the computer instructions. Several programming activities exist for children, e.g., for drawing—"Delta Drawing" and "EZ Logo"; for programming the movements of a face or object— "Facemaker," "Creature Creator."

pull-down menu—A visual method of making on-screen selections. A mouse is used to move a pointer to an icon or word. Clicking the mouse then causes a related list of options to appear.

scan mode—A method of entering information into a computer by following a cursor that constantly moves among possible responses. When the cursor highlights a desired response, one key (such as the spacebar) must be pressed.

shareware—Software that you are encouraged to copy and give to others at no cost and on a noncommercial basis. A message is included in the program, with the address of the producer, asking for a contribution if the user finds the program of value. Also called *freeware*.

simulation—A program that models a real-life situation, such as the operation of a lemonade stand, the flying of an airplane, or the exploration of a volcano. Simulations are frequently designed to allow children to practice skills or concepts in a life-like situation.

single switch—A computer attachment. Has a single button or switch that can be used to enter responses into the computer. Commonly used in special education settings. Produced by Developmental Equipment, Inc.

Slotbuster II—A card for the Apple IIe that includes a modem, a clock/calendar, and a speech synthesizer that will say anything that can be printed. Costs around $230 and is available from RC Systems, Inc.

software—The information that controls the computer. This information is usually stored on an electromagnetic medium such as a disk or tape. See *program*.

spell checker program—A program that checks the spelling of word processor stories. Some include such features as a built-in thesaurus, a list of optional spellings, or the ability to add words to the dictionary.

Sound Source, The—A computer attachment for IBM-compatible computers that produces digitized music or speech. Produced by Walt Disney Computer Software, Inc., this attachment is designed especially for Disney software titles. It plugs into the printer port, requires a battery, and costs $34.95.

TouchWindow—A touch-sensitive transparent screen that fits over a computer monitor, allowing information to be entered into the computer by touching screen images with a finger or stylus. It requires specially designed software. Produced by Edmark Corporation, it costs about $240.

tutorial—A computer program, or part thereof, demonstrating a process or skill, such as matching objects one-to-one, with provisions for children to model or try the same process or skill on their own.

Unicorn Board, The—An expanded keyboard that works with the Apple IIe or Apple IIGS computer and an Adaptive Firmware Card. For more information, contact Unicorn Engineering, Inc. (800/899-6687).

WonderWorker—See *PowerPad*.

word-processing program—A program that enables a child to use the computer to write, as with a typewriter. Word-processing programs usually have additional features, such as ability to edit, save, and recall written material; ability to reformat written material; and ability to choose print style.

ABOUT THE AUTHOR

Warren Buckleitner has been an educational consultant and computer specialist at the High/Scope Educational Research Foundation in Ypsilanti, Michigan, since 1984. A national speaker and workshop leader, Mr. Buckleitner trains parents, teachers, and college educators in successful techniques for using computers with young children. Identifying an unmet need through his training and speaking engagements, Mr. Buckleitner first developed the *High/Scope Buyer's Guide to Children's Software* in 1984. This publication is now in its eighth edition.